Berlitz®

KT-492-336

Italian
phrase book

Berlitz Publishing Company, Inc.

Princeton Mexico City Dublin Eschborn Singapore

Copyright © 1998 by Berlitz Publishing Company, Inc.

400 Alexander Park, Princeton, NJ 08540 USA
9-13 Grosvenor St., London W1X 9FB UK

All rights reserved. No part of this book may be reproduced or transmitted in any form or by any means, electronic or mechanical, including photocopying, recording or by any information storage and retrieval system without permission in writing from the publisher.

Berlitz Trademark Reg. US Patent Office and other countries
Marca Registrada

Cover photo: Copyright©Juan Alvarez/The Image Bank 1998

ISBN 2-8315-6241-4
Eighth printing–August 2000
Printed in Spain.

Developed and produced for Berlitz Publishing Company by:
G&W Publishing Services, Oxfordshire, U.K.

Contents

Pronunciation 6

Basic Expressions 10

Greetings/Apologies 10
Communication difficulties 11
Questions 12
Where? 12
When? 13
What kind of? 14
How much/many? 15
Why? 15
Who?/Which?/Whose? 16
How? 17
Is it/Are there ...? 17
Can/May? 18
What do you want? 18
Other useful words 19
Exclamations 19

Accommodations 20

Reservations/Booking 21
Reception 22
Requirements 26
Renting 28
Youth hostel 29
Camping 30
Checking out 32

Eating Out 33

Restaurants 33
Italian cuisine 34
Finding a place to eat 35
Reservations 36
Ordering 37
Fast food/Café 40
Complaints 41
Paying 42
Course by course 43
Breakfast 43
Appetizers/Starters 43
Pizza/Soups 44
Pasta/Fish 45
Meat 46
Vegetables/Salads 47
Cheese/Fruit 48
Dessert 48
Drinks 49
Beer/Wine 49
Other drinks 51
Non-alcoholic drinks 51
Menu reader 52

Travel 65

Safety 65
Arrival 66
Plane 68
Train 72
Long-distance bus [Coach] 78
Bus 78
Subway [Metro] 80
Ferry 81
Bicycle/Motorbike 82
Hitchhiking 83
Taxi/Cab 84
Automobile [Car] 85
Car rental 86
Gas [Petrol] Station 87
Breakdown 88
Accidents 92
Legal matters 93
Asking directions 94

Sightseeing 97

Tourist information 97
Excursions 98
Sights 99
Admission 100
Impressions 101
Tourist glossary 102
Who/What/When? 104
In the countryside 106

Leisure 108

Tickets 109
Movies [Cinema] 110
Theater 110
Opera/Ballet/Dance 111
Music/Concerts 111
Nightlife 112
Children 113
Sports 114
At the beach 116
Skiing 117

Making Friends 118

Introductions 118
Where are you from? 119
Who are you with? 120
What do you do? 121
Enjoying your trip? 123
Invitations 124
Encounters 126
Telephoning 127

Stores & Services 129

Hours 132
Service 133
Paying 136
Complaints 137
Repairs/Cleaning 137
Bank/Changing money 138
Pharmacy 140
Clothing 143
Health and beauty 147
Household articles 148
Jeweler 149
Newsstand [News-agent]/Tobacconist 150
Photography 151
Police 152
Lost property/Theft 153
Post office 154
Souvenirs/Gifts 156
Antiques 157
Supermarket 158

Health 161

Doctor (general) 161
Accident and injury 162
Symptoms/Conditions 163
Doctor's inquiries 164
Parts of the body 166
Gynecologist 167
Hospital 167
Optician 167
Dentist 168
Payment and Insurance 168

English–Italian dictionary & index 169

Italian–English dictionary 202

Reference 216

Numbers 216
Days/Months/Dates 218
Greetings 219
Public holidays 219
Time 220
Maps 222
Quick reference 224
Emergency 224

Pronunciation

This section is designed to make you familiar with the sounds of Italian using our simplified phonetic transcription. You'll find the pronunciation of the Italian letters and sounds explained below, together with their "imitated" equivalents. This system is used throughout the phrase book: simply read the pronunciation as if it were English, noting any special rules below.

The Italian language

There are approximately 64 million speakers of Italian. These are the countries where you can expect to hear Italian spoken (figures are approximate):

Italia Italy

Italian is the national language, spoken by almost the entire population (59 million). Other languages: Sardinian in Sardinia (1.5 million); Rhaeto-Romanic in Friuli, near the border with Slovenia and Austria.

Svizzera Switzerland

Italian is one of the four official languages, spoken by about 800,000 people in the southern part of the country, particularly the canton of Ticino (capital: Bellinzona). Other languages: German in the north (5 milllion); French in the west (1.3 million); Romansch in the east (50,000).

Italian is also spoken amongst large Italian emigré communities, particularly in the United States (**Stati Uniti**), with almost 1.5 million speakers, and Canada (**Canada**), with over half a million speakers.

The Italian alphabet is the same as English, with the addition of accents which indicate stress only (see below). However, the letters **j**, **k**, **w**, **x** and **y** only appear in foreign words.

English has absorbed numerous Italian words, for example: **balcony**, **studio**, **umbrella**, **volcano** as well as many terms in the fields of food (e.g. **broccoli**, **macaroni**, **pizza**, **spaghetti**) and music (e.g. **concerto**, **piano**, **solo**, **trio**, **viola**).

Consonants

Letter	Approximate pronunciation	Symbol	Example	
b, d, f, k, l, m, n, p, q, t, v	as in English			
c	1) before **e** and **i**, like *ch* in *ch*ip	*ch*	**cerco**	*chayrko*
	2) elsewhere, like *c* in *c*at	*k*	**conto**	*konto*
ch	like *c* in *c*at	*k*	**che**	*kay*
g	1) before **e** and **i**, like *j* in *j*et	*j*	**valigia**	*valeeja*
	2) elsewhere, like *g* in *g*o	*g*	**grande**	*granday*
gh	like *g* in *g*o	*g*	**ghiaccio**	*geeacho*
gl	like *lli* in mi*lli*on	*ly*	**gli**	*lyee*
gn	like *ni* in o*ni*on	*ñ*	**bagno**	*baño*
h	always silent		**ha**	*ah*
r	trilled like a Scottish *r*	*r*	**deriva**	*dehreeva*
s	1) generally like *s* in *s*it	*s*	**questo**	*kwaysto*
	2) sometimes like *z* in *z*oo	*z*	**viso**	*veezo*
sc	1) before **e** and **i**, like *sh* in *sh*ut	*sh*	**uscita**	*oosheeta*
	2) elsewhere, like *sk* in *sk*in	*sk*	**scarpa**	*skarpa*
z/zz	1) generally like *ts* in hi*ts*	*ts*	**grazie**	*graatseeay*
	2) sometimes like *ds* in roa*ds*	*dz*	**romanzo**	*romandzo*

Vowels

a	1) short, like *a* in c*a*t	*a*	**gatto**	*gatto*
	2) long, like *a* in f*a*ther	*aa*	**casa**	*kaasa*
e	1) can always be pronounced like *ay* in w*ay*, but without moving tongue or lips	*ay*	**sera**	*sayra*
	2) in correct speech, it is sometimes pronounced like *e* in g*e*t or, when long, more like *ai* in h*ai*r	*eh*	**bello**	*behllo*
i	like *ee* in m*ee*t	*ee*	**vini**	*veenee*
o	can always be pronounced like *o* in g*o*	*o*	**sole**	*solay*
u	1. like *oo* in f*oo*t	*oo*	**fumo**	*foomo*
	2. like *w* in *w*ell	w	**buono**	*bwono*

Two or more vowels

In groups of vowels **a**, **e** and **o** are strong, and **i** and **u** are weak vowels. The following combinations occur:

two strong vowels	pronounced as two separate syllables	**beato**	*bay-aato*
a stong vowel and a weak vowel	1) the weak one is pronounced more quickly and with less stress than the strong one; such sounds are diphthongs and constitute only one syllable:	**piede**	*peeayday*
	2) if the weak vowel is stressed, then it is pronounced as a separate syllable	**due**	*doo-ay*
two weak vowels	pronounced as a diphthong; it is generally the second one that is more strongly stressed	**guida**	*gweeda*

Stress

Stress has been indicated in the phonetic transcription by underlining the letters that should be pronounced louder than the others.

Generally, the vowel of the next to last syllable is stressed. When a final vowel is stressed, it has an accent written over it (**caffè**). Normally, when the stress falls on the syllable before the next to last one, it is not indicated by an accent.

Pronunciation of the Italian alphabet

A	*ah*	**N**	*ehnnay*
B	*bee*	**O**	*o*
C	*chee*	**P**	*pee*
D	*dee*	**Q**	*koo*
E	*ay*	**R**	*ehrray*
F	*ehffay*	**S**	*ehssay*
G	*jee*	**T**	*tee*
H	*aaka*	**U**	*oo*
I	*ee*	**V**	*voo*
J	*ee loongga*	**W**	*voo doppeea*
K	*kaappa*	**X**	*eeks*
L	*ehllay*	**Y**	*ee grayka*
M	*ehmmay*	**Z**	*dzaytah*

Basic Expressions

Greetings/ Apologies 10
Communication difficulties 11
Questions 12
Where? 12
When? 13
What kind of ...? 14
How much/many? 15
Why? 15
Who?/Which? 16
Whose? 16
How? 17
Is it ...?/Are there ...? 17
Can/May? 18
What do you want? 18
Other useful words 19
Exclamations 19

ESSENTIAL

Yes.	**Sì.** *see*
No.	**No.** *no*
Okay.	**D'accordo./Va bene.** *daakordo/va baynay*
Please.	**Per favore.** *pehr favoray*
Thank you (very much).	**(Mille) grazie.** *(meellay) graatseeay*

Greetings/Apologies Saluti e scuse

Hello/Hi!	**Salve./Ciao!** *saalvay/chaao*
Good morning.	**Buongiorno.** *bwon jorno*
Good afternoon.	**Buonasera.** *bwona sayra*
Good evening.	**Buonasera.** *bwona sayra*
Good night.	**Buonanotte.** *bwona nottay*
Good-bye.	**Arrivederci.** *arreevaydehrchee*
Excuse me! *(getting attention)*	**Scusi!** *skoozee*
Excuse me. *(May I get past?)*	**Permesso?** *pehrmehsso*
Excuse me!/Sorry!	**Scusi!/Sono spiacente!** *skoozee/sono speeachehntay*
It was an accident.	**È stato un incidente.** *eh staato oon eencheedehntay*
Don't mention it.	**Prego.** *praygo*
Never mind.	**Non importa.** *non eemporta*

Communication difficulties
Difficoltà di comunicazione

Do you speak English?	**Parla inglese?** *parla eengglaysay*
Does anyone here speak English?	**C'è qualcuno qui che parla inglese?** *cheh kwalkoono kwee kay parla eengglaysay*
I don't speak (much) Italian.	**Non parlo italiano (molto bene).** *non parlo eetaleeaano (molto baynay)*
Could you speak more slowly?	**Può parlare più lentamente?** *pwo parlaaray peeoo layntamayntay*
Could you repeat that?	**Può ripetere?** *pwo reepehtayray*
Pardon?/What was that?	**Prego?/Cosa ha detto?** *praygo/kosa ah daytto*
Could you spell it?	**Come si scrive?** *komay see skreevay*
Please write it down.	**Lo scriva, per piacere.** *lo skreeva pehr peeachayray*
Can you translate this for me?	**Può tradurre questo?** *pwo tradoorray kwaysto*
What does this/that mean?	**Cosa significa questo/quello?** *kosa seeñeefeeka kwaysto/kwayllo*
Please point to the phrase in the book.	**Per piacere, indichi la frase nel libro.** *pehr peeachayray eendeekee la fraazay nel leebro*
I understand	**Capisco.** *kapeesko*
I don't understand.	**Non capisco.** *non kapeesko*
Do you understand?	**Capisce?** *kapeeshay*

– Fa tredicimila cinquecento lire.
(That's 13,500 lire.)
– Non capisco. (I don't understand.)
– Fa tredicimila cinquecento lire. (That's 13,500 lire.)
– Lo scriva, per piacere …
Ah, tredicimila cinquecento lire. Ecco.
(Please write it down. … Ah, 13,500 lire.
Here you are.)

Questions Domande

GRAMMAR

Questions can be formed in Italian:

1 by adding interrogatory intonation (letting the voice rise at the end of the sentence)

Parlo* italiano.	I speak Italian.
Parla* italiano?	Do you speak Italian?

2 by using a question word (➤12–17) and inverting the order of the subject and the verb

Quando apre il museo?	When does the museum open?

* Note that the personal pronoun (I, you, etc.) is rarely used.

Where? Dove?

Where is it?	**Dov'è?** *doveh*
Where are you going?	**Dove va?** *dovay va*
to the meeting place [point]	**al punto d'incontro** *al poonto deenkontro*
downstairs	**al piano inferiore** *al peeaano eenfayreeoray*
from the U.S.	**dagli Stati Uniti** *daalyee staatee ooneetee*
here	**qui** *kwee*
in the car	**in automobile** *een owtomobeelay*
in Italy	**in Italia** *een eetaaleea*
inside	**dentro** *dayntro*
near the bank	**vicino alla banca** *veecheeno alla banka*
next to the apples	**accanto alle mele** *akkanto allay maylay*
opposite the market	**di fronte al mercato** *dee frontay al mayrkaato*
on the left/right	**a sinistra/a destra** *ah seeneestra/ah daystra*
there	**là** *la*
to the hotel	**all'albergo** *allalbehrgo*
toward Florence	**verso Firenze** *vehrso feerehnzay*
outside the café	**fuori del bar** *fworee dayl baar*
upstairs	**al piano superiore** *al peeaano soopayreeoray*

When? Quando?

When does the museum open? **Quando apre il museo?**
kwando apray eel moozeho

When will the train arrive? **Quando arriva il treno?**
kwando arreeva eel trayno

in 10 minutes **In dieci minuti.**
een dee-ehchee meenootee

after lunch **dopo pranzo** *dopo prandzo*

around midnight **verso mezzanotte** *vehrso mehdzanottay*

at 7 o'clock **alle sette** *allay sehttay*

before Friday **prima di venerdì** *preema dee vaynayrdee*

by tomorrow **entro domani** *ayntro domaanee*

early **di buon'ora** *dee bwonora*

every week **ogni settimana/tutte le settimane**
oñee saytteemaana/toottay lay saytteemaanay

for 2 hours **per due ore** *pehr doo-ay oray*

from 9 a.m. to 6 p.m. **dalle nove alle diciotto**
dallay novay allay deechotto

immediately **immediatamente** *eemaydeeatamayntay*

in 20 minutes **in venti minuti** *een vayntee meenootee*

always **sempre** *sehmpray*

never **non mai** *non maee*

not yet **non ancora** *non ankora*

now **ora/adesso** *ora/adehsso*

often **sovente/spesso** *sovayntay/spehsso*

on March 8 **l'otto marzo** *lotto martso*

on weekdays **nei giorni feriali**
nayee jornee fehreeaalee

sometimes **qualche volta** *kwalkay volta*

soon **presto/fra poco** *prehsto/fra poko*

then **poi** *poee*

within 2 days **entro due giorni** *ayntro doo-ay jornee*

What kind of ...? Che tipo di ...?

I'd like something ... **Vorrei qualcosa ...** *vorrehee kwalkosa*

It's ... **È ...** *eh*

beautiful/ugly	**bello(-a)/brutto(-a)** *behllo(-a)/brootto(-a)*
better/worse	**migliore/peggiore** *meelyoray/paydjoray*
big/small	**grande/piccolo(-a)** *granday/peekkolo(-a)*
cheap/expensive	**a buon prezzo/caro(-a)** *a bwon pretso/kaaro(-a)*
clean/dirty	**pulito(-a)/sporco(-a)** *pooleeto(-a)/sporko(-a)*
dark/light	**scuro(-a)/chiaro(-a)** *skooro(-a)/keeahro(-a)*
delicious/revolting	**delizioso(-a)/disgustoso(-a)** *dehleetzeeozo(-a)/deesgoostozo(-a)*
easy/difficult	**facile/difficile** *faacheelay/deeffeecheelay*
empty/full	**vuoto(-a)/pieno(-a)** *vwoto(-a)/peeayno(-a)*
good/bad	**buono(-a)/cattivo(-a)** *bwono(-a)/katteevo(-a)*
heavy/light	**pesante/leggero(-a)** *paysantay/laydjehro(-a)*
hot/warm/cold	**molto caldo(-a)/caldo(-a)/freddo(-a)** *molto kaldo(-a)/kaldo(-a)/frayddo(-a)*
modern/old-fashioned	**moderno(-a)/antiquato(-a)** *modayrno(-a)/anteekwato(-a)*
narrow/wide	**stretto(-a)/largo(-a)** *straytto(-a)/lahrgo(-a)*
old/new	**vecchio(-a)/nuovo(-a)** *vehkkeeao(-a)/nwovo(-a)*
open/shut	**aperto(-a)/chiuso(-a)** *apehrto(-a)/keeooso(-a)*
pleasant/nice/unpleasant	**gradevole/bello(-a)/sgradevole** *grahdayvolay/behllo(-a)/zgradayvolay*
quick/slow	**veloce/lento(-a)** *vaylochay/laynto(-a)*
right/wrong	**guisto(-a)/sbagliato(-a)** *joosto(-a) zbalyaato(-a)*
tall/short	**alto(-a)/basso(-a)** *alto(-a)/basso(-a)*
vacant/occupied	**libero(-a)/occupato(-a)** *leebayro(-a)/okoopaato(-a)*

GRAMMAR

Nouns in Italian are either masculine or feminine and the adjectival endings change accordingly. See page 169 for more explanation.

How much/many? Quanto/quanti?

How much is that?	**Quanto costa?** *kwanto kosta*
How many are there?	**Quanti ce ne sono?** *kwantee cheh neh sono*
1/2/3	**uno(-a)/due/tre** *oono(-a)/doo-ay/tray*
4/5	**quattro/cinque** *kwattro/cheenkway*
none	**nessuno(-a)** *nayssoono(-a)*
about 10,000 lire	**circa diecimila lire** *cheerka dee-ehcheemeela leeray*
a little	**un poco** *oon poko*
a lot of traffic	**molto traffico** *molto traffeeko*
enough *(adv./adj.)*	**abbastanza/sufficiente** *abbastantsa/soffeecheeayntay*
few/a few of them	**alcuni(-e)/alcuni(-e) di loro** *alkoonee(-ay)/alkoonee(-ay) dee loro*
more than that	**più di quello(-a)** *peeoo dee kwayllo(-a)*
less than that	**meno di quello(-a)** *mayno dee kwayllo(-a)*
much more	**molto di più** *molto dee peeoo*
nothing else	**nient'altro** *neeayntaltro*
too much	**troppo(-a)** *troppo(-a)*

Why? Perchè?

Why is that?	**Perchè?** *pehrkay*
Why not?	**Perchè no?** *pehrkay no*
because of the weather	**a causa del tempo** *a kowsa dayl tehmpo*
because I'm in a hurry	**perchè ho fretta** *pehrkay o fraytta*
I don't know why	**non so perchè** *non so pehrkay*

Who? / Which? Chi? / Quale?

Who's there?	**Chi è?** *kee eh*
It's me!	**Sono io!** *sono eeo*
It's us!	**Siamo noi!** *seeamo noee*
someone	**qualcuno** *kwalkoono*
no one	**nessuno** *nayssoono*
Which one do you want?	**Quale vuole?** *kwalay vwolay*
one like that	**uno(-a) come quello(-a)** *oono(-a) komay kwayllo(-a)*
that one / this one	**quello(-a)/questo(-a)** *kwayllo(-a)/kwaysto(-a)*
not that one	**non quello(-a)** *non kwayllo(-a)*
something	**qualcosa** *kwalkosa*
nothing	**nulla** *noolla*
none	**nessuno(-a)** *nayssoono(-a)*

Whose? Di chi?

Whose is that?	**Di chi è quello(-a)?** *dee kee eh kwayllo(-a)*
It's …	**È … eh**
mine / ours	**mio(-a)/nostro(-a)** *meeo(-a)/nostro(-a)*
yours (*formal*) / yours (*familiar*)	**Suo(-a)/tuo(-a)** *soo-o(-a)/too-o(-a)*
his / hers / theirs	**suo(-a)/di lui (di lei)/loro** *soo-o(-a)/dee looee(di layee)/loro*

GRAMMAR

Possessive adjectives and pronouns

	masculine singular	*masculine plural*	*feminine singular*	*feminine plural*
my, mine	**il mio**	**i miei**	**la mia**	**le mie**
your, yours	**il tuo**	**i tuoi**	**la tua**	**le tue**
his, her, hers, its	**il suo**	**i suoi**	**la sua**	**le sue**
our, ours	**il nostro**	**i nostri**	**la nostra**	**le nostre**
your, yours	**il vostro**	**i vostri**	**la vostra**	**le vostre**
their, theirs,	**il loro**	**i loro**	**la loro**	**le loro**
*your, yours (sing.)	**il Suo**	**i Suoi**	**la Sua**	**le Sue**
*your, yours (plur.)	**il Loro**	**i Loro**	**la Loro**	**le Loro**

*These are the formal forms – used when addressing people you do not know well.

How? Come?

How would you like to pay? **Come desidera pagare?** *komay dayzeedayra pagaaray*

by cash **in contanti** *een kontantee*

by credit card **con carta di credito** *kon karta dee kraydeeto*

How are you getting here? **Come arriva qui?** *komay arreeva kwee*

by car **in automobile/macchina** *een owtomobeelay/makkeena*

by bus **in autobus** *een owtobooss*

on foot **a piedi** *a peeaydee*

extremely **estremamente** *aystraymamayntay*

quickly **presto** *prehsto*

slowly **lentamente** *lehntamayntay*

too fast **troppo veloce** *troppo vehlochay*

totally **totalmente** *totalmayntay*

very **molto** *molto*

with a friend **con un amico/un'amica** *kon oon ameeko/ameeka*

Is it ...?/Are there ...? È ...?/Ci sono ...?

Is it ...? **È ...?** *eh*

Is it free? *(unoccupied)* **È libero(-a)?** *eh leebayro(-a)*

It isn't ready. **Non è pronto(-a).** *non eh pronto(-a)*

Is there ...? **C'è ...?** *cheh*

Are there ...? **Ci sono ...?** *chee sono*

Is there a bus into town? **C'è un autobus per il centro?** *cheh oon owtobooss pehr eel chayntro*

Are there buses to the airport? **Ci sono autobuse per l'aeroporto?** *chee sono owtobooseh pehr la-ayroporto*

Here it is/they are. **Eccolo(-a)/eccoli(-e).** *ehkkolo/ehkkolee*

There it is/they are. **È là/sono là** *eh la/sono la*

Can/May? Potere?

May I have ...?	**Posso avere ...?** *posso avayray*
May we have ...?	**Possiamo avere ...?** *posseeamo avayray*
Can you tell me?	**Può dirmi ...?** *pwo deermee*
Can you help me?	**Può aiutarmi?** *pwo aeeootaarmee*
Can I help you?	**Posso aiutare?** *posso aeeootaaray*
Can you direct me to ...?	**Può indicarmi la via per ...?** *pwo eendeekaarmee la veea pehr*
I can't.	**Non posso.** *non posso*

What do you want? Cosa desidera?/vuole?

I'd like ...	**Vorrei ...** *vorrehee*
Do you have ...?	**Ha ...?** *ah*
We'd like ...	**Vorremmo ...** *vorrehmmo*
Give me ...	**Mi dia ...** *mee deea*
I'm looking for ...	**Cerco ...** *chayrko*
I need to ...	**Ho bisogno di ...** *o beezoño dee*
go ...	**andare ...** *andaaray*
find ...	**trovare ...** *trovaaray*
see ...	**vedere ...** *vaydayray*
speak to ...	**parlare a ...** *parlaaray ah*

– Scusi. (Excuse me.)
– Sì? (Yes?)
– Può aiutarmi? (Can you help me?)
– Sì, certamente. (Yes, certainly.)
– Ho bisogno di parlare al Signor Gambetti.
(I would like to speak to Mr. Gambetti.)
– Un momento, per favore.
(One moment, please.)

Other useful words
Altre parole utili

fortunately	**fortunatamente** *fortoonatamayntay*
hopefully	**con (la) speranza di** *kon (la) spayrantsa dee*
of course	**naturalmente** *natooralmayntay*
perhaps/possibly	**forse/possibilmente** *forsay/posseebeelmayntay*
probably	**probabilmente** *probabeelmayntay*
unfortunately	**sfortunatamente** *sfortoonatamayntay*

Exclamations Esclamazioni

At last!	**Finalmente!** *feenalmayntay*
Damn!	**Maledizione!** *malaydeetseeonay*
Go on.	**Continui.** *konteenooee*
Good Heavens!	**Santo Cielo!** *santo cheeaylo*
I can't believe it!	**Incredibile!** *eenkraydeebeelay*
I don't mind.	**Mi è indifferente.** *mee eh eendeeffayrayntay*
No way!	**Assolutamente no.** *assolootamayntay no*
Really?	**Davvero?** *davvayro*
Rubbish.	**Stupidaggini.** *stoopeedadjeenee*
That's enough!	**Basta!** *basta*
That's true.	**É vero.** *eh vayro*
How are things?	**Come vanno le cose?** *komay vanno lay kosay*
Fine, thanks.	**Bene, grazie.** *baynay graatseeay*
great/brilliant	**magnifico** *mañeefeeko*
great	**benissimo** *bayneesseemo*
fine	**bene** *baynay*
not bad	**non male** *non malay*
okay	**abbastanza bene** *abbastantza baynay*
not good	**non bene** *non baynay*

Accommodations

Reservations	21	Requirements	26
Reception	22	Renting	28
Price	24	Youth hostel	29
Decisions	24	Camping	30
Problems	25	Checking out	32

Early reservations are essential in most major tourist centers, especially during the high season and at festival time. If you haven't booked, most towns and arrival points have a tourist information office (**azienda di promozione turistica** or **ufficio turistico**).

The Italian tourist organization **E.N.I.T.** publishes an annual directory of all the 37,000 hotels in Italy, with details of minimum and maximum prices and facilities.

There is a wide range of accommodation options available, from **locande** (country inns) and **rifugi alpini** (mountain huts) to converted historic buildings, and the following:

albergo/hotel *albayrgo/otehl*

Hotels in Italy are classified as **di lusso** (luxury class), or **prima**, **seconda**, **terza**, **quarta categoria** (first, second, third, fourth class).

Note: especially near railway stations, one often finds **alberghi diurni** ("daytime hotels"). These have no sleeping accommodations, but provide bathrooms, rest rooms, hairdressers, and other similar services. Most close at midnight.

motel *motehl*

Increasing in number and improving in service; the Automobile Association of Italy has a list of recommended motels.

pensióne *paynseeonay*

Corresponds to a guest house; it usually offers **pensióne completa** (full board) or **mezza pensióne** (half board). Meals are likely to be from a set menu. **Pensioni** are classified first, second, and third class.

ostello della gioventù *ostehllo daylla jovayntoo*

Youth hostel. They are open to holders of membership cards issued by the International Youth Hostel Association. The Italian Association of Youth Hostels (**AIG**) publishes a complete guide of youth hostels in Italy. Information can also be obtained from any **CTS** (**Centro Turistico Studentesco**). Reservations are advisable.

Reservations Prenotazioni

In advance In anticipo

Can you recommend a hotel in ...?	**Può consigliarmi un albergo a ...?** *pwo konsilyarmee oon albayrgo ah*
Is it near the center of town?	**È vicino al centro città?** *eh veecheeno al chayntro cheetta*
How much is it per night?	**Quanto costa per notte?** *kwanto kosta pehr nottày*
Is there anything cheaper?	**C'è qualcosa di più economico?** *cheh kwalkosa dee peeoo aykonomeeko*
Could you reserve me a room there, please?	**Può prenotarmi una camera lì, per piacere?** *pwo prehnotaarmee oona kamayra lee pehr peeachayray*
How do I get there?	**Come ci arrivo?** *komay chee arreevo*

At the hotel All'albergo

Do you have a room?	**Ha camere libere?** *ah kamayray leebayray*
I'm sorry. We're full.	**Mi dispiace, siamo al completo.** *mee deespeegchay seeamo al komplayto*
Is there another hotel nearby?	**C'è un altro albergo qui vicino?** *cheh oon altro kwee veecheeno*
I'd like a single/double room.	**Vorrei una camera singola/doppia.** *vorrehee oona kamayra seengola/doppeea*
A room with ...	**Una camera con ...** *oona kamayra kon*
twin beds	**due letti** *doo-ay lehttee*
a double bed	**un letto matrimoniale** *oon lehtto matreemoneeaalay*
a bath/shower	**un bagno/una doccia** *oon baaño/oona dotcha*

– Ha camere libere? Vorrei una camera doppia.
(Do you have any vacancies? I'd like a double room.)
– Mi dispiace, siamo al completo. (Sorry, we're full.)
– C'è un altro albergo qui vicino?
(Is there another hotel nearby?)
– Sì, l'albergo "La Giara" è vicino.
(Yes, the Giara Hotel is nearby.)

Reception Ricezione

I have a reservation. **Ho una prenotazione.** *o oona praynotatseeonay*

My name is ... **Il nome è ...** *eel nomay eh*

We've reserved a double and a single room. **Abbiamo prenotato una camera doppia e una camera singola.** *abbeeaamo praynotaato oona kamayra doppeea ay oona kamayra seengola*

I confirmed my reservation by mail. **Ho confermato la prenotazione per lettera.** *o konfehrmaato la praynotatseeonay pehr lehttayra*

Could we have adjoining rooms? **Possiamo avere camere adiacenti?** *posseeamo avayray kamayray adjachehntee*

Amenities and facilities Amenità e servizi

Is there (a) ... in the room? **C'è ... nella camera?** *cheh naylla kamayra*

air conditioning **l'aria condizionata** *lareea kondeetseeonaata*

TV/telephone **la televisione/il telefono** *la taylayveezeeonay/ eel taylayfono*

Does the hotel have a(n)...? **L'albergo ha ...** *lalbayrgo ah*

laundry service **il servizio di lavanderia** *eel sayrveetseeo dee lavandayreea*

satellite TV **la televisione via satellite** *la taylayveezeeonay veea sataylleetay*

solarium **il solarium** *eel solareeoom*

swimming pool **la piscina** *la peesheena*

Could you put ... in the room? **Può mettere ... nella camera?** *pwo mayttehrray ... naylla kamayra*

an extra bed **un letto supplementare** *oon lehtto soopplaymayntaray*

a crib [child's cot] **una culla** *oona koolla*

Do you have facilities for children/the disabled? **È attrezzato per i bambini/i clienti disabili?** *eh attraytsaato pehr ee bambeenee/ ee kleeehntee deesabeelee*

How long? Quanto si ferma?

We'll be staying …	**Ci fermeremo …** *chee fehrmayraymo*
overnight only	**solo per una notte** *solo pehr oona nottay*
a few days	**per alcuni giorni** *pehr alkoonee jornee*
a week (at least)	**una settimana (minimo)** *oona sayteemaana (meeneemo)*
I don't know yet.	**Non so ancora.** *non so ankora*
I'd like to stay an extra night.	**Vorrei fermarmi per un'altra notte.** *vorrehee fehrmaarmee pehr oonaaltra nottay*

– Buona sera. Il nome è John Newton.
(Hello. My name is John Newton.)
– Buona sera, Signore Newton.
(Good afternoon, Mr. Newton.)
– Vorrei fermarmi per due giorni.
(I'd like to stay for two days.)
– Ah sì. Per piacere compili questo modulo.
(Very good. Please fill out this form.)

Posso vedere il suo passaporto, per piacere?	May I see your passport, please?
Per piacere compili questo modulo/firmi qui.	Please fill out this form/sign here.
Qual'è il suo numero di targa?	What's your license plate [registration] number?

SOLO CAMERE … LIRE	room only … lire
COLAZIONE COMPRESA	breakfast included
RISTORANTE	meals available
IL COGNOME/IL NOME	last name/first name
L'INDIRIZZO/IL DOMICILIO/ LA VIA/IL NUMERO	home address/street/ number
LA NAZIONALITÀ/LA PROFESSIONE	nationality/profession
LA DATA/IL LUOGO DI NASCITA	date/place of birth
IL NUMERO DI PASSAPORTO	passport number
IL NUMERO DI TARGA DEL VEICOLO	license plate [registration] number
IL LUOGO/LA DATA	place/date (of signature)
LA FIRMA	signature

Price Il prezzo

How much is it ...? **Quant'è ...?** *kwanteh*

per night/week **per notte/per settimana** *pehr nottay/pehr saytteemaana*

for bed and breakfast **per il pernottamento e la colazione** *pehr eel pehrnottamaynto ay la kolatseeonay*

excluding meals **pasti esclusi** *paastee ayskloozee*

for American Plan (A.P.) [full board] **per la pensione completa** *pehr la paynseeonay komplayta*

for Modified American Plan (M.A.P.) [half board] **per la mezza pensione** *pehr la mehdza paynseeonay*

Does the price include ...? **Il prezzo include ...?** *eel prehtso eengklooday*

breakfast **la colazione** *la kolatseeonay*

sales tax [VAT] **l'IVA (Imposta Valore Aggiunto)** *leeva (eemposta valoray adjoonto)*

Do I have to pay a deposit? **Devo pagare un anticipo?** *dayvo pagaaray oon anteecheepo*

Is there a reduction for children? **Ci sono sconti per i bambini?** *chee sono skontee pehr ee bambeenee*

Decisions Decisioni

May I see the room? **Posso vedere la camera?** *posso vaydayray la kamayra*

That's fine. I'll take it. **Va bene. La prendo.** *va baynay. la prayndo*

It's too ... **È troppo ...** *eh troppo*

dark/small **buia/piccola** *booeea/peekola*

noisy **rumorosa** *roomoroza*

Do you have anything ...? **Ha qualcosa di ...?** *ah kwalkoza dee*

bigger/cheaper **più grande/più economico** *peeoo granday/peeoo aykonomeeko*

quieter/warmer **più tranquillo/più caldo** *peeoo trankweello/peeoo kaldo*

No, I won't take it. **No, non la prendo.** *no non la prehndo*

Problems Problemi

The ... doesn't work. **... non funziona.** *non foontseeona*

air conditioning **L'aria condizionata** *laareea kondeetseeonaata*

fan **Il ventilatore** *eel vaynteelatoray*

heat **Il riscaldamento** *eel reeskaldamaynto*

light **La luce** *la loochay*

I can't turn the heat [heating] on/off. **Non posso accendere/spegnere il riscaldamento.** *non posso atchaynedehray/spayñehray eel reeskaldamaynto*

There is no hot water/toilet paper. **Non c'è acqua calda/carta igienica.** *non cheh akwa kalda/karta eejayneeka*

The faucet [tap] is dripping. **Il rubinetto perde.** *eel roobeenehto pehrday*

The sink/toilet is blocked. **Il lavello/gabinetto è bloccato.** *eel lavehllo/ga-bee-nay-to eh blokaato*

The window/door is jammed. **La finestra/porta è bloccata.** *la feenaystra/porta eh blokaata*

My room has not been made up. **La mia camera non è stata rifatta.** *la meea kamayra non eh staata reefatta*

The ... is broken. **... è rotto(-a).** *eh rotto(-a)*

blind **la tapparella** *la tapparehlla*

lock **la serratura** *la sehrratoora*

There are insects in our room. **Ci sono insetti nella nostra camera.** *chee sono eensehtee naylla nostra kamayra*

Action Azione

Could you have that taken care of? **Può farlo(-a) controllare?** *pwo farlo(-a) kontrollaaray*

I'd like to move to another room. **Vorrei cambiare camera.** *vorrehee kambeeaaray kamayra*

I'd like to speak to the manager. **Vorrei parlare con il direttore.** *vorrehee parlaaray kon eel deeraytoray*

Requirements Richieste

In the hotel In albergo

Where's the ...?	**Dov'è ...?** *doveh*
bar	**il bar** *eel baar*
restroom [toilet]	**la toeletta** *la toehlehta*
parking lot [car park]	**il parcheggio** *eel parkaydjo*
dining room	**la sala da pranzo** *la sala da prandzo*
elevator [lift]	**l'ascensore** *lashaynsoray*
shower	**la doccia** *la dotchaa*
swimming pool	**la piscina** *la peesheena*
tour operator's bulletin board	**la bacheca dell'agente di viaggio** *la bakayka dayllajayntay dee veeadjo*
Does the hotel have a garage?	**L'albergo ha un garage?** *lalbayrgo ah oon garazh*
What time is the front door locked?	**A che ora chiude la porta d'ingresso?** *ah kay ora keeooday la porta deegngrehsso*
What time is breakfast served?	**A che ora è servita la colazione?** *a kay ora eh sayrveeta la kolatseeonay*
Is there room service?	**C'è servizio camera?** *cheh sayrveetseeo kamayra*

SOLO PER RASOI	shavers only
USCITA D'EMERGENZA	emergency exit
PORTA ANTINCENDIO	fire door
NON DISTURBARE	do not disturb
FARE ... PER OTTENERE LA LINEA ESTERNA	dial ... for an outside line

Personal needs Richieste personali

The key to room ..., please.	**La chiave della camera ..., per piacere.** *la keeaavay daylla kamayra ... pehr peeaachayray*
I've lost my key.	**Ho perso la mia chiave.** *o pehrso la meeaa keeaavay*
I've locked myself out of my room.	**Mi sono chiuso(-a) fuori della camera.** *mee sono keeooso(-a) fworee daylla kamayra*
Could you wake me at ...?	**Può svegliarmi alle ...?** *pwo zvaylyaarmee allay*
I'd like breakfast in my room.	**Vorrei la colazione in camera.** *vorrehee la kolatseeonay een kamayra*
Can I leave this in the safe?	**Vorrei mettere questo in cassaforte.** *vorrehee mayttehray kwaysto een kassafortay*
Could I have my things from the safe?	**Vorrei ritirare le mie cose dalla cassaforte.** *vorrehee reeteeraaray lay meeay kosay daylla kassafortay*
Where is ...?	**Dov'è ...?** *doveh?*
a maid	**una cameriera** *oona kamareeehra*
a bellman [porter]	**un portiere** *oon porteeayray*
our tour representative	**il nostro rappresentante?** *eel nostro rappraysayntaantay*
May I have a(n)/some ...?	**Ha ...?** *ah*
bath towel	**un asciugamano** *oon ashoogamaano*
blanket	**una coperta** *oona kopehrta*
hangers	**grucce portabiti** *grootchay portabeetee*
pillow	**un cuscino** *oon koosheeno*
soap	**del sapone** *dayl saponay*
Is there any mail for me?	**C'è posta per me?** *cheh posta pehr meh*
Are there any messages for me?	**Ci sono messaggi per me?** *chee sono mayssadjee pehr meh*

BREAKFAST ➤ 43; CHANGING MONEY ➤ 138

Renting In affitto

We've reserved an apartment/cottage in the name of ...
Abbiamo prenotato un appartamento/una villa a nome di ... *abbeegmo praynotato oon oon appartamaynto/oona veella ah nomay dee*

Where do we pick up the keys?
Dove passiamo a prendere le chiavi? *dovay passeegmo a praynderay lay keeaavee*

Where is the ...?
Dov'è ...? *doveh*

electric meter
il contatore dell'elettricità *eel kontatoray dayll aylehttreecheeta*

fuse box
i fusibili *ee foozeebeelee*

stopcock
il rubinetto di arresto *eel roobeenehtto dee arraysto*

water heater
lo scaldaacqua *low skalda-akwa*

Are there any spare ...?
Ci sono ... di ricambio? *chee sono ... dee reekambeeo*

fuses
fusibili *foozeebeelee*

gas bottles
bombole di gas *bombolay dee gaz*

sheets
lenzuola *layntsoo-ola*

Which day does the maid come?
In che giorno viene la cameriera? *een kay jorno veeaynay la kamareeayra*

Where/When do I put out the trash?
Dove/Quando si mettono fuori i rifiuti? *dovay/kwando see mehttono fworee ee reefeeootee*

Problems? Problemi?

Where can I contact you?
Dove posso contattarla? *dovay posso kontattaarla*

How does the stove [cooker]/water heater work?
Come funziona la stufa/lo scaldaacqua? *komay foontseeona la stoofa/lo skalda-akwa*

The ... is dirty.
Il ... è sporco. *eel ... eh sporko*

The ... has broken down.
La ... non funziona. *la ... non foontseeona*

We accidentally broke/lost ...
Abbiamo accidentalmente rotto/perso ... *abbeegmo acheedayntalmayntay rotto/pehrso*

Useful terms Espressioni utili

dishes [crockery]	**le stoviglie** *lay stoveelyay*
freezer	**il congelatore** *eel konjaylatoray*
frying pan	**la padella** *la padehlla*
kettle	**il bollitore** *eel bolleetoray*
lamp	**la lampada** *la lampada*
refrigerator	**il frigorifero** *eel freegoreefayro*
saucepan	**la pentola** *la payntola*
stove [cooker] (gas/electric)	**la cucina a gas/elettrica** *la koocheena a gaz/aylehttreeka*
utensils [cutlery]	**le posate** *lay posatay*
washing machine	**la lavatrice** *la lavatreechay*
water heater	**lo scaldaacqua** *lo skalda-akwa*

Rooms Camere

balcony	**il balcone** *eel balkonay*
bathroom	**il bagno** *eel baaño*
bedroom	**la camera da letto** *la kamayra da lehtto*
dining room	**la sala da pranzo/il tinello** *la saala da prandzo/eel teenehllo*
kitchen	**la cucina** *la koocheena*
living room	**il soggiorno** *eel sodjorno*
bathroom [toilet]	**la toeletta/il gabinetto** *la toaylehtta/eel gabeenehtto*

Youth hostel L'ostello della gioventù

Do you have any places left for tonight?	**Avete posti liberi per questa notte?** *avaytay postee leebayree pehr kwaysta nottay*
Do you rent bedding?	**Noleggiate la biancheria da letto?** *nolehdjatay la beeankayreea da lehtto*
What time are the doors locked?	**A che ora chiudete?** *a kay ora keeoodaytay*

REQUIREMENTS ➤ 26; CAMPING ➤ 30

Camping Il campeggio

Reservations Prenotazioni

Is there a campsite near here?	**C'è un campeggio qui vicino?** *cheh oon kampaydjo kwee veecheeno*
Do you have space for a tent/trailer [caravan]?	**Avete un posto per una tenda/una roulotte?** *avaytay oon posto pehr oona tehnda/oona roolot*
What is the charge ...?	**Quanto costa ...?** *kwanto kosta*
per day/week	**al giorno/alla settimana** *al jorno/alla saytteemaana*
for a tent/a car	**per una tenda/un'auto(mobile)** *pehr oona tehnda/oonowto (oon owtomobeelay)*
for a trailer [caravan]	**per una roulotte** *pehr oona roolot*

Facilities Attrezzature

Are there cooking facilities on site?	**Ci sono attrezzature per cucinare?** *chee sono attraytsatooray pehr koocheenaaray*
Are there any electrical outlets [power points]?	**Ci sono delle prese di corrente?** *chee sono dayllay prayzay dee korrayntay*
Where is/are the ...?	**Dov'è/Dove sono ...?** *doveh/dovay sono*
drinking water	**l'acqua potabile** *lakwa potabeelay*
trash cans [dustbins]	**i cassettoni per i rifiuti** *ee kassayttonee pehr ee reefeeootee*
laundry facilities	**la lavanderia (sing.)** *la lavandayreea*
showers	**le docce** *lay dotchay*
Where can I get some butane gas?	**Dove si compra il campingaz?** *dovay see kompra eel campingaz*

CAMPEGGIO VIETATO	no camping
ACQUA POTABILE	drinking water
VIETATO ACCENDERE FUOCHI/ CUCINARE ALL'APERTO	no fires/barbeques

Complaints Reclami

It's too sunny. **È troppo esposto al sole.**
eh troppo aysposto al solay

It's too shady/crowded. **È troppo ombreggiato/affollato.**
eh troppo ombraydjaato/affollaato

The ground's too hard/uneven. **Il terreno è troppo duro/in dislivello.**
eel tayrrayno eh troppo dooro/een deesleevehllo

Do you have a more level spot? **C'è uno spazio su terreno più livellato?**
cheh oono spatseeo soo tayrrayno peeoo leevehllaato

You can't camp here. **Qui non può campeggiare.**
kwee non pwo kampaydjaaray

Camping equipment Attrezzatura per campeggio

air mattress **materasso di gomma**
eel matayrasso dee gomma

butane gas **il campingaz** *eel campingaz*

campbed **il lettino da campeggio**
eel lehtteeno da kampaydjo

charcoal **il carbone** *eel karbonay*

flashlight [torch] **la torcia** *la torcheea*

groundcloth [groundsheet] **il telone impermeabile**
eel taylonay eempehrmeeaabeelay

hammer **il martello** *eel martehllo*

kerosene [primus] stove **il fornello da campeggio**
eel fornayllo da kampaydjo

knapsack **lo zaino** *lo dzaaeeno*

mallet **il maglio** *eel malyo*

matches **i fiammiferi** *ee feeammeefayree*

sleeping bag **il sacco a pelo** *eel sakko a paylo*

tent **la tenda** *la taynda*

tent pegs **i picchetti** *ee peekkehttee*

tent pole **il palo della tenda** *eel palo daylla taynda*

Checking out Partenza

Customers are required by law to have a receipt (**ricevuta fiscale**) for any services or goods purchased in hotels, shops, and restaurants.

Tipping: a service charge is generally included in hotel and restaurant bills. However, if the service has been particularly good, you may want to leave an extra tip.

What time do we have to check out?	**A che ora dobbiamo lasciare libere le camere?** *a kay ora dobbeeaamo lashaaray leebayray lay kamayray*
Could we leave our baggage here until …	**Possiamo lasciare i nostri bagagli qui fino alle …?** *posseeaamo lashaaray ee nostree bagalyee kwee feeno allay …*
I'm leaving now.	**Parto ora.** *parto ora*
Could you call me a taxi, please?	**Può chiamarmi un tassì, per piacere?** *pwo keeamaarmee oon tassee pehr peeachayray*
It's been a very enjoyable stay.	**È stato un soggiorno molto piacevole.** *eh staato oon sodjorno molto peeachayvolay*

Paying Pagare

May I have my bill, please?	**Vorrei il conto, per favore.** *vorrehee eel konto pehr favoray*
I think there's a mistake on this bill.	**Penso che ci sia un errore in questo conto.** *paynso kay chee seea oon ayrroray een kwaysto konto*
I've made … telephone calls.	**Ho fatto … telefonate.** *oh fatto … taylayfonatay*
I've taken … from the minibar.	**Ho preso … dal minibar.** *oh prayzo … dal minibar*
Can I have an itemized bill?	**Vorrei un conto dettagliato, per favore.** *vorrehee oon konto dayttalyaato pehr favoray*

Bellman [Porter]	*Hotel maid (per week)*	*Waiter*
1,500 lire	1,000–2,000 lire	5–10%

TIME ➤ 220

Eating Out

Restaurants	33	Pizza/Soups	44
Italian cuisine	34	Pasta/Fish	45
Finding a place to eat	35	Meat	46
Reservations	36	Vegetables/Salads	47
Ordering	37	Cheese/Fruit	48
Fast food/Café	40	Dessert	48
Complaints	41	Drinks	49
Paying	42	Beer/Wine	49
Breakfast	43	Other drinks	51
Appetizers/Starters	43	Non-alcoholic drinks	51
		Menu Reader	52

Restaurants Ristoranti

Autogrill *owtogreel*
A large restaurant on an expressway [motorway]; usually table and cafeteria service available.

Bar *bar*
Bar; can be found on virtually every street corner; coffee and drinks served. In most of them you first have to get a ticket from the cashier. Then you go to the counter and order what you want.

Caffè *kaffeh*
Coffee shop; generally food isn't served there except for breakfast. If it offers **panini** (sandwiches) or toast you'll be able to get a snack. Coffee shops always serve alcoholic beverages.

Gelateria *jaylatayreea*
Ice cream parlor; Italian ice cream is very tasty, rich and creamy, often reminiscent of old-fashioned, homemade ice cream. Ice cream and pastries can also be bought and consumed in a **sala da tè.**

Locanda *lokanda*
Simple restaurant serving local dishes.

Osteria *ostayreea*
Inn; wine and simple food are served.

Paninoteca *paneenotayka*
A sort of coffee shop where you can find a great variety of sandwiches (**panini**) served hot or cold.

Ristorante *reestorantay*
You'll encounter restaurants classified by stars or forks and knives and endorsed by everyone including travel agencies, automobile associations and gastronomic guilds. Bear in mind that any form of classification is relative. Some restaurants are judged according to their fancy décor while others – linen and chandeliers aside – are rated merely by the quality of their cooking.

Trattoria *trattoreea*
A medium-priced restaurant serving meals and drinks. The food is simple but can be surprisingly good if you happen to hit upon the right place. A more modest type of **trattoria** is the **taverna.** Bear in mind that some very expensive restaurants may call themselves **Osteria, Trattoria** or **Taverna.**

Most restaurants display a menu in the window. Many offer a tourist menu (**menù turistico**), a fixed-price three- or four-course meal with limited choice, or the specialty of the day (**piatto del giorno**).
All restaurants, no matter how modest, must issue a formal bill (**la ricevuta fiscale**) with VAT, or sales tax (**I.V.A.**). A customer may actually be stopped outside the premises and fined if he or she cannot produce this receipt. The bill usually includes cover (**il coperto**) and service (**il servizio**) charges as well.

You may have difficulty finding a restaurant with a non-smoking area.

Meal times Orari dei pasti

la colazione *la kolatseeonay*
Breakfast is usually served at the hotel from 7 to 10 a.m. Hotels usually offer coffee or tea, bread, butter and jam. Italians usually have just a cappuccino and a brioche for breakfast.

il pranzo *eel prandzo*
Lunch is served from 12.30 to 2 p.m.

la cena *la chayna*
Dinner begins at 7 or 8 p.m., but hotels tend to open their dining rooms earlier for foreign tourists. The names of meals can be confusing. Lunch is sometimes called **colazione** and dinner **pranzo**, especially in towns. If you are invited out, make sure of the time, so you don't turn up at the wrong meal.

Italian cuisine Cucina italiana

Italian cuisine consists of a lot more than just pasta. You will be amazed at the rich variety available: tasty hors d'œuvres, long-simmered soups, traditional meat dishes, fresh fish and shellfish, high-quality poultry, an incredible number of cheeses, not to mention the magnificent cakes and ice cream.

Each of Italy's 18 regions has its own specialty, never lacking in flavor or originality, inspired by sun-drenched fruit and vegetables. Italian cooking is like the country itself: colorful, happy, generous, exuberant.

ESSENTIAL

A table for …	**Un tavolo per …** *oon tavolo pehr*
1/2/3/4	**uno(-a)/due/tre/quattro** *oono(-a)/doo-ay/tray/kwattro*
Thank you.	**Grazie.** *graatseeay*
The bill, please.	**Il conto, per piacere.** *eel konto pehr peeachayray*

Finding a place to eat Trovare un ristorante

Can you recommend a good restaurant?	**Può consigliare un buon ristorante?** *pwo konseelyaaray oon bwon reestorantay*
Is there a … near here?	**C'è … qui vicino?** *cheh … kwee veecheeno*
traditional local restaurant	**un ristorante con cucina tradizionale** *oon reestorantay kon koocheena tradeetseeonaalay*
Chinese/Greek restaurant	**un ristorante cinese/greco** *oon reestorantay cheenaysay/grayko*
inexpensive restaurant	**una trattoria** *oona trattoreea*
Turkish restaurant	**un ristorante turco** *oon reestorantay toorko*
vegetarian restaurant	**un ristorante vegetariano** *oon reestorantay vayjaytareeaano*
Where can I find …?	**Dove si trova …?** *dovay see trova*
burger stand	**un chiosco dove vendono hamburger** *oon keeosko dovay vayndono hamburger*
café	**un bar** *oon bar*
café with terrace/garden	**un bar con terrazza/giardino** *oon bar kon tayrratsa/jardeeno*
fast-food restaurant	**una tavola calda (un self-service)** *oona tavola kalda (oon self-service)*
ice cream parlor [parlour]	**una gelateria** *oona jaylatayreea*
pizzeria	**una pizzeria** *oona peettsayreea*
steak house	**ristorante specializzato in bistecche** *reestorantay spaychaleedzato een beestaykkay*

DIRECTIONS ➤ 94

Reservations Prenotare

I'd like to reserve a table for 2.
Vorrei prenotare un tavolo per due.
vorrehee praynotaaray oon tavolo pehr doo-ay

For this evening/tomorrow at ...
Per questa sera/domani alle ...
pehr kwaysta sayra/domanee allay

We'll come at 8:00.
Arriveremo alle venti.
arreevayraymo allay vayntee

A table for 2, please.
Un tavolo per due, per piacere. *oon tavolo pehr doo-ay pehr peeachayray*

We have a reservation.
Abbiamo una prenotazione.
abbeeamo oona praynotatseeonay

A che nome, prego?	What's the name, please?
Mi dispiace. Siamo al completo.	I'm sorry. We're very busy/full.
Avremo un tavolo libero fra ... minuti.	We'll have a free table in ... minutes.
Dovrà ritornare fra ... minuti.	You'll have to come back in ... minutes.

Where to sit Dove sedersi

Could we sit ...?
Vorremmo sederci...
vorrehmmo saydayrchee

over there
là *la*

in a non-smoking area
in una zona per non fumatori
een oona dzona pehr non foomatoree

by the window
vicino alla finestra
veecheeno alla feenaystra

– Vorrei prenotare un tavolo per questa sera.
(I'd like to reserve a table for this evening.)
– Per quante persone? (For how many people?)
– Per quattro. (For four.)
– A che ora arriva? (What time are you coming?)
– Arriveremo alle venti. (We'll come at 8 p.m.)
– E il nome, per favore? (And the name, please?)
– Evans. E-V-A-N-S. (Evans.)
– Bene. A questa sera. (Good. See you tonight.)

TIME ➤ 220; NUMBERS ➤ 216

Ordering Ordinare

Waiter!/Waitress!	**Cameriere!/Cameriera!** *kamayreeehray/-a*
May I see the wine list, please?	**Posso vedere la lista dei vini, per piacere?** *posso vedayray la leesta dehee veenee pehr peeachayray*
Do you have a set menu?	**Ha un menù fisso?** *ah oon maynoo feesso*
Can you recommend some typical local dishes?	**Può consigliare dei piatti tipici della regione?** *pwo konseelyaarmee dehee peeattee teepeechee daylla rayjonay*
Could you tell me what ... is?	**Cos'è ...?** *kozay*
I'd like ...	**Vorrei ...** *vorrehee*
a bottle/glass/carafe of ...	**una bottiglia/un bicchiere/una caraffa di ...** *oona botteelya/oon beekkeeehray/oona karaffa dee*

E' pronto(-a) per ordinare?	Are you ready to order?
Cosa prende/desidera?	What would you like?
Vuole ordinare prima le bibete?	Would you like to order drinks first?
Consiglio ...	I recommend ...
Non abbiamo ...	We haven't got ...
Ci vogliono ... minuti.	That will take ... minutes.
Buon appetito!	Enjoy your meal.

– E' pronto per ordinare? (Are you ready to order?)
– Può consigliare qualcosa di tipicamante italiano?
(Can you recommend some typical Italian dishes?)
– Sì, consiglio il saltimbocca alla romana.
(Yes, I recommend the "saltimbocca alla romana".)
– D'accordo. Prendo quello e insalata di contorno, per piacere. (Good. I'll have that, with a side order of salad, please.)
– Benissimo. E cosa vuole bere?
(Very good. And what would you like to drink?)
– Una caraffa di vino rosso, per favore.
(A carafe of red wine, please.)
– Certo. (Certainly.)

WHAT SORT OF ... ? ➤ 14; DRINKS ➤ 49

Side dishes Contorni

I prefer ... without the ...	**Preferisco ... senza ...** *prayfayreesko ... sayntsa*
With a side order of ...	**Con un contorno di ...** *kon oon kontorno dee*
Could I have salad instead of vegetables, please?	**Si può avere insalata al posto dei legumi?** *see pwo avayray eensalaata al posto dehee laygoomee*
Does the meal come with vegetables/potatoes?	**Il piatto include legumi/patate?** *eel peeatto eenklooday laygoomee/ patatay*
Do you have any sauces?	**Ha delle salse?** *ah dayllay salsay*
Would you like ... with your dish?	**Vuole ... con il Suo piatto?** *vwolay kon eel soo-o peeatto*
vegetables	**legumi/verdure** *laygoomee/vayrdooray*
mixed salad	**insalata mista** *eensalaata meesta*
potatoes/French fries [chips]	**patate/patatine fritte** *patatay/patateenay freettay*
sauce	**la salsa** *la salsa*
ice	**il ghiaccio** *eel geeatcho*
May I have some ...?	**Mi può dare ...?** *mee pwo daray*
bread	**del pane** *dayl panay*
butter	**del burro** *dayl boorro*
lemon	**del limone** *dayl leemonay*
mustard	**della senape** *daylla saynapay*
pepper	**del pepe** *dayl paypay*
salt	**del sale** *dayl salay*
seasoning (oil/vinegar)	**dei condimenti (olio/aceto)** *dehee kondeemayntee (olyo/achayto)*
sugar	**dello zucchero** *dayllo tsookkayro*
(artificial) sweetener	**dello zucchero dietetico** *dayllo tsookkayro deeaytayteeko*

General requests Richieste generali

Could you bring a(n) (clean) ..., please?	**Può portare ... (pulito), per piacere?** *pwo portaaray (pooleeto) pehr peeachayray*
ashtray	**un portacenere** *oon portachaynayray*
cup/glass	**una tazza/un bicchiere** *oona tattsa/oon beekkeeehray*
fork/knife	**una forchetta/un coltello** *oona forkehtta/oon koltehllo*
napkin	**un tovagliolo** *oon tovalyolo*
plate/spoon/little spoon	**un piatto/un cucchiaio/un cucchiaino** *oon peeatto/oon kookkeeageeo/oon kookkeeaeeno*
I'd like some more ..., please.	**Vorrei ancora un pò di ..., per piacere.** *vorrehee ankora oon poh dee ... pehr peeachayray*
Nothing more, thanks.	**Nient'altro, grazie.** *neeehntaltro gratseeay*
Where are the restrooms [toilets]?	**Dove sono le toelette?** *dovay sono lay toylayttay*

Special requirements Richieste particolari

I can't eat food containing ...	**Non devo mangiare piatti che contengono ...** *non dayvo manjaaray peeattee kay kontayngono*
salt/sugar	**sale/zucchero** *salay/tsookkayro*
Do you have meals/drinks for diabetics?	**Ha piatti/bevande per diabetici?** *ah peeattee/bayvanday pehr deeabayteechee*
Do you have vegetarian dishes?	**Ha piatti vegetariani?** *ah peeattee vayjaytareeanee*

For the children Per i bambini

Do you have children's portions?	**Fate porzioni per bambini?** *fatay portseeonee pehr bambeenee*
Could you bring a child's seat, please?	**Può portare una seggiola per bambini, per piacere?** *pwo portaaray oona saydjola pehr bambeenee pehr peeachayray*

Fast food / Café Bar/Tavola calda

Bars and cafés play an important part in Italian life; there is one on almost every corner. They are an ideal place to meet people, revive weary feet, write postcards, study maps, or just watch the world go by while sipping a cappuccino or beer. Bar staff are usually friendly and a great source of local information.

Something to drink Qualcosa da bere

I'd like ...	**Vorrei ...** *vorrehee*
a beer	**una birra** *oona beerra*
coffee	**un caffè/un espresso** *oon kaffeh/oon ehspraysso*
with milk	**lungo con latte** *loongo kon lattay*
tea	**un tè** *oon teh*
red/white wine	**del vino rosso/bianco** *dayl veeno rosso/beeanko*

And to eat ... E da mangiare ...

A piece/slice of ..., please.	**Un pezzo/una fetta di ... , per piacere** *oon pehtso/oona fehtta dee ... pehr peeachayray*
I'd like two of those.	**Vorrei due di quelli(e).** *vorrehee doo-ay dee kwehllee (ay)*
burger/French fries	**un hamburger/delle patatine fritte** *oon hamburger/dayllay patateenay freettay*
cake/sandwich	**una torta/un panino** *oona torta/ oon paneeno*
bun/pastry	**una pasta** *oona pasta*
an ice cream	**un gelato** *oon jaylaato*

Ice cream; flavors include: **alla vaniglia** or **alla crema** (vanilla), **al cioccolato** (chocolate), **alla fragola** (strawberry), **al limone** (lemon), **misto** (mixed).

a sandwich	**un panino imbottito** *oon paneeno eembotteeto*

Sandwich; you may want yours **al formaggio** (cheese), **al prosciutto cotto** (ham), **al prosciutto crudo** (Parma ham) or **al salame** (salami).

A ... portion, please.	**Una porzione ... , per piacere.** *oona portseeonay ... pehr peeachayray*
small/medium/large	**piccola/regolare/grande** *peekkola/raygolaaray/granday*

OTHER DRINKS ➤ 49–51

– Cosa prende? (What would you like?)
– Due caffè, per piacere.
(Two coffees, please.)
– Espresso? Cappuccino?
(Espresso? Cappuccino?)
– No, caffè lunghi con latte, per piacere.
(No, regular coffee with milk, please.)
– Nient'altro? (Anything else?)
– No, nient'altro, grazie. (No, that's all, thanks.)

Complaints Reclami

I have no knife/fork/spoon.	**Non ho il coltello/la forchetta/il cucchiaio.** *non oh eel koltayllo/la forkaytta/eel kookeegeeo*
There must be some mistake.	**Deve esserci un errore.** *dayvay ehssayrchee oon ehrroray*
That's not what I ordered.	**Non ho ordinato questo.** *non oh ordeenaato kwaysto*
I ordered ...	**Ho ordinato ...** *oh ordeenaato*
The meat is ...	**La carne è ...** *la karnay eh*
overdone	**troppo cotta** *troppo kotta*
underdone	**non abbastanza cotta** *non abbastantsa kotta*
too tough	**troppo dura** *troppo doora*
This is too ...	**Questo è troppo ...** *kwaysto eh troppo*
bitter/sour	**amaro/acido** *amaaro/acheedo*
This ... is cold.	**Questo ... è freddo.** *kwaysto ... eh frehddo*
This isn't fresh.	**Questo non è fresco.** *kwaysto non eh fraysko*
How much longer will our food be?	**Quanto dobbiamo aspettare ancora?** *kwanto dobbeeaamo aspayttaray ankora*
We can't wait any longer. We're leaving.	**Non possiamo più aspettare. Andiamo via.** *non posseeaamo peeoo aspehttaaray andeeaamo veea*
This isn't clean.	**Questo non é pulito.** *kwaysto non eh pooleeto*
I'd like to speak to the head waiter/manager.	**Vorrei parlare con il capocameriere/ il direttore.** *Vorrehee parlaaray kon eel kapokamayree-ehray/eel deeraytoray*

Paying Pagare

A service charge (**il servizio**) is generally included in restaurant bills, but if the service has been especially good, an extra tip (**la mancia**) is appropriate and appreciated: 5–10%. You may also find the following items added to your bill: **coperto** (cover charge), **supplemento** (surcharge).

The check [bill], please.	**Il conto, per piacere.** *eel konto pehr peeachayray*
We'd like to pay separately.	**Vorremmo pagare separatamente.** *vorrehmmo pagaaray sayparatamayntay*
It's all together, please.	**Un conto unico, per piacere.** *oon konto ooneeko pehr peeachayray*
I think there's a mistake on this check [bill].	**Penso ci sia un errore in questo conto.** *paynso chee seea oon ehrroray een kwaysto konto*
What is this amount for?	**Per cosa è questa cifra?** *pehr kosa eh kwaysta cheefra*
I didn't order that. I had …	**Non ho ordinato questo. Ho preso …** *non oh ordeenaato kwaysto. oh prayzo*
Is service included?	**È compreso il servizio?** *eh komprayzo eel sayrveetseeo*
I would like to pay with this credit card.	**Vorrei pagare con questa carta di credito.** *vorrehee pagaaray kon kwaysta karta dee kraydeeto*
I've forgotten my wallet.	**Ho dimenticato il portafoglio.** *oh deemaynteekaato eel portafolyo*
I haven't got enough cash.	**Non ho abbastanza contanti.** *non oh abbastantsa kontantee*
Could I have a receipt?	**Vorrei una ricevuta.** *vorrehee oona reechayvoota*

– Cameriere! Il conto, per piacere. (Waiter! The bill, please.)
– *Certamente. Ecco a Lei. (Certainly. Here you are.)*
– È compreso il servizio? (Is service included?)
– *Sì. (Yes.)*
– Vorrei pagare con questa carta di credito.
(I'd like to pay with this credit card.)
– *Naturalmente. (Certainly.)*
– Grazie. Che pranzo eccelente!
(Thank you. That was a very good meal.)

PAYING ➤ 32; NUMBERS ➤ 216

Course by course Portate

Breakfast Colazione

I'd like ...	**Desidero ...** *dayzeedayro*
bread	**del pane** *dayl paanay*
butter	**del burro** *dayl boorro*
eggs	**delle uova** *dayllay wova*
fried/scrambled	**fritte/strapazzate** *freettay/strapattsaatay*
fruit juice	**un succo di frutta** *oon sookko dee frootta*
grapefruit/orange	**un pompelmo/un'arancia** *oon pompaylmo/oon arancheea*
milk	**del latte** *dayl lattay*
jam	**della marmellata** *daylla marmayllaata*
marmalade	**della marmellata d'arance** *daylla marmayllaata daranchay*
honey	**del miele** *dayl mee-aylay*
rolls	**dei panini** *dehee paneenee*
toast	**del pane tostato** *dayl paanay tostaato*

Appetizers/Starters Antipasti

anchovies	**acciughe** *achoogay*
assorted appetizer	**antipasto assortito** *anteepasto assorteeto*
artichoke hearts in olive oil	**carciofini sottolio** *karchofeenee sottolyo*
cured pork shoulder	**coppa** *koppa*
Bologna sausage	**mortadella** *mortadehlla*
cured ham from Parma	**prosciutto crudo di Parma** *proshootto kroodo dee parma*
pickled vegetables	**sottaceti** *sottachaytee*

bagna cauda *baaña kaooda*
raw vegetables accompanied by a hot sauce made from anchovies, garlic, oil, butter and sometimes truffles (Northern Italy)

Pizza Pizza

Pizza (plural **pizze**) is one of Italy's best-known culinary exports. The variety of toppings is endless. A **calzone** has basically the same ingredients, but the pastry forms a sealed sandwich, with the filling inside.

ai funghi	*ai foonggee*	with mushrooms
capricciosa	*kapreetchosa*	the cook's specialty
siciliana	*seecheeleeaana*	with black olives, capers and cheese

margherita *margayreeta*
named after Italy's first queen, the pizza ingredients (tomato, cheese and basil) reflect the national colors

napoletana *napolaytaana*
the classic pizza with anchovies, ham, capers, tomatoes, cheese and oregano

quattro formaggi *kwattro formadjee*
pizza with four different types of cheese, usually including **gorgonzola** and **caciotta**

quattro stagioni *kwattro stajonee*
"four seasons", containing a variety of vegetables: tomatoes, artichokes, mushrooms, olives; plus cheese, ham and bacon

Soups Minestre, zuppe

An Italian meal always includes a **pastasciutta** or a soup; some of them are sufficient for a main course.

brodo di manzo	*brodo dee manzo*	beef broth
busecca	*boozaykka*	thick tripe, vegetable and bean soup
cacciucco	*kachookko*	spicy seafood chowder/stew
crema di legumi	*krehma dee laygoomee*	vegetable cream soup
minestrone	*meenehstronay*	vegetable soup (sometimes with noodles) sprinkled with parmesan cheese
passato di verdura	*passaato dee vehrdoora*	mashed vegetable soup, generally with croutons
zuppa alla pavese	*tsooppa alla pavayzay*	consommé with poached egg, croutons and grated cheese
zuppa di vongole	*tsooppa dee vonggolay*	clams and white wine soup

Pasta Pasta

Pasta (or **pastasciutta**) constitutes the traditional Italian first course. In addition to the well-known **spaghetti**, pasta comes in a bewildering variety of sizes and shapes– **penne** (quills), **tagliatelle** (flat noodles), and the following examples:

cannelloni *kanaylonee*
tubular dough stuffed with meat, cheese or vegetables, covered with a white sauce and baked

cappelletti *kapaylayttee*
small ravioli filled with meat, herbs, ham, cheese and eggs

fettuccine *faytoocheenay*
narrow flat noodles

lasagne *lazaañay*
thin layers of white or green (**lasagne verdi**) dough alternating with tomato sauce and sausage meat, white sauce and grated cheese; baked in the oven

tortellini *tortehlleenee*
rings of dough filled with seasoned ground meat and served in broth or with a sauce

Fish and seafood Pesci e frutti di mare

acciughe	*atchoogay*	anchovies
anguilla	*anggooella*	eel
bianchetti	*beeangkayttee*	herring/whitebait
gamberi	*gambayree*	prawns
granchi	*grangkee*	crabs
merluzzo	*mayrloottso*	cod
orata	*oraata*	type of sea bream
polipo	*poleepo*	octopus
sogliola	*solyola*	sole

Fish specialties Specialità di pesce

anguilla alla veneziana *anggooella alla vaynaytseeaana*
eel cooked in sauce made from tuna and lemon

fritto misto *freetto meesto*
fry of small fish and shellfish

lumache alle milanese *loomaakay allay meelanaysay*
snails with anchovy, fennel and wine sauce

stoccafisso *stokkafeesso*
dried cod cooked with tomatoes, olives and artichoke

Meat Carne

Among small fowl considered gourmet dishes in Italy are lark (**allodola**), thrush (**tordo**) and ortolan (**ortolano**). They are usually grilled or roasted.

Vorrei ...	*vorrehee*	I'd like some ...
della pancetta	*daylla panchehtta*	bacon
del manzo	*dayl mandzo*	beef
del pollo	*dayl pollo*	chicken
dell'anatra	*dayllaanatra*	duck
dell'oca	*daylloka*	goose
del prosciutto	*dayl proshootto*	ham
dell'agnello	*dayllañehllo*	lamb
del maiale	*dayl maeeaalay*	pork
della salsicce	*daylla salseetchay*	sausages
della bistecca	*daylla beestaykka*	steak
del vitello	*dayl veetehllo*	veal

Meat dishes Piatti di carne

bistecca alla fiorentina *beestaykka alla feeoraynteena*
grilled steak flavored with pepper, lemon juice and parsley

cima alla genovese *cheema alla jaynovaysay*
rolled veal stuffed with eggs, sausage and mushrooms

cotoletta alla milanese *kostolaytta alla meelanaysay*
breaded veal cutlet, flavored with cheese

fegato alla veneziana *faygato alla vaynaytseeaana*
thin slices of calf's liver fried with onions

filetto al pepe verde *feelaytto al paypay vehrday*
filet steak in a creamy sauce with green peppercorns

galletto amburghese *gallaytto amboorgaysay*
young tender chicken, oven-roasted

involtini *eenvolteenee*
thin slices of meat rolled and stuffed

polenta e coniglio *polehnta ay koneelyo*
rabbit stew with cornmeal mush

pollo alla romana *pollo alla romaana*
diced chicken with tomato sauce and sweet peppers

saltimbocca alla romana *salteembokah alla romaana*
veal escalope braised in marsala wine with ham and sage

Vegetables/Salads Verdure/Insalate

You'll recognize: **asparagi**, **broccoli**, **carote**, **patate**, **spinaci**, **zucchini**.

cavolo	*kaavolo*	cabbage
cipolle	*cheepollay*	onions
funghi	*foonggee*	mushrooms
insalata mista	*eensalaata meesta*	mixed salad
lattuga	*lattooga*	lettuce
piselli	*peesehllee*	peas
pomodoro	*pomodoro*	tomatoes
radicchio	*radeekeeo*	bitter red and white lettuce
verdura mista	*vehrdoora meesta*	mixed vegetables

carciofi alla giudea *karchofee alla jeeoodeea*
a delicious, crispy, deep-fried artichoke, originally a specialty of the old Jewish quarter in the heart of Rome

carciofi alla romana *karchofee alla romaana*
whole lightly stewed artichokes stuffed with garlic, salt, olive oil, wild mint (**mentuccia**) and parsley

fagioli alla toscana *fajolee alla toskana*
Tuscan-style beans, simmered for hours and seasoned with salt, black pepper and crude olive oil

fagioli in umido *fajolee een oomeedo*
all types of haricot beans cooked in tomato sauce and spices

funghi porcini arrosti *foonggee arrosto*
boletus mushrooms roasted or grilled with garlic, parsley and chili peppers

peperoni ripieni *paypayronee reepeeaynee*
stuffed sweet peppers (usually containing ground meat); similarly, zucchini is also served this way (**zucchini ripieni**)

Sauces Salse

Italian cooks are masters at making the sauces that make spaghetti and macaroni taste so delicious.

al burro	*al boorro*	butter, grated parmesan
bolognese	*boloñayzay*	tomatoes, ground meat, onions, herbs
carbonara	*karbonaara*	smoked ham, cheese, eggs, olive oil
pesto	*paysto*	basil leaves, garlic, cheese
pommarola	*pommarola*	tomatoes, garlic, basil

Cheese Formaggio

Bel Paese	smooth cheese with delicate taste
caciotta	firm, usually mild cheese; some sharper varieties can be found
caciocavallo	firm, slightly sweet cheese from cow's or sheep's milk
gorgonzola	most famous of the Italian blue-veined cheese, rich with a tangy flavor
grana	a grained cheese similar to parmesan originating from Padova usually grated on pasta dishes
mascarpone	a thick, full-fat creamy cheese mostly used for desserts; similar to clotted cream
mozzarella	soft, unripened cheese with a bland, slightly sweet flavor, made from buffalo's milk in southern Italy, elsewhere with cow's milk
parmigiano (-reggiano)	parmesan (also called **grana**), a hard cheese generally grated for use in hot dishes and pasta but also eaten alone
pecorino	a hard cheese with a strong flavor made from sheep's milk usually grated on certain pasta dishes such as **Pasta all'amatriciana** and **Trippa alla romana**
provolone	a firm, tasty cheese
ricotta	soft cow's or sheep's milk cheese

Fruit Frutta

You'll recognize: **banana**, **datteri**, **limone**, **melone**, **pera**.

ciliege	*cheelee-ehjay*	cherries
uva	*oova*	grapes
bianca/nera	*beeanka/nayra*	white/black
arancia	*arancha*	orange
pesca	*pehska*	peach
prugna	*prooña*	plum
lamponi	*lamponee*	raspberries
fragole	*fraagolay*	strawberries
anguria	*angoorreea*	watermelon (northern Italy)
cocomero	*kokomayro*	watermelon (Rome & southern Italy)

Dessert Dolce

cassata siciliana *kassaata seecheeleeaana*
sponge cake garnished with sweet cream cheese, chocolate and candied fruit

tiramisù *teerameesoo*
mascarpone, eggs and lady fingers

Drinks Bevande

Aperitifs Aperitivi

Often bittersweet, some aperitifs have a wine and brandy base with herbs and bitters, while others may have a vegetable base.

Americano *amayreekaano*: vermouth with bitters, brandy and lemon peel
Aperol *apayrol:* a non-alcoholic bitters
bitter analcolico *beettehr analkoleeko:* a non-alcoholic aperitif
Campari *kampaaree:* reddish-brown bitters with orange peel and herbs
Campari soda *kampaaree soda:* Campari diluted with soda
Cynar *cheenaar:* produced from artichoke
Gingerino *jeenjehreeno*: ginger-flavored aperitif
Martini *marhteenee*: brand-name vermouth, sweet or dry

neat/straight	**liscio** *leesho*
on the rocks	**con ghiaccio** *kon geeacho*
with (seltzer or soda) water	**con acqua (di seltz)** *kon akwa (dee sehltz)*

Beer Birra

Do you have ... beer?	**Avete della birra ...?** *avayta daylla beerra*
bottled/draft/draught	**in bottiglia/alla spina** *een botteelya/alla speena*

Wine Vino

Italy is one of the most important wine producers in Europe, with vineyards found all over the Italian peninsula and islands. Some of the country's best come from northwestern Italy (like *Barbaresco*, *Barbera* and *Barolo*). Italy's best-known wine abroad is Chianti, particularly **classico** and **riserva** (superior quality); the best is produced between Florence and Siena.

More sophisticated restaurants have wine lists, while others list their wines in a corner of the menu or have them marked up on the wall. Good quality bottled wine from the various regions is now easily available all over Italy in restaurants and specialized wine shops (*enoteche*).

Don't expect a trattoria to offer more than a few types of wine. In smaller places you may find **vino sfuso** (unbottled wine usually served as house wine) at a moderate price, served in one-quarter, one-half or one-liter carafes.

I'd like a bottle of white/red wine.	**Vorrei una bottiglia di vino bianco/rosso.** *vorrehee oona botteelya dee veeno beeanko/rosso*
I'd like the house wine, please.	**Desidero il vino della casa, per favore.** *dayzeedayro eel veeno dayllya kassa pehr favoray*

There is no standard labeling of Italian wines, which may be named by place (e.g. *Chianti, Orvieto, Frascati, Asti*), descriptive term (e.g. **classico**, **dolce**, **liquoroso**, **riserva**, **superiore**), grape (e.g. **Barbera**, **Dolcetto**, **Moscato**, **Pinot nero**), proprietary name or a combination of these elements. However, the table below will help you with some important terms.

Reading the Label

abboccato semi-dry
amabile slightly sweet
bianco white
DOC guarantee of origin (240 regions)
DOCG highest quality wine complying with most stringent regulations (13 wines)
dolce sweet
IGT higher quality than "**vino tipico**"
imbottigliato dal produttore all'origine bottled by producers at source
leggero light
pieno full-bodied
rosato/rosatello rosé
rosso red
secco dry
spumante sparkling
vino del paese local wine

Type of wine	*Examples*
sweet white wine	**Aleatico, Vino Santo (Tuscany); Marsala and Malvasia (Sicily), Moscato, Passito di Pantelleria**
dry white wine	**Frascati (Latium), Verdicchio dei Castelli di Jesi (Adriatic Marches), Orvieto (Umbria), Vermentino (Sardinia), Corvo bianco, Colombo Platino (Sicily); Cortese di Gavi (Liguria) Gavi dei Gavi (Piedmont) Chardonnay, Pino bianco, Pino grigio (Friuli); local white wine generally falls into this category**
rosé	**Lagrein (Trentino-Alto Adige)**
light-bodied red wine	**Bardolino, Valpolicella (Lake Garda); Vino Novello (in the Autumn, mostly from Tuscany); local red wine, including Italian-Swiss Merlot, usually fits into this category**
full-bodied red wine	**Barolo, Barbera, Barbaresco, Dolcetto, Gattinara, Nebbiolo (Piedmont); Amarone (Veneto); Brunello di Montalcino (one of the most famous wines in Italy), Chianti Classico, Vino Nobile di Montepulciano (Tuscany); Corvo Rosso (Sicily).**
sparkling sweet white wine	**Asti Spumante**
sparkling dry white wine	**Prosecco, Ferrari Brut Spumante; metodo champenoise in general**
sparkling sweet red wine	**Braghetto d'Acqui (Piedmont); Fragolino (made from "uva fragola" with a distinct strawberry flavour, Veneto region)**

Other drinks Altre bevande

You'll certainly want to take the opportunity to sip an after-dinner drink. If you'd like something that approaches French cognac try **Vecchia Romagna etichetta nera** or **Carpene Malvolta Stravecchio**.

If you feel like an after-dinner drink (**un digestivo**), why not try the following:

amaro *amaaro*
Bitter; three of the most popular being *Amaro Averna*, *Amaro Lucano* or *Amaro Montenegro* (bittersweet), or a glass of *Fernet-Branca* (very bitter) should fit the bill.

liquore *leekworay*
Popular liqueurs include *Strega* (sweet herb), *Sambuca* (aniseed-flavored), *Amaretto* (almond), *Millefiore* (herb and alpine flower), *Silvestro* (herb and nut).

You'll recognize: **un brandy**, **un cognac**, **un gin e tonico**, **un porto**, **un rum**, **una vodka**.

Non-alcoholic drinks Bevande analcoliche

I'd like ...	**Vorrei ...** *vorrehee*
hot chocolate	**una cioccolata calda** *oona chokkolaata kalda*
lemonade	**una limonata** *oona leemonaata*
milk shake	**un frullato di latte** *oon froollaato dee lattay*
mineral water	**dell'acqua minerale** *dayllakwa meenayraalay*
carbonated/non-carbonated	**gassata/naturale** *gassaata/natooraalay*
tonic water	**dell'acqua tonica** *dayllakwa toneeka*

un caffè *oon kaffeh*
Any coffee drinker will be spoiled in Italy; try un (**caffè**) **espresso**, strong and dark with a rich aroma, served in demi-tasses, or **un ristretto** (concentrated espresso); alternatively, ask for **un caffè lungo** (weaker coffee), which can be **con panna** (with cream), or **con latte** (with milk). **Un cappuccino** (coffee and hot milk, dusted with cocoa) is also a must; while in summer, **un caffè freddo** (iced coffee) is popular.

un succo di frutta *oon sookko dee frootta*
Common fruit juices include: **un succo di limone** (lemon), **di pompelmo** (grapefruit), **di pomodoro** (tomato) and **d'arancia** (orange); for a freshly squeezed fruit juice ask for **una spremuta**.

Menu Reader

Italian cooking is essentially regional. Although there are many well-known dishes that are common to the whole of Italy, the terminology may vary from place to place. (There are at least half a dozen names for octopus or squid!) So, be prepared for regional variations to the terms appearing in this Menu Reader.

How it is cooked

baked	**al forno**	*al forno*
breaded	**impanato(-a)**	*eempanaato(-a)*
boiled	**bollito(-a)**	*bolleeto(-a)*
braised	**stufato(-a)**	*stoofaato(-a)*
diced	**tagliato(-a) a cubetti**	*talyaato(-a) a koobayttee*
fried	**fritto(-a)**	*freetto(-a)*
grilled	**alla griglia**	*alla greelya*
roasted	**arrosto(-a)**	*arrosto(-a)*
poached	**in camicia**	*een kameecha*
marinated	**marinato(-a)**	*mareenaato(-a)*
sautéed	**saltato(-a)**	*saltaato(-a)*
smoked	**affumicato(-a)**	*affoomeekaato(-a)*
spicy	**speziato(-a)/piccante**	*spaytsaato(-a)/peekkantay*
steamed	**al vapore**	*al vaporay*
stewed	**in umido**	*een oomeedo*
stuffed	**ripieno(-a)**	*reepeeayno(-a)*
creamed	**in purè**	*een pooreh*

very rare	**quasi crudo(-a)**	*kwasee kroodo(-a)*
rare/underdone	**al sangue**	*al sanway*
medium	**a puntino**	*a poonteeno*
well-done	**ben cotto(-a)**	*behn kotto (a)*

A

a puntino medium
a scelta choice
abbacchio roast lamb; **~ al forno con patate** with potatoes; **~ alla cacciatora** "hunting style": diced and cooked with white wine, garlic, rosemary, anchovy paste and hot peppers
abbacchio alla scottadita tender grilled lamb cutlets
(all')abruzzese Abruzzi style; with red peppers and sometimes ham
acciughe anchovies
aceto vinegar
acetosella sorrel
acqua water; **~ calda** hot water; **~ minerale** mineral water; **~ tonica** tonic water

acquacotta soup of bread and vegetables, sometimes with egg and cheese
affettati cold cuts; **~ misti** mixed cuts of pork
affogato poached
affumicato smoked
aglio garlic; **~ olio, peperoncino** sauce of garlic, olive oil, sweet peppers, anchovies and parmesan
agnello lamb; **~ abbacchio** very young lamb
agnolotti round-filled pasta
(all')agro dressing of lemon juice and oil
agrodolce sweet-sour dressing of caramelized sugar, vinegar and flour
aguglie garfish
ai ferri grilled
ai funghi (pizza) with mushrooms
ai funghi porcini sauce of boletus mushrooms
al burro with butter and grated parmesan
al forno baked
al sangue rare/underdone
al sugo with tomato sauce and grated parmesan
al tartufo sauce of grated truffle
al, all', alla in the style of; with
ala wing
albicocca apricot
alfredo dairy sauce
alice anchovy
alici al limone baked anchovies with lemon juice
all'Amatriciana with bacon (**pancetta**), tomatoes and hot pepper
alla boscaiola with eggplant, mushrooms and tomato sauce
alla carrettiera "cart driver style"; with hot peppers and pork
alla graticola barbequed
alla griglia grilled
alla milanese with marrow, white wine, saffron and parmesan (risotto)
alla Norma with spices and tomato sauce *(Sicily)*
alla pescatora with tomatoes and seafood
alla rustica with garlic, anchovies and oregano
alla spina draft/draught (beer)
alle vongole sauce of clams, garlic, parsley, pepper, olive oil, sometimes tomatoes
allo spiedo broiled; spit-roasted
allodola lark
alloro bay leaf
amaro after-dinner drink/digestive ➤ 51
amatriciana sauce of tomatoes, red peppers, bacon, onions, garlic and white wine (Latium)
Americano a vermouth ➤ 49
ananas pineapple
anelli small egg-pasta rings
anguilla eel; **~ alla veneziana** cooked in sauce made from tuna and lemon
anguria watermelon (*northern Italy*)
animelle di vitello calf's sweetbreads fried in butter and Marsala
anitra duck; **~ selvatica** wild duck
annegati slices of meat in white wine or Marsala
antipasti appetizers, hors d'oeuvres ➤ 43; **~ a scelta** of one's choice; **~ assortiti** assorted; **~ di mare** seafood

aperitivi aperitifs ➤ 49
Aperol a non-alcoholic bitters
arachidi peanuts
aragosta lobster
arancia orange
aranciata orangeade
arancini very popular and tasty Italian rice snack specialties
aringa herring
arista loin of pork; **~ alla fiorentina** roast with garlic, cloves and rosemary
arrosto roast(ed)
arselle scallops
asparagi asparagus; **~ alla Fiorentina** with fried eggs and cheese
assortito assorted
astice lobster
attesa: 15 minuti waiting time: 15 minutes

B

baccalà dried salt cod; **~ alla romana** cooked with tomato sauce, garlic and parsley; **~ alla vicentina** cooked in milk
bagna cauda raw vegetables with a hot sauce (*northern Italy*)
barbabietola beet
basilico basil
bavette type of spaghetti
beccaccia woodcock
beccaccino snipe
Bel Paese smooth cheese with delicate taste
ben cotto well-done
ben fritto deep-fried
bevande drinks ➤ 49; **~ analcoliche** non-alcoholic drinks
bianchetti herring/whitebait
bianco white (wine)
bibita soft drink
bicchiere glass
bieta swiss chard
bionda light (beer)
birra beer; **~ rossa** stout (dark beer)
biscotti cookies/biscuits
bistecca steak; **~ di cinghiale** wild boar in a sweet-sour sauce; **~ alla fiorentina** grilled and flavored with pepper, lemon juice and parsley; **~ di filetto** rib steak
bitter analcolico a non-alcoholic aperitif
bollito boiled
bollito misto sausages with other boiled meats
bologna smooth, mild, slightly smoked sausage, usually of pork or beef, occasionally of veal or chicken
bolognese sauce of tomatoes, ground meat, onions and herbs
bottiglia bottle
braciola chop or cutlet
branzino (sea) bass
brasato braised
briciolata olive oil, black pepper and crisp breadcrumb sauce
broccoli broccoli; **~ al burro e formaggio** with butter and cheese; **~ alla romana** sauteed in olice oil and braised in wine
brodo bouillon, broth, soup
bruidda fish soup
bucatini thick spaghetti; **~ con le sarde alla Palermitana** with fresh sardines
budino pudding; **~ di ricotta** souffle with ricotta cheese and candied fruits
burrida fish stew with dogfish and skate (*Sardinia*)

burro butter; **~ e salvia** butter and sage sauce
busecca thick tripe, vegetable and bean soup

C

cacciagione game
cacciucco spicy seafood chowder/stew
cachi persimmon
caciocavallo firm, slightly sweet cheese ➤ 48
caciotta firm, mild cheese ➤ 48
caffè coffee ➤ 51
caffè freddo iced coffee
calamaretti baby squid
calamari squid
caldo hot
camoscio chamois
Campari reddish-brown bitters, flavored with orange peel and herbs; has a quinine taste; **~ soda** *campari* diluted with soda, one of the most common Italian apertifis
canederli bread, ham and salami dumplings
cannariculi fried honey biscuits
cannella cinnamon
cannelloni stuffed tubular pasta baked with a white sauce ➤ 45; **~ alla partenopea** with ricotta, mozzarella and ham
cannoli sweetened ricotta cheese stuffed in deep-fried pastry shells
canoe di mele canoe-shaped pastry boats with rum pastry cream and glazed apples
canoe salate savory canoes
capellini type of spaghetti
caponata olives, eggplants and anchovies *(Sicily)*
capone apparecchiate mahi mahi fish fried with tomatoes, capers, olives *(Sicily)*
cappelletti "little hats" filled pasta ➤ 45; **~ di Romagna** with cheese
capperi capers
cappone capon
capretto kid goat; **~ ripieno al forno** stuffed with herbs and oven-roasted
capricciosa the cook's specialty (pizza)
capriolo roebuck
carbonara sauce of smoked ham, cheese, eggs and olive oil
carciofi artichokes; **~ alla giudea** deep-fried ➤ 47; **~ alla romana** lightly stewed and stuffed
carciofini sottolio artichoke hearts in olive oil
carne meat ➤ 46; **~ ai ferri** grilled
carota carrot; **~ rossa** beet
carpa carp
carrettiera sauce of tuna, mushrooms, tomato purée, freshly ground pepper
cassata ice cream with candied fruit (spumoni); **~ siciliana** garnished sponge cake ➤ 48
castagna chestnut
castagnaccio chestnut cake with sultanas and pine nuts *(Tuscany)*
caviale caviar
cavolfiore cauliflower; **~ stracciato** boiled and fried in olive oil and garlic
cavolini di Bruxelles Brussels sprouts
cavolo cabbage
ceci chickpeas
cedro citron
cereali cereal
cervello brains
cervo deer

cetriolini pickles/gherkins
cetriolo cucumber
chiodi di garofano cloves
cicoria chicory
ciliege cherries
cima alla genovese rolled veal stuffed with eggs, sausage and mushrooms
cima genovese cold veal stuffed with onions, herbs and calf's brains
cinghiale wild boar
cioccolata (calda) (hot) chocolate
cipolle onions
cipollina spring onion
clementino seedless mandarin orange
cocomero watermelon (*Rome, southern Italy*)
colazione breakfast ➤ 43
con with
con acqua (di seltz) with (seltzer or soda) water
con briciolata with toasted breadcrumbs
con funghi with mushrooms
con ghiaccio on the rocks (with ice)
con il sugo di melanze e peperoni with peppers and eggplant
con latte with milk
con le lumache with snails and parsley
con limone with lemon
con panna with cream
con polpettine with tiny meatballs
con porchetta with tasty cold pork (sandwich)
con salsa di noci with walnut sauce
conchiglie conch shell-shaped pasta
coniglio rabbit; **~ ai capperi** cooked with capers
contorno a scelta choice of vegetables
coppa cured pork shoulder
cosciotto leg
costata al prosciutto filled chop
costola rib
costolette di maiale al finocchio braised pork chops with white wine and fennel seed
cotechino con lenticchie sausage-like spicy pork mix
cotogna quince
cotoletta cutlet; **~ alla milanese** breaded veal cutlet, flavored with cheese
cotto cooked; **~ a vapore** steamed
cozze mussels
crema custard; **~ di legumi** vegetable cream soup; **~ di pomodori** tomato cream soup
crespelle di farina dolce chestnut-flour crepes with ricotta and rum
crostacei shellfish
crostata pie; **~ di mele** apple pie; **~ di ricotta** cheesecake with raisins and Marsala
crudo di Parma cured ham from Parma
cumino cumin
cuscus couscous
Cynar aperitif produced from artichoke

D

d', di of, with
datteri dates
decaffeinato decaffeinated
dentice type of sea bream
digestivo after-dinner drink/digestive
ditali pasta thimbles
dolce cake; dessert ➤ 48; mild (cheese); sweet (wine)
doppio double (a double shot)

E

elicoidali short, twisted pasta tubes
eperlano smelt

F

fagiano pheasant; **~ al tartufo** stuffed with truffles
fagioli (haricot) beans; **~ all'uccelletto** cooked in tomatoes and black olives; **~ in umido** cooked in tomato sauce
fagioli alla toscana Tuscan-style beans, simmered for hours and garnished with salt, black pepper and crude olive oil
fagiolini French (green) beans
faraona guinea fowl
farcito stuffed
farfalle butterfly-shaped pasta
farfallini small bow-shaped egg-pasta
favata beans and port stew *(Sardinia)*
fave broad beans
fazzoletti salati savory turnovers
fegato liver; **~ alla veneziana** thin slices fried with onions; **~ alla salvia** with tomatoes, garlic and sage
fesa round cut from the rump
fetta di pizza slice of pizza
fettuccine egg-pasta ribbons ➤ 45; **~ Alfredo** with parmesan and cream
fico fig
filetto fillet; **~ al pepe verde** fillet steak served in a creamy sauce with green peppercorns
finocchio fennel
focaccia savory flatbread; **~ alla salvia** sage bread; **~ alla salsiccia** sausage bread; **~ alle noci** walnut bread; **~ genovese** savory bread with sage and olive oil
focaccia al Gorgonzola warm yeast flatbread topped with cheese
fonduta hot dip of Fontina cheese, egg yolks and truffles
formaggio cheese ➤ 48
fragole strawberries
fragoline di bosco wild strawberries
freddo cold
frittata omelet; **~ campagnola** with onion, grated cheese, milk and cream; **~ primaverile** with vegetables
fritte al buro nero brains with black butter
fritte alla fiorentina marinated, breadcrumbed, fried brains served with spinach
fritto fried
fritto misto a fry of various small fish and shellfish
frullato di latte milk-shake
frustenga cornmeal fruit cake
frutta fruit ➤ 48
frutti di mare seafood
funghi mushrooms; **~ alla parmigiani** stuffed with breadcrumbs, Parmesan, garlic, herbs; **~ porcini arrosti** roasted or grilled with chili peppers
fusilli pasta twists

G

galletto amburghese young tender chicken, oven-roasted
gallina stewing fowl
gallo cedrone grouse
gamberetti shrimps
gamberi prawns
gassata carbonated/fizzy (water)
gelato ice cream

gianduia cold chocolate pudding
gin e tonico gin and tonic
gingerino ginger-flavored aperitif (also sold in small bottles)
gnocchi alla genovese dumplings with pesto sauce
gnocchi di patate potato dumplings
gorgonzola blue-veined cheese ➤ 48
granchi crabs
granita coarse sorbet ice cream
gronghi conger eel

I

i nostri piatti di carne sono serviti con contorno our meat dishes are accompanied by vegetables
in bianco without tomato sauce
in bottiglia bottled (beer)
in casseruola in casserole
in umido stewed
indivia endive
insalata salad
insalata di frutti di mare prawns and squid with lemon, pickles and olives
insalata di pollo chicken salad with green salad, lemon and cream
insalata mista mixed salad
insalata russa diced boiled vegetables in mayonnaise
involtini thin slices of meat (beef, veal or pork) rolled and stuffed

L

lamponi raspberries
lamprede lampreys
lasagne thin layers of pasta lined with meat and tomato sauce with Bel Paese and Mozzarella cheeses ➤ 45; **~ al forno** oven baked lasagna; **~ con anitra** with duck; **~ con le verdure** vegetable lasagna
lasagnette del lucchese lasagna with sauce of spinach, ricotta, chicken livers
lattaiolo cinnamon custard
latte milk
lattuga lettuce
lauro bay
leggero light (wine)
lenticchie lentils
lepre hare; **~ in agrodolce** with pine kernels, sultanas and chocolate; **~ piemontese** cooked in Barbera wine, sprinkled with herbs and bitter chocolate
lesso boiled
limonata lemonade
limone lemon
lingua tongue
linguine type of thick spaghetti
liquore liqueur ➤ 51
liscio straight/neat
lo chef consiglia the chef recommends ...
lombata/lombo loin
lombo di maiale al forno garlic-roasted pork loin
lombo di maiale al prosciutto grilled pork loin with prosciutto
luccio pike
luganeghe fresh pork sausages sold by the length
lumache snails; snail shell-shaped pasta
lumache alle milanese snails with anchovy, fennel and wine sauce
lumache di mare sea snails
lunette half-moon-shaped stuffed pasta

M **maccheroni alla chitarra** handmade pasta cut into strips
macchiato with milk
maggiorana marjoram
maiale pork
malfade thin pasta strips
mandarino tangerine
mandorle almonds
manzo beef
margherita tomato, cheese and basil pizza ➤ 44
marinara sauce of tomatoes, olives, garlic, clams and mussels
marinato marinated
marmellata jam; **~ d'arance** marmalade
mascarpone a thick, full-fat creamy cheese mostly used for desserts, similar to clotted cream
Martini a brand-name vermouth, sweet or dry; not to be confused with a martini cocktail
medaglioni round fillet
mela apple
melanzane eggplant/aubergine
mele apples
melone melon
menta mint
menù a prezzo fisso set menu
merlano whiting
merluzzo cod
metà pollo arrosto half a roasted chicken
midollo marrow
miele honey
minestra soup ➤ 44; **~ di funghi** cream of mushroom soup; **~ di sedano e riso** celery and rice; **~ in brodo** with noodles or rice
minestrone a thick vegetable soup (sometimes with noodles) sprinkled with parmesan cheese
mirtilli blueberries
misto mixed
molle soft (egg)
montone mutton
more blackberries
mortadella Bologna sausage
mostaccioli chocolate biscuits
mozzarella soft, unripened cheese ➤ 48; **~ con pomodori** with tomatoes

N **napoletana** anchovies, ham, tomatoes, cheese (pizza topping) ➤ 44
nasello coal-fish
naturale still (water)
nero black (coffee)
nocciole hazelnuts
noce di cocco coconut
noce moscata nutmeg
noci walnuts
nodini veal chops

O **oca** goose
odori herbs
olio (d'oliva) (olive) oil
olive olives
orata type of sea bream
orecchiette ear-shaped pasta
origano oregano
ortolano ortolan
osso buco braised veal knuckles and shins
ostriche oysters

P **palombacce allo spiedo** wood pigeon, spit-roasted
pan di Spagna honey and rum sponge cake
pancetta affumicata smoked bacon
pandorato alla crema di formaggio fried bread with cream cheese

pandoro large, sponge cake served with powdered vanilla on top

pane bread; **~ al latte** milk bread: **~ all'olio** olive oil white bread: **~ tostato** toast

pane, grissini e coperto bread, breadsticks (**grissini**) and table cover charge

panettone butter-enriched Christmas bread with candied fruit, sultanas and raisins

panforte similar to **pangiallo**

pangiallo fairly hard nut and honey cake

panini rolls

panino imbottito sandwich

panna cotta delicious Italian adaptation of blancmange and creme brulé

panpepato very spicy nut cake

pansotti con salsa di noci alla ligure triangles stuffed with greens in walnut sauce

pappardelle fat ribbons of egg-pasta; **~ alla lepre** with hare sauce

papriot thick spinach soup

parmigiana breaded veal escalopes with tomato sauce and mozzarella

parmigiano (-reggiano) parmesan ➤ 48

passato di verdura mashed vegetable soup, generally with croutons

pasta pasta, noodles ➤ 45; **~ e ceci** with chickpeas; **~ e fagioli** with beans

pasta Maddalena plain génoise cake

pastasciutta pasta

pasticcini pastries

pasticcio macaroni, white sauce, meat and tomato

pastiera ricotta cake with wheat berries

pastina small pasta pieces; **~ in brodo** in broth

patate potatoes

patatine fritte French fries, chips

pecorino hard cheese ➤ 48

penne pasta quills

peperonata peppers sauteed with tomato and onion

peperoni peppers; **~ ripieni** stuffed ➤ 47

pera pear

pernice partridge

pesca peach

pescanoce nectarine

pesce all'acqua pazza fish cooked in seawater

pesce persico perch

pesce spada swordfish

pescespada grilled swordfish stuffed with Mozzarella, brandy and herbs

pesche peaches

pesci fish ➤ 45; **~ al cartoccio** baked in a parchment envelope; **~ in carpione** boiled and cooked in vinegar, served cold with lemon

pestingolo rich fruit cake with figs and honey

pesto sauce of basil leaves, garlic, cheese and sometimes pine kernels *(Liguria)* and marjoram

piatti di carne meat dishes

piatti freddi cold dishes

piatto del giorno dish of the day

piccante sharp (cheese)

piccata al marsala thin veal escalope braised in marsala sauce

piccione pigeon

pieno full-bodied (wine)

pinoli pine nuts
piselli peas; **~ al prosciutto** cooked slowly with Parma ham and bacon
piviere plover
pizelle thin waffle cones with cream or ice cream
pizza pizza ➤ 44
polenta mush made from cornmeal; **~ alla piemontese** layered with meat; **~ e coniglio** with rabbit stew; **~ e uccelli** with roasted small birds *(northern Italy)*
pollame poultry
pollo chicken; **~ all'abruzzese** with sweet peppers; **~ alla romana** diced and served with tomato sauce and sweet peppers; **~ alla diavola** highly spiced and grilled chicken; **~ novello** spring chicken
polpette meatballs
polpettone meat loaf of seasoned beef or veal
polpo octopus
pommarola sauce of tomatoes, garlic, basil *(Campania)*
pomodori tomatoes
pomodori e capperi salad with capers
pompelmo grapefruit
porcellino da latte suckling pig
porcetto arrosto suckling spit-roasted pig *(Sardinia)*
porchetta roasted whole pig with fennels and sausages
porchetta very spicy cooked pork served cold
porcini boletus mushrooms
porrata bacon and leeks in yeast dough crust
porro leek
porto port
prezzemolo parsley
primo piatto first course
prosciutto ham
prosciutto crudo con melone/con fichi sliced melon or figs with cured ham from Parma
provolone firm cheese ➤ 48
prugna plum
prugna secca prune
puttanesca sauce of capers, black olives, parsley, garlic, olive oil, black pepper

Q

quaglia quail
quattro formaggi four types of cheese (pizza topping) ➤ 44
quattro stagioni vegetables, cheese, ham and bacon (pizza topping) ➤ 44

R

radicchio a kind of bitter red and white lettuce
ragù sauce like bolognese
ravanelli radishes
ravioli alla piemontese ravioli with beef and vegetable stuffing
razza ray
ribes red currants
ribes nero black currants
ricci sea urchins
ricciarelli delicate honey and almond biscuit *(Tuscany)*
ricotta soft cow's or sheep's milk cheese
rigatoni short, wide pasta tubes; **~ alla pagliata** with veal guts
risi e bisi rice with peas and bacon
riso rice ➤ 44
riso con le seppie rice cooked with the ink from squid

riso in bianco boiled rice with butter and grated parmesan
risotto rice casserole; **~ con fegatini** with chicken livers; **~ con gamberetti in bianco** with prawns and red wine
rognoncini trifolatti kidneys sauteed with Marsala
rognoni kidneys
rombo turbot
rosato rosé (wine)
rosbif roast beef
rosmarino rosemary
rosso red (wine)
ruoti wheel-shaped pasta

S

salame salami
salami spicy sausages made with uncooked beef or pork, often flavored with pepper and garlic
salciccia small sausage, country-style pork mixture
sale salt
salmone salmon
salse sauces ➤ 47
salsicce sausages
saltimbocca veal escalopes with prosciutto ham; **~ alla romana** braised in marsala wine with sage
salumi assorted pork products
salvia sage
sardine sardines; **~ all'olio** in oil
sauersuppe sour tripe soup marinated in white wine vinegar
scalogno shallot
scaloppina veal escalope; **~ alla Valdostana** filled with cheese and ham; **~ al Marsala** with Marsala wine
scampi prawns
sciule pieuno onions stuffed with macaroons, breadcrumbs, cheese, spices and sultanas
scorfano sea-scorpion, sculpin
scura dark (beer)
secco dry (wine)
secondo piatto second (main) course
sedano celery
selvaggina venison
semi-freddo ice cream cake
senape mustard
seppia cuttlefish
seppie con piselli baby squid and peas
sfogliatelle sweet Ricotta cheese turnovers
sgombri in umido stewed mackerel in white wine with green peas
sgombro mackerel
siciliana with black olives, capers and cheese (pizza)
sodo hard (egg)
sogliola sole
sogliole alla mugnaia sole sautéed in butter, garnished with parsley and lemon
solubile instant (coffee)
sottaceti pickled vegetables
spaghetti all'amatriciana spaghetti with tomato, bacon and Pecorino cheese sauce
spalla shoulder
specialità della casa specialties of the house
specialità di pesce fish specialties
specialità locali local specialties
spezie spices
spezzatino meat or poultry stew
spezzatino di cinghiale alla cacciatora diced wild boar stewed in white wine with garlic and bay leaves

spezzato di tacchino turkey casserole with olives *(Umbria)*
spiedino pieces of meat grilled or roasted on a skewer
spigola sea bass
spinaci spinach
spremuta di ... freshly squeezed (juice)
spumante sparkling (wine)
stecca di cioccolato chocolate bar
stelline small pasta stars
stoccafisso dried cod cooked with tomatoes, olives and artichoke
storione sturgeon
stracciatella clear egg and cheese soup
stracotto meat stew with sausages, beef and vegetables in white wine, slowly cooked for several hours *(Tuscany)*
strangola-preti bread and spinach dumpling
straniera foreign (beer)
su ordinazione made to order
succo di frutta fruit juice ➤ 51
supplemento extra charge
suppli very popular and tasty Italian rice croquettes with Mozzarella cheese and minced meat, breadcrumbed and fried
susina plum (yellow) or greengage

T

tacchino turkey
tagliatelle egg-pasta ribbons
tartufi truffles
tartufi di cioccolata chocolate truffles
timballo con le sarde macaroni, sardines, pine nuts, fennel, raisins
timo thyme
tiramisù sponge cake, custard, cream and chocolate dessert ➤ 48
tisana herb tea
tonno tuna
tonno alla livornese fried tuna in slices, stewed in garlic and tomato
tordo thrush
Torrone delicious Italian nougat which can be found hard and crispy or soft, also chocolate flavored.
torta cake; pie
torta di cioccolata chocolate cake
torta di frutta fruit cake
torta di mandorle almond pie
torta di mele apple pie
torta di ricotta delicious pie made with ricotta cheese (roughly similar to cheese cake)
torta manfreda liver pate with Marsala and Parmesan
torta Margherita layered cake with meringue, fresh fruit and whipped cream
tortelli di zucca tortellini with pumpkin stuffing
tortellini stuffed egg-pasta rings ➤ 45; **~ alla panna con tartufi** with cream and truffles; **~ di piccioncello** with pigeon stuffing
tortino di zucchine zucchini with white sauce
triglie red mullet; **~ alla livornese** baked; **~ alla siciliana** grilled with orange peel and white wine
trippa tripe; **~ alla fiorentina** and beef braised in a tomato sauce and served with cheese *(Tuscany)*; **~ verde** in green sauce
trota trout: **~ alla brace** grilled
tutto mare seafood sauce
tè tea; **~ freddo** iced tea

U **uova** eggs
uova alla Romana omelet with beans, onions and herbs
uova e pancetta bacon and eggs
uova e prosciutto ham and eggs
uova fritte fried eggs
uova strapazzate scrambled eggs
uovo alla coque boiled egg
uva bianca/nera white/black grapes
uva passa raisins
uva spina gooseberries

V **vaniglia** vanilla
veneziana sweet bread with whole almonds
verde with creamed green vegetables
verdura mista mixed vegetables
verdure vegetables ➤ 47; **~ di stagione** vegetables in season
vermicelli thin spaghetti
verza green cabbage
vincigrassi cooked pasta with cream sauce and gravy
vino wine ➤ 49–50
vitello veal; **~ alla bolognese** cutlet cooked with Parma ham and cheese; **~ tonnato** cold with tuna fish sauce; **~ valdostana** stuffed with soft cheese
vongole clams

WX YZ **whisky (e soda/con seltz)** whisky (and soda)
Würstel frankfurters
zabaglione egg yolks, sugar and Marsala wine
zafferano saffron
zampone pig's foot/trotter filled with seasoned pork, boiled and served in slices
zenzero ginger
ziti long, solid eggless-pasta tubes
zucca pumpkin, gourd; **~ gialla al forno** baked and served with parmesan cheese (winter only)
zucchero sugar
zucchini ripieni stuffed zucchini (usually containing mince meat)
zuppa soup ➤ 44; **~ alla cacciatora** meat soup with mushrooms; **~ alla marinara** spicy fish chowder/stew; **~ alla pavese** consommé with poached egg, croutons and grated cheese; **~ alla senese** sausages with lentils; **~ alla veneta** vegetable soup with white wine and noodles; **~ di bue con spaghettini** spaghetti in beef soup; **~ di cipolle** onion soup with brandy; **~ di cozze** mussels soup; **~ di datteri di mare** sea dates (kind of mussel) soup; **~ di frutti di mare** seafood soup; **~ di pesce** spicy fish chowder/stew; **~ di vongole** clams and white wine soup
zuppa inglese sponge cake steeped in rum with candied fruit and custard or whipped cream

Travel

Safety	65	Hitchhiking	83
Arrival	66	Taxi/Cab	84
Plane	68	Car/Automobile	85
Train	72	Car rental	86
Long-distance bus [Coach]	78	Gas [Petrol] station	87
Bus	78	Breakdown	88
Subway [Metro]	80	Car parts	90
Ferry	81	Accidents	92
Bicycle/Motorbike	82	Legal matters	93
		Asking directions	94

ESSENTIAL

1/2/3 for ...	**Uno/due/tre per** *oono/doo-ay/tray pehr*
A ticket to ...	**Un biglietto per ...** *oon beelyaytto pehr*
one-way [single]	**solo andata** *solo andaata*
round-trip [return]	**andata e ritorno** *andaata ay reetorno*
How much ...?	**Quanto ... ?** *kwanto*

Safety Sicurezza

Would you accompany me ...?	**Le spiace accompagnarmi?** *lay speeachay akkompañaarmee*
to the bus stop	**alla fermata dell'autobus** *alla fayrmaata dayllowtobooss*
to my hotel	**al mio albergo** *al meeo albayrgo*
I don't want to ... on my own.	**Non voglio ... da solo(-a).** *non volyo ... da solo(-a)*
stay here	**rimanere qui** *reemanayray kwee*
walk home	**rientrare a piedi** *reeayntraaray ah peeaydee*
I don't feel safe here.	**Non mi sento sicuro(-a) qui.** *non me saynto seekooro(-a) kwee*

POLICE ➤ 152; EMERGENCY PHONE NUMBERS ➤ 224

Arrival Arrivo

Most visitors, including citizens of all EU{European Union} countries, the US, Canada, Eire, Australia and New Zealand, require only a valid passport for entry to Italy.

Import restrictions between EU countries have been relaxed on items for personal use or consumption which are bought duty-paid within the EU. Suggested maximum: 90L. wine or 60L. sparkling wine, 20L. fortified wine, 10L. spirits and 110L. beer.

There are duty-free shops at the following airports: Bologna, Genova, Milan, Naples, Pisa, Rimini, Rome Ciampino, Rome Fiumicino, Turin, and Venice.

Passport control Il controllo passaporti

We have a joint passport.
Abbiamo un passaporto congiunto.
abbeeamo oon passaporto konjoonto

The children are on this passport.
I bambini sono su questo passaporto.
ee bambeenee sono soo kwaysto passaporto

I'm here on vacation [holiday]/business.
Sono qui per vacanza/per lavoro.
sono kwee pehr vakantsa/pehr lavoro

I'm just passing through.
Sono solo di passaggio.
sono solo dee passadjo

I'm going to ...
Vado a ...
vado a

I'm ...
Sono ...
sono

on my own
da solo(-a)
da solo(-a)

with my family
con la mia famiglia
kon la meea fameelya

with a group
con un gruppo
kon oon groopo

FAMILY ➤ 120

Customs Dogana

I have only the normal allowances. — **Ho solo beni in esenzione fiscale.** *oh solo baynee een ayzentseeonay feeskalay*

It's a gift. — **È un regalo.** *eh oon raygaalo*

It's for my personal use. — **È per mio uso personale.** *eh pehr meeo oozo pehrsonaalay*

Ha qualcosa da dichiarare?	Do you have anything to declare?
Deve pagare il dazio per questo.	You must pay duty on this.
Dove l'ha comprato?	Where did you buy this?
Apra questa borsa, per favore.	Please open this bag.
Ha altri bagagli?	Do you have any more luggage?

I would like to declare … — **Vorrei dichiarare ..** *vorrehee deekeearaaray*

I don't understand. — **Non capisco.** *non kapeesko*

Does anyone here speak English? — **C'è qualcuno qui che parla inglese?** *cheh kwalkoono kwee kay parla eengglaysay*

IL CONTROLLO PASSAPORTI	passport control	
LA FRONTIERA	border crossing	
LA DOGANA	customs	
NULLA DA DICHIARARE	nothing to declare	
MERCI DA DICHIARARE	goods to declare	
ESENTE DA DAZIO	duty-free	

Duty-free shopping Comprare al negozio duty-free

What currency is this in? — **In che valuta è questo?** *een kay valoota eh kwaysto*

Can I pay in … — **Posso pagare in …** *posso pagaaray een*

dollars — **dollari** *dollaree*

lira — **lire** *leeray*

pounds — **sterline** *stayrleenay*

Plane L'aereo

Italian cities and major islands are well connected by air. This includes a shuttle service (**Arcobaleno**) between Rome and Milan every 20 minutes. Domestic flights can be expensive. However, cheaper rates can be obtained off-peak, and special fares are generally available for family groups, young people/students and senior citizens.

Tickets and reservations Biglietti e prenotazioni

When is the ... flight to ...?	**Quando parte il volo ... per ...?** *kwando partay eel volo ... pehr*
first/next/last	**il primo/il prossimo/l'ultimo** *eel preemo/eel prosseemo/loolteemo*
I'd like 2 ... tickets to ...	**Vorrei due biglietti ... per ...** *vorrehee doo-ay beelyayttee ... pehr*
one-way [single]	**di andata** *dee andaata*
round-trip [return]	**di andata e ritorno** *dee andaata ay reetorno*
first class	**di prima classe** *dee preema klassay*
economy class	**in classe turistica** *een klassay tooreesteeka*
business class	**business class**
How much is a flight to ...?	**Quanto costa il volo per ...?** *kwanto kosta eel volo pehr*
I'd like to ... my reservation for flight number ...	**Vorrei ... la mia prenotazione per il volo numero ...** *vorrehee ... la meea praynotatseeonay pehr eel volo noomayro*
cancel	**annullare** *annoollaaray*
change	**cambiare** *kambeeaaray*
confirm	**confermare** *konfayrmaaray*

Enquiries about the flight Informazioni sul volo

How long is the flight?	**Quanto dura il volo?** *kwanto doora eel volo*
What time does the plane leave?	**A che ora decolla l'aereo?** *ah kay ora daykolla la-ayrayo*
What time will we arrive?	**A che ora arriveremo?** *ah kay ora arreevayraymo*
What time do I have to check in?	**A che ora devo registrare i bagagli?** *ah kay ora dayvo rayjeestraaray ee bagaalyee*

NUMBERS ➤ 216; TIME ➤ 220

Checking in Accettazione

Where is the check-in counter for flight ...?	**Dov'è il banco accettazione per il volo ...?** *dovay ell banko achaytatseeonay pehr eel volo*
I have ...	**Ho ...** *oh*
3 suitcases to check in	**tre valige da registrare** *treh valeejay da rayjeestraaray*
2 pieces of hand luggage	**due borse a mano** *doo-ay borsay ah mano*

Il suo biglietto/passaporto/ carta d'imbarco, per favore.	Your ticket/passport/ boarding card, please.
Preferisce un posto vicino al finestrino o nel corridoio?	Would you like a window or an aisle seat?
Fumatori o non fumatori?	Smoking or non-smoking?
Si accomodi nella sala partenze.	Please go through to the departure lounge.
Quanti pezzi/quante valige ha?	How many pieces of luggage do you have?
Ha un eccesso di bagaglio.	You have excess luggage.
Deve pagare un supplemento di ... lire per ogni chilo in più.	You'll have to pay a supplement of ... lire per kilo of excess luggage.
Questo bagaglio a mano è troppo pesante/grande.	That's too heavy/ large for hand luggage.
Ha fatto i bagagli personalmente?	Did you pack these bags yourself?
Ci sono articoli elettrici o taglienti?	Do they contain any sharp or electrical items?

ARRIVI	arrivals
PARTENZE	departures
I CONTROLLI DI SICUREZZA	security check
TENERE CON SÈ I BAGAGLI	do not leave luggage unattended

Information Informazioni

Is there any delay on flight ...? **C'è un ritardo sul volo ...?** *cheh oon reetardo sool volo*

How late will it be? **Di quanto ritarderà?** *dee kwanto reetardayra*

Has the flight from ... landed? **È atterrato il volo da ...?** *eh attayrraato eel volo da*

Which gate does flight ... leave from? **Da quale uscita parte il volo ...?** *da kwalay oosheeta partay eel volo*

Boarding/In-flight L'imbarco/In volo

Your boarding pass, please. **La sua carta d'imbarco, per favore.** *la sooa karta deembarko pehr favoray*

Could I have a drink/something to eat, please? **Può portarmi qualcosa da bere/da mangiare, per favore?** *pwo portaarmee kwalkosa da bayray/da manjaaray pehr favoray*

Please wake me for the meal. **Mi svegli per il pasto, per favore.** *mee svaylyee pehr eel pasto pehr favoray*

What time will we arrive? **A che ora arriveremo?** *ah kay ora arreevayraymo*

An airsick bag, quick, please. **Un sacchetto di carta, presto, per favore.** *oon sakkaytto dee karta praysto pehr favoray*

Arrival L'arrivo

Where is/are ...? **Dov'è/Dove sono ...?** *doveh/dovay sono*

currency exchange **l'ufficio cambio** *looffeecho kambeeo*

buses **gli autobus** *lyee owtobooss*

car rental **il noleggio auto** *eel nolaydjo owto*

exit **l'uscita** *loosheeta*

taxis **i tassì** *ee tassee*

Is there a bus into town? **C'è un autobus per il centro città?** *cheh oon owtobooss pehr eel chayntro cheetta*

How do I get to the ... Hotel? **Come si arriva all' albergo ...?** *komay see arreeva allalbayrgo*

LUGGAGE/BAGGAGE ➤ 71; CUSTOMS ➤ 66–67

Luggage/Baggage Il bagaglio

Tipping: The suggested rate for the porter is Lit. 2,000-5,000 per bag; in railway stations, tariffs are generally displayed.

Porter! Excuse me!	**Facchino! Scusi!** *fakkeeno. skoozee*
Could you take my luggage to ...?	**Può portarmi i bagagli fino ...?** *pwo portaarmee ee bagalyee feeno*
a taxi/bus	**al tassì/alla fermata dell'autobus** *al tassee/ alla faymaata daylowtobooss*
Where is/are ...?	**Dov'è/Dove sono ...?** *doveh /dovay sono*
luggage carts [trolleys]	**i carrelli portabagaglio** *ee karrayllee portabagaalyo*
baggage lockers	**il deposito bagagli automatico** *eel dayposeeto bagalyee owtomateeko*
baggage check [left-luggage office]	**il deposito bagagli** *eel dayposeeto bagalyee*
Where is the luggage from flight ...?	**Dove sono i bagagli del volo ...?** *dovay sono ee bagalyee dayl volo*

Loss, damage and theft Smarrimento, danni e furti

My luggage has been lost.	**Ho smarrito i bagagli.** *oh smarreeto ee bagalyee*
My luggage has been stolen.	**Il mio bagaglio è stato rubato.** *eel meeo bagaalyo eh staato roobaato*
My suitcase was damaged.	**La mia valigia è stata danneggiata** *la meea valeeja eh staata dannaydjaata*

Può descrivere i suoi bagagli?	What does your luggage look like?
Ha l'etichetta di ricupero bagagli?	Do you have the claim check/ reclaim tag?
I suoi bagagli ...	Your luggage ...
potrebbero essere stati mandati a ...	may have been sent to ...
potrebbero arrivare oggi più tardi	may arrive later today
Ritorni domani, per favore.	Please come back tomorrow.
Chiami questo numero per controllare se i suoi bagagli sono arrivati.	Call this number to check if your luggage has arrived.

POLICE ➤ 152; COLORS ➤ 143

Train Treno

EuroCity (EC) *ayoorosseetee*
International express connecting main European cities; first and second class. A supplement is payable and reservations are obligatory.

Pendolino-ETR 450 (P) *pehndoleeno*
High-speed train connecting major Italian cities. Luxury first class and second class; tickets include hostess service and a meal. Reservations are obligatory.

Rapido *raapeedo*
Long-distance express train stopping at major cities only; first and second class.

Intercity (IC) *"intercity"*
Intercity express with very few stops; luxury, international service with first and second class. Seat reservations are essential and a special supplement is charged.

Espresso (EXP) *aysprehsso*
Long-distance express train, stopping at major stations.

Diretto (D) *deerehtto*
Slower than the Espresso, it stops at most stations.

Interregionale (IR) *eentehrrayjeeonalay*
Train stopping at main stations within a region.

Regionale (R) *rayjeeonalay*
Local train stopping at many smaller locations. Not very fast, but an excellent means of visiting small hilltop towns that abound in Italy. Marked by a white "**R**" on a black background (to distinguish it from the **Rapido**).

carrozza ristorante *karrottsa reestorantay*
Dining car; attached to most international and long-distance trains. Some services include self-service restaurant cars. In addition, most trains have snacks and refreshments available.

vagone letto *vagonay lehtto*
Sleeping car with individual compartment and washing facilities. Sleeping cars containing berths with blankets and pillows (**carrozza cuccette**) are also available on some lines. First and second class are distinguished by the number of berths per compartment.

The National Railways (**Ferrovie dello Stato – FS**) publishes a free, easy-to-consult pocket timetable of the major trains running throughout Italy. Italy's trains can be crowded; if you haven't booked, it's wise to arrive at the station at least 30 minutes before departure to be sure of a seat.

Check out the various reductions and travel cards available. These include: **Biglietto turistico libera circolazione** (for extensive "travel-at-will," only available outside Italy); and **Chilometrico** (for groups of up to five people, valid for 2 months).

To the station Alla stazione ferroviaria

How do I get to the (main) rail station? **Come si arriva alla stazione ferroviaria (principale)?** *komay see arreeva alla statseeonay fayrroveeaareea (preencheepaalay)*

Do trains to … leave from … Station? **I treni per … partono dalla stazione di …?** *ee traynee pehr … partono dalla statseeonay dee*

Is it far? **È lontano?** *ay lontano*

Can I leave my car there? **Posso lasciare la mia macchina là?** *posso lashaaray la meea makkeena la*

At the station Alla stazione ferroviaria

Where is/are …? **Dov'è/Dove sono …?** *doveh /dovay sono*

currency exchange office **l'ufficio cambio** *looffeecho kambeeo*

information desk **lo sportello informazioni** *lo sportayllo eenformatseeonay*

baggage check [left-luggage office] **il deposito bagagli** *eel dayposeeto bagaalyee*

lost-and-found [lost property office] **l'ufficio oggetti smarriti** *looffeecho odjayttee smarreetee*

luggage lockers **il deposito bagagli automatico** *eel dayposeeto bagaalyee owtomaateeko*

platforms **i binari** *ee beenaaree*

snack bar **il bar** *eel bar*

ticket office **la biglietteria** *la beelyayttayreea*

waiting room **la sala d'aspetto** *la sala daspaytto*

ENTRATA	entrance	
USCITA	exit	
AI BINARI	to the platforms	
INFORMAZIONI	information	
PRENOTAZIONI	reservations	
ARRIVI	arrivals	
PARTENZE	departures	

DIRECTIONS ➤ 94

Tickets Biglietti

It is **very important** to validate tickets before commencing your journey by inserting them in machines (generally yellow) positioned on platforms; otherwise you will be liable for a fine.

I'd like a … ticket to …	**Vorrei un biglietto … per …** *vorrehee oon beelyayto … pehr*
one-way [single]	**di andata** *dee andaata*
round-trip [return]	**di andata e ritorno** *dee andaata ay reetorno*
first/second class	**di prima/di seconda classe** *dee preema/dee saykonda klassay*
I'd like to reserve a …	**Vorrei prenotare …** *vorrehee praynotaaray*
window/aisle seat	**un posto vicino al finestrino/al corridoio** *oon posto veecheeno al feenaystreeno/al korreedoyo*
Is there a sleeping car [sleeper]?	**C'è un vagone letto?** *cheh oon vagonay laytto*
I'd like a … berth.	**Vorrei una cuccetta …** *vorrehee oona koochaytta*
upper/lower	**superiore/inferiore** *soopayreeoray/eenfayreeoray*

Price Tariffe

How much is that?	**Quant'è?** *kwanteh*
Is there a discount for …?	**C'è una riduzione per …?** *cheh oon reedootseeonay pehr*
children/families	**bambini/famiglie** *bambeenee/fameelyay*
senior citizens	**anziani** *antseeanee*
students	**studenti** *stoodayntee*
Do you offer a cheap same-day round-trip ticket?	**Avete una tariffa economica per una andata e ritorno in giornata?** *avaytay oona tareeffa aykonomeeka pehr oona andaata ay reetorno een jornaata*

NUMBERS ➤ 216; DAYS OF THE WEEK ➤ 218

Queries Richieste d'informazione

Do I have to change trains?	**Devo cambiare treno?** *dayvo kambeeaaray trayno*
You have to change at …	**Deve cambiare a …** *dayvay kambeeaaray ah*
How long is this ticket valid for?	**Per quanto tempo è valido questo biglietto?** *pehr kwanto taympo eh valeedo kwaysto beelyayto*
Can I return on the same ticket?	**Posso ritornare con lo stesso biglietto?** *posso reetornaaray kon lo staysso beelyaytto*
Which car [coach] is my seat in?	**In quale carrozza è il mio posto?** *een kwalay karrotsa eh eel meeo posto*
Is there a dining car on the train?	**C'è un vagone ristorante sul treno?** *cheh oonh vagonay reestorantay sool trayno*

– Vorrei un biglietto per Siena, per favore.
(I'd like a ticket to Siena, please.)
– Andata o andata e ritorno?
(One-way or round-trip?)
– Andata e ritorno, per favore. (Round-trip, please.)
– Fa ventitre mille lire. (That's 23,000 lire.)
– Devo cambiare treno? (Do I have to change trains?)
– Si, deve cambiare a Poggibonsi.
(Yes, you have to change in Poggibonsi.)

Train times L'orario ferroviario

Could I have a timetable, please?	**Ha un orario, per favore?** *ah oon orareeo pehr favoray*
When is the … train to … ?	**Quando parte … treno per …** *kwando paartay … trayno pehr*
first/next/last	**il primo/il prossimo/l'ultimo** *eel preemo /eel prosseemo/ loolteemo*

How frequent are the trains to ...?
Che frequenza hanno i treni per ...?
kay fraykwayntsa anno ee traynee pehr

once/twice a day
una volta/due volte al giorno
oona volta/doo-ay voltay al jorno

5 times a day
cinque volte al giorno
cheenkweh voltay al jorno

every hour
ogni ora
oñee ora

What time do they leave?
A che ora partono?
ah kay ora partono

on the hour
ad ogni ora precisa
ad oñee ora praycheesa

What time does the train stop at ...?
A che ora si ferma il treno a ...?
ah kay ora see fayrma eel trayno ah

What time does the train arrive in ...?
A che ora arriva il treno a ...?
ah kay ora arreeva eel trayno ah

How long is the trip [journey]?
Quanto dura il viaggio?
kwanto doora eel veeadjo

Is the train on time?
Il treno è in orario?
eel trayno eh een orareeo

Departures Partenze

Which platform does the train to ... leave from?
Da quale binario parte il treno per ...?
da kwalay beenaareeo partay eel trayno pehr

Where is platform 4?
Dov'è il binario quattro?
doveh eel beenaareeo kwattro

over there
laggiù
ladjoo

on the left/right
a sinistra/a destra
ah seeneestra/ah daystra

Where do I change for ...?
dove cambio per ...?
dovay kambeeo pehr

How long will I have to wait for a connection?
Quanto devo aspettare per la coincidenza?
kwanto dayvo aspayttaaray pehr la koeencheedayntsa

BASIC EXPRESSIONS ➤ 12-18; TIME ➤ 220

Boarding Salire a bordo

Is this the right platform for the train to ...?
È questo il binario del treno diretto a ...?
eh kwaysto eel beenadreeo dayl trayno deeraytto ah

Is this the train to ...?
È questo il treno diretto a ...?
eh kwaysto eel trayno deeraytto ah

Is this seat taken?
È occupato questo posto?
eh okoopaato kwaysto posto

I think that's my seat.
Questo è il mio posto, credo.
kwaysto eh eel meeo posto kraydo

Are there any seats/berths available?
Ci sono posti liberi/cuccette libere?
chee sono postee leebayree/ koochayttay leebayray

Do you mind ...?
Le spiace ...? *lay speeachay*

if I sit here
se mi siedo qui *say mee seeaydo kwee*

if I open the window
se apro la finestra
say apro la feenaystra

During the trip Durante il viaggio

How long are we stopping here?
Per quanto tempo ci fermiamo a ...? *pehr kwanto taympo che fayrmeeaamo ah*

When do we get to ...?
Quando arriviamo a ...?
kwando arreeveeaamo ah

Have we passed ...?
Abbiamo passato ...?
abbeeaamo passaato

Where is the dining/ sleeping car?
Dov'è la carrozza ristorante/il vagone letto? *doveh la karrotsa reestorantay/eel vagonay lehtto*

Where is my berth?
Dov'è la mia cuccetta?
doveh la meea koo\chaytta

I've lost my ticket.
Ho perso il biglietto.
oh payrso eel beelyaytto

FRENI D'EMERGENZA	emergency brake	
PORTE AUTOMATICHE	automatic doors	
SEGNALE D'ALLARME	alarm signal	

Long-distance bus Corriera

Bus travel can be a convenient way of traveling to smaller towns and a cheaper way to reach major cities. You'll find information on destinations and timetables at bus terminals, usually situated near railway stations. Main companies include *A.M.T.* (Genoa), *Appian Line* (Rome), *Autostradale, Lazzi, Pesci, Sadem, Sita.*

Where is the bus [coach] station?	**Dov'è la stazione delle corriere/ dei pullman?** *doveh la statseeonay dayllay korreeehray/dayee pullman*
When's the next bus [coach] to ...?	**Quando parte la prossima corriera per ...?** *kwando partay la prosseema korreeehra pehr*
Which terminal does it leave from?	**Da quale piazzola parte?** *da kwalay piatsola partay*
Where are the bus [coach] stops?	**Dove sono le piazzole di sosta?** *dovay sono ley piatsolay dee sosta*
Does this bus [coach] stop at ...?	**Questa corriera ferma a ...?** *kwaysta korreeehra fayrma ah*
How long does the trip [journey] take?	**Quanto dura il viaggio?** *kwanto doora eel veeadjo*

Bus Autobus

Many cities have introduced an automatic system of fare-paying. Instructions are usually also given in English. Most machines now give change, though usually limited to L.2,000.

In most towns, bus or subway tickets are valid for 75 minutes and the fare is standard, irrespective of distance. If you're planning to travel extensively in one city, enquire about special runabout tickets, such as **biglietto giornaliero** (one-day ticket).

Deve andare a quella fermata lì	You need that stop over there.
Deve prendere quella strada.	You need to go down that road.
Deve prendere l'autobus numero ...	You need bus number ...
Deve cambiare autobus a ...	You must change buses at ...

LA FERMATA D'AUTOBUS	bus stop	
LA FERMATA A RICHIESTA	request stop	
VIETATO FUMARE	no smoking	
USCITA (D'EMERGENZA)	(emergency) exit	

DIRECTIONS ➤ 94; TIME ➤ 220

Buying tickets Comprare i biglietti

Where can I buy tickets?	**Dove si comprano i biglietti?** *dovay see komprano ee beelyaytee*
A ... ticket to ..., please.	**Un bigletto per ..., per favore.** *oon beelyaytto pehr ... pehr favoray*
one-way/round-trip [single/return]	**di corsa semplice/circolare** *dee korsa saympleechay/cheerkolaaray*
bus pass	**per corse multiple** *pehr korsay moolteeplay*
day/weekly/monthly	**giornaliero/settimanale/mensile** *jornaleeehro/saytteemanaalay/maynseelay*
A book of tickets, please.	**Un blocchetto di biglietti, per favore.** *oon blokkaytto dee beelyaytee pehr favoray*
How much is the fare to ...?	**Quant'è il biglietto per ...?** *kwanteh eel beelyaytto pehr*

Traveling In viaggio

Is this the right bus/tram to ...?	**È questo l'autobus/il tram per ...?** *eh kwaysto lowtobooss/eel tram pehr*
Could you tell me when to get off?	**Può dirmi quando devo scendere?** *pwo deermee kwando dayvo shayndayray*
Do I have to change buses?	**Devo cambiare autobus?** *dayvo kambeeaaray owtobooss*
How many stops are there to ...?	**Quante fermate ci sono per ...?** *kwantay fayrmaatay chee sono pehr*
Next stop, please!	**La prossima fermata, per favore!** *lah prosseema fayrmaata pehr favoray*

– Scusi. E' questo l'autobus per il Municipio?
(Excuse me, is this the right bus to the town hall?)
– No. Deve prendere l'autobus numero otto. Eccolo, laggiù.
(No, you'll need number 8, over there.)
– Dove si comprano i biglietti?
(Where can I buy tickets?)
– In un'edicula. (At a kiosk.)
– Quando devo scendere?
(When do I need to get off?)
– Fra quattro fermate. (Four stops from here.)

BUYING TICKETS ➤ 74; DIRECTIONS ➤ 94

Subway La metropolitana

The **metropolitana** in Rome and Milan provide big maps in every station to make the system easy to use. The fare is standard, irrespective of the distance traveled.

General Inquiries Richieste di informazioni generali

Where's the nearest subway [metro] station?
Dov'è la fermata della metropolitana più vicina? *doveh la fayrmaata daylla maytropoleetaana peeoo veecheena*

Where can I buy a ticket?
Dove si comprano i biglietti? *dovay see komprano ee beelyayttee*

Could I have a map of the subway [metro]?
Ha una carta/mappa della rete metropolitana? *ah oona karta/mappa daylla raytay maytropoleetaana*

Traveling In viaggio

Which line should I take for ...?
Che linea devo prendere per ...? *kay leeneea dayvo praynday ray pehr*

Is this the right line for ...?
È questa la linea per ...? *eh kwaysta la leeneea pehr*

Which stop is it for ...?
Che fermata è per ...? *kay fayrmaata eh pehr*

How many stops is it to ...?
Quante fermate ci sono per arrivare a ...? *kwantay fayrmaatay chee sono pehr arreevaaray ah*

Is the next stop ...?
La prossima/fermata è ...? *la prosseema (fayrmaata) eh*

Where are we?
Dove siamo? *dovay seeaamo*

Where do I change for ...?
Dove devo cambiare per ...? *dovay dayvo kambeeaaray pehr*

What time is the last train to ...?
A che ora è l'ultimo treno per ...? *ah kay ora eh loolteemo trayno pehr*

PER ALTRE LINEE/ COINCIDENZE to other lines/transfer

NUMBERS ➤ 216; BUYING TICKETS ➤ 79, 74

Ferry Il traghetto

Regular boat, ferry and hydrofoil services run to the Italian islands. In addition to the large state-owned services such as *Tirrenia* (esp. services to Sicily and Sardinia), there are many other operators that access islands such as Capri, Ischia, Ponza, Ventotene, the Tremiti Islands, Elba and Giglio.

When is the ... car ferry to ...? **Quando c'è ... traghetto auto per ...?**
kwando cheh tragaytto owto pehr

first/next/last **il primo/il prossimo/l'ultimo**
eel preemo/ eel prosseemo/ loolteemo

hovercraft **l'aliscafo** *laleeskaafo*

ship **la nave** *la navay*

A round-trip [return] ticket for ... **Un biglietto di andata e ritorno per ...** *oon beelyaytto andaata ay reetorno pehr*

1 car and 1 trailer [caravan] **un'auto e una roulotte**
oonowto ay oona roolot

2 adults and 3 children **due adulti e tre bambini**
doo-ay adooltee ay tray bambeenee

I want to reserve a ... cabin. **Vorrei prenotare una cabina ...** *vorrehee praynotaaray oona kabeena*

single/double **singola/doppia** *seenggola/ doppeea*

ⓘ	**VIETATO L'ACCESSO AL PONTE AUTO**	no access to car decks	⊘
	LA SCIALUPPA DI SALVATAGGIO	life boat	
	LA CINTURA DI SALVATAGGIO	life preserver [life belt]	
⊖	**PUNTO DI RACCOLTA**	meeting point	⊘

Boat trips Gite in barca

Travelers to Venice can take tours on a myriad of canals, organized by the *Gondola Cooperative Service*. The price is usually quoted per gondola, which can seat 6 to 8 people, per 45 minutes, but you may be able to bargain. A cheaper, but less romantic, way of getting around are the water bus services: **Vaporetti** (slow) and **Diretti** (express).

Is there a ...? **C'è ...?** *cheh*

boat trip **una gita in barca** *oona jeeta een baarka*

Where can we buy tickets? **Dove si comprano i biglietti?**
dovay see komprano

NUMBERS ➤ 216; TIME ➤ 220

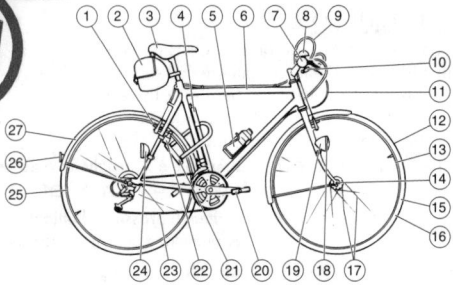

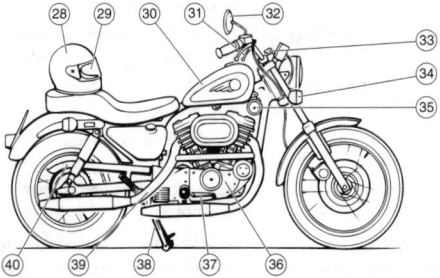

1 brake pad **il pattino/la pastiglia**
2 bicycle bag **il borsello**
3 seat [saddle] **il sellino**
4 pump **la pompa**
5 water bottle **la bottiglia dell'acqua**
6 frame **il telaio**
7 handlebars **il manubrio**
8 bell **il campanello**
9 brake cable **il cavo dei freni**
10 gear shift [lever] **la leva del cambio**
11 gear [control] cable **il cambio**
12 inner tube **la camera d'aria**
13 front/back wheel **la ruota anteriore/posteriore**
14 axle **l'asse**
15 tire **il pneumatico**
16 wheel **la ruota**
17 spokes **i raggi**
18 bulb **la lampadina**
19 headlamp **il fanalino anteriore**
20 pedal **il pedale**
21 lock **la serratura**
22 generator [dynamo] **la dinamo**
23 chain **la catena**
24 rear light **il fanalino posteriore**
25 rim **il cerchione**
26 reflectors **il catarinfrangente**
27 fender [mudguard] **il parafango**
28 helmet **il casco**
29 visor **l'antiabbagliante**
30 fuel tank **il serbatoio**
31 clutch **la leva della frizione**
32 mirror **lo specchietto**
33 ignition switch **la leva dell'avviamento**
34 turn signal [indicator] **l'indicatore di posizione**
35 horn **il claxon**
36 engine **il motore**
37 gear shift **la leva del cambio**
38 kick stand **il cavalletto**
39 exhaust pipe **la marmitta**
40 chain guard **il paracatena**

Bicycle / Motorbike
Bicicletta/Motocicletta

I'd like to rent a …	**Vorrei noleggiare …** *vorrehee nolaydjaaray*
3-/10-gear bicycle	**una bici(cletta) a tre/dieci marce** *oona beechee(beecheeklaytta) ah tray/deeaychee marchay*
moped	**un motorino** *oon motoreeno*
mountain bike	**una MTB** *oona ehmmayteebee*
motorbike	**una moto(cicletta)** *oona moto (motocheeklaytta)*
How much does it cost per day/week?	**Quanto costa al giorno/alla settimana?** *kwanto kosta al jorno/alla saytteemaana*
Do you require a deposit?	**Vuole una caparra?** *vwolay oona kaparra*
The brakes don't work.	**I freni non funzionano.** *ee fraynee non foontseeonano*
There are no lights.	**Non ci sono i fanalini.** *non chee sono ee fanaleenee*
The front/rear tire has a flat [puncture].	**il pneumatico anteriore/posteriore è bucato.** *eel pnayoomateeko antayreeoray/postayreeoray ay bookato*

Hitchhiking Fare l'autostop

Where are you heading?	**In che direzione va?** *een kay deeraytseeonay va*
I'm heading for …	**Vado verso …** *vado vayrsoh*
Is that on the way to …?	**È sulla strada per …?** *eh soolla straada pehr*
Could you drop me off …?	**Può farmi scendere …?** *pwo faarmee shayndayray*
here	**qui** *kwee*
at the … exit	**all'uscita** *alloosheeta*
in the town center	**in centro città** *een chayntro cheetta*
Thanks for the lift.	**Grazie per il passaggio.** *gratseeay pehr eel passadjeeo*

DIRECTIONS ➤ 94; NUMBERS ➤ 216

Taxi/Cab Il tassì

All cabs must be metered by law, but it is still wise to ask the fare for longer trips. All rates, including supplements for Sundays, holidays, night trips (11 p.m. – 6 a.m.), airport trips, baggage, are indicated on an official chart, which should be posted inside the taxi. Before getting into an argument with your driver when arriving at or from an airport, remember there is a return trip surcharge to be added to what you read on the meter.

Beware of unlicensed cabs ("**abusivi**") touting for business at airports and stations – they charge greatly over the normal tariffs.

Tipping suggestions: 10-15% for the taxi driver.

Where can I get a taxi?	**Dove si trovano i tassì?** *dovay see trovano ee tassee*
Do you have the number for a taxi?	**Ha il numero dei tassì?** *ah eel noomayro dayee tassee*
I'd like a taxi ...	**Vorrei un tassì ...** *vorrehee oon tassee*
now	**subito** *soobeeto*
in an hour	**fra un'ora** *fra oonora*
for tomorrow at 9:00 am	**per domani alle nove** *pehr domaanee allay novay*
The address is ...	**L'indirizzo è ...** *leendeereetzo eh ...*
Please take me ...	**Per favore, mi porti ...** *pehr favoray mee portee*
to the airport	**all'aeroporto** *allaayroporto*
to the train station	**alla stazione ferroviaria** *alla statseeonay fayrrooveeareea*
this address	**a questo indirizzo** *ah kwaysto eendeereetso*
How much will it cost?	**Quanto costerà?** *kwanto kostayra*
On the meter it's ...	**Sul tassametro è segnato ...** *sool tasseemaytroa eh sayñaato*

– Può portarmi alla stazione, per favore?
(Please take me to the train station.)
– *Certo. (Certainly.)*
– Quanto tempo impiegherà?
(How long will it take?)
– *Circa dieci minuti... Eccoci.*
(About 10 minutes... Here we are.)
– Grazie. Quant'è? (Thank you. How much is it?)

NUMBERS ➤ 216; DIRECTIONS ➤ 94

Car/Automobile Automobile

While driving, the following documents must be carried at all times: valid full driver's license, vehicle registration document and insurance documentation. If you don 't hold an EC format license, a translation of the license is also required. Visitors must carry their vehicle registration book/logbook and, if it is not their car, written consent from the owner.

Insurance for minimum Third Party risks is compulsory in Europe. It is recommended that you take out International motor insurance (or a "*Green Card*") through your insurer.

The most common crime against tourists in Italy is theft from rental cars. Always look for secure parking areas overnight and never leave valuables in your car at any time.

Essential equipment: warning triangle, nationality plate. Wearing seat-belts is compulsory. Children under 13 must travel in seats with special restraints.

Traffic on main roads has priority; where 2 roads of equal importance merge, traffic from the right has priority. On 3-lane roads, the central lane is for passing.

Minimum driving age: 18.

Tolls (**il pedaggio**) are payable on expressways [motorways] (**autostrada**) in Italy.

Traffic police can give on-the-spot fines (ask for a receipt).

The use of horns is prohibited in built-up areas except for emergencies.

Alcohol limit in blood: max. 80mg/100ml. Note that any alcohol may impair concentration.

Conversion Chart

km	1	10	20	30	40	50	60	70	80	90	100	110	120	130
miles	0.62	6	12	19	25	31	37	44	50	56	62	68	74	81

Road network

Italy	**autostrada** – toll expressway [motorway]; **superstrada** – non-toll expressway [motorway]; **strata statale** – main road; **strada provinciale** – secondary road; **stada comunale** – local road
Switzerland	**A** – expressway [motorway] toll free; **N** – main road; **E** – secondary road

Speed limits *mph (kmph)*	**Built-up area**	**Outside built-up area**	**(Toll) expressway/ highway [motorway]**
Italy	31 (50)	69 (110) main roads 55 (90) sec. roads	81 (130)
car with trailer/ caravan	31 (50)	44 (70)	50 (80)
Switzerland	31 (50)	50 (80)	62–74 (100–120)

Car rental L'autonoleggio

Third-party insurance (**R.C.A.**) is included in the basic rental charge, usually with a Collision Damage Waiver.

If you are traveling by air or train, you may want to take advantage of special inclusive arrangements for car rental. Small local firms are generally cheaper than international or major Italian rental companies, but cars can only be booked locally. Some firms require a minimum age of 21; a valid license held for at least one year is a standard requirement.

Where can I rent a car?	**Dove posso noleggiare un'auto(mobile)?** *dovay posso nolaydjaaray oonowto (oonowtomobeelay)*
I'd like to rent a(n) ...	**Vorrei noleggiare ...** *vorrehee nolaydjaaray*
2-/4-door car	**un'auto a due/a quattro porte** *oonowto ah doo-ay/ah kwattro portay*
an automatic	**con cambio automatico** *kon kambeeo owtomaateeko*
with air conditioning	**con aria condizionata** *kon areea kondeetseeonaata*
I'd like it for a day/a week.	**Vorrei noleggiarla per un giorno/una settimana.** *vorrehee nolaydjaaray pehr oon jorno/oona saytteemaana*
How much does it cost per day/week?	**Quanto costa al giorno/alla settimana?** *kwanto kosta al jorno/ alla saytteemaana*
Are mileage and insurance included?	**Il chilometraggio e l'assicurazione sono inclusi?** *eel keelomaytradjo ay lasseekooratseeonay sono eengkloosee*
Can I leave the car at ...?	**Posso lasciare la macchina a ...?** *posso lashaaray la makkeena ah*
What kind of fuel does it take?	**Che tipo di benzina prende?** *kay teepo dee bayndzeena praynday*
Where is the high/ low beam?	**Dove sono gli abbaglianti/anabbaglianti?** *dovay sono lyee abbalyeeantee/ anabbalyeeantee*
Could I have full insurance, please?	**Vorrei una polizza di assicurazione completa.** *vorrehee oona poleetsa dee asseekooratseeonay komplayta*

DAYS OF THE WEEK ➤ 218; PAYING ➤ 89

Gas station La stazione di servizio

Where's the next gas [petrol] station, please?	**Dov'è la prossima stazione di servizio?** *doveh la prosseema statseeonay dee sayrveetseeo*
Is it self-service?	**È un distributore automatico?** *eh oon deestreebootoray owtomateeko*
Fill it up, please.	**Il pieno, per favore.** *eel peeayno pehr favoray*
... liters of ... , please.	**... litri di benzina ..., per favore.** *leetree dee bayndzeena ... pehr favoray*
super/regular	**super/normale** *super/normaalay*
lead-free/diesel	**verde/il diesel** *vayrday/eel diesel*
Where is the air pump/water?	**Dov'è la pompa per l'aria/l'acqua?** *doveh la pompa pehr lareea/lakwa*

⊘	**PREZZO AL LITRO**	price per liter/litre	⊖

Parking Parcheggio

Most street parking is limited in town centers. Tokens (**dischi di sosta**) for parking (up to 1 hour) in blue zones are obtained from tourist organizations, automobile clubs and service stations. Set the disc to show when you arrived and when you must leave.

In Rome, central parking (in the **zona tutelata**) on weekdays is prohibited; punishable by a fine and prison sentence.

Is there a parking lot [car park] nearby?	**C'è un parcheggio qui vicino?** *cheh oon parkaydjo kwee veecheeno*
What's the charge per hour/per day?	**Quanto costa all'ora/al giorno?** *kwanto kosta allora/ al jorno*
Do you have some change for the parking meter?	**Ha moneta per il parchimetro?** *ah monayta pehr eel parkeemaytro*
My car has been booted [clamped]. Who do I call?	**La mia auto è stata bloccata con ceppo bloccaruote. A chi devo rivolgermi?** *la meea owto ay staata blokkaata kon chayppo blokkaroo-otay. a kee dayvo reevoljayrmee*

NUMBERS ➤ 216; DIRECTIONS ➤ 94

Breakdown Guasti

For help in the event of a breakdown:
refer to your breakdown assistance documents; or contact the **ACI** (**Automobile Club d'Italia**) breakdown service:
Italy: ☎ 116.

Where is the nearest garage?	**Dov'è l'autorimessa più vicina?** *doveh lowtoreemaysssa peeoo veecheena*
I've had a breakdown.	**Ho un guasto all'automobile.** *o oon goosto allowtomobeelay*
Can you send a mechanic/ tow [breakdown] truck?	**Può mandare un meccanico/un carro attrezzi?** *pwo mandaaray oon maykkaneeko/ oon karro attraytzee*
I belong to … rescue service.	**Sono socio del servizio soccorso stradale …** *sono socho dayl sayrveetseeo sokkorso stradaalay*
My license plate number is …	**La mia targa è …** *la meea targa eh*
The car is …	**L'auto è …** *lowto eh*
on the highway [motorway]	**sull'autostrada** *soollowtostraada*
2 km from …	**a due chilometri da …** *ah doo-ay keelomaytree da*
How long will you be?	**Fra quanto tempo arriva?** *fra kwanto taympo arreeva*

What's wrong? Che guasto ha?

My car won't start.	**L'auto non parte.** *lowto non partay*
The battery is dead.	**La batteria è scarica.** *la battayreea eh skareeka*
I've run out of gas [petrol].	**Ho finito la benzina.** *oh feeneeto la bayndzeena*
I have a flat [pucture].	**Ho forato.** *oh foraato*
There is something wrong with …	**C'è qualcosa che non funziona con …** *cheh kwalkosa kay non foontseeona kon*
I've locked the keys in the car.	**Ho chiuso le chiavi dentro la macchina.** *o keeoozo lay keeaavee dayntro la makkeena*

TELEPHONING ➤ 127; CAR PARTS ➤ 90–91

Repairs Riparazioni

Do you do repairs?	**Fa riparazioni?** *fa reeparatseeonee*
Can you repair it (temporarily)?	**Può fare una riparazione (provvisoria)?** *pwo faaray oona reeparatseeonay (provveezoreea)*
Please make only essential repairs.	**Faccia solo le riparazioni essenziali, per favore.** *fatcha solo lay reeparatseeonay ayssayntseeaalee pehr favoray*
Can I wait for it?	**Posso aspettare?** *posso aspayttaaray*
Can you repair it today?	**Può ripararla oggi?** *pwo reeparaarla odjee*
When will it be ready?	**Quando sarà pronta?** *kwando sara pronta*
How much will it cost?	**Quanto costerà?** *kwanto kostayra*
That's outrageous!	**Non esageriamo!** *non aysajayreeaamo*
Can I have a receipt for the insurance?	**Mi dia una ricevuta per l'assicurazione, per favore.** *mee deea oona reechayvoota pehr lasseekooratseeonay pehr favoray*

... non funziona.	The ... isn't working.
Non ho i pezzi di ricambio necessari.	I don't have the necessary parts.
Devo ordinare i pezzi di ricambio.	I will have to order the parts.
Posso solo fare una riparazione provvisoria.	I can only repair it temporarily.
La sua macchina è inservibile.	Your car is totaled/a write-off.
Non si può riparare.	It can't be repaired.
Sarà pronta ...	It will be ready ...
oggi più tardi	later today
domani	tomorrow
fra ... giorni.	in ... days

TIME ➤ 220; NUMBERS ➤ 216

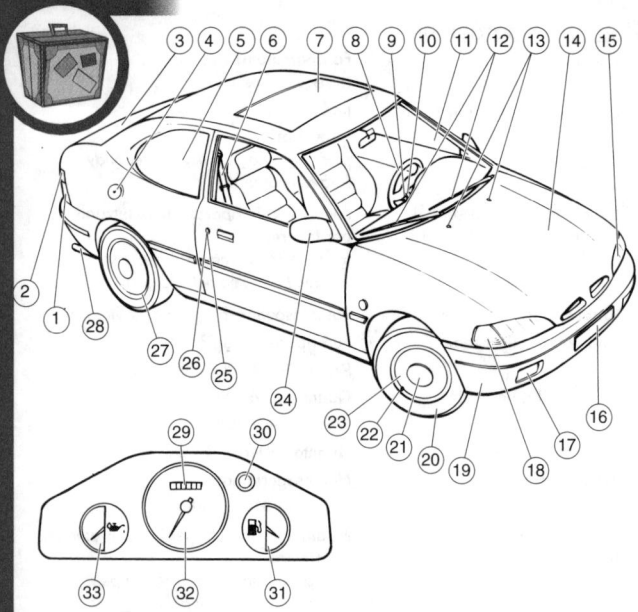

1 tail lights [back lights]
i fanali posteriori
2 brakelights **le luci dei freni**
3 trunk [boot] **il portabagagli**
4 gas cap
il tappo del serbatoio
5 window **il lunotto**
6 seat belt **la cintura di sicurezza**
7 sunroof **il tetto apribile**
8 steering wheel **il volante**
9 ignition/starter **l'accensione**
10 ignition key
la chiave dell'accensione
11 windshield **il parabrezza**
12 windshield [windscreen] wipers
il tergicristallo
13 windshield [windscreen] washers
i lavacristalli
14 hood **il cofano**
15 headlights **i fari/gli abbaglianti**
16 license plate **la targa**
17 fog lamp **il fanale antinebbia**
18 turn signals [indicators]
gli indicatori di posizione
19 bumper **il paraurti**
20 tires **i pneumatici**
21 hubcap **la coppa**
22 valve **la valvola**
23 wheels **le ruote**
24 outside mirror
lo specchietto retrovisore esterno
25 automatic locks
la chiusura centralizzata
26 lock **la chiusura**
27 wheel rim **il cerchione**
28 exhaust pipe **il tubo di scappamento**
29 odometer **il contachilometri**

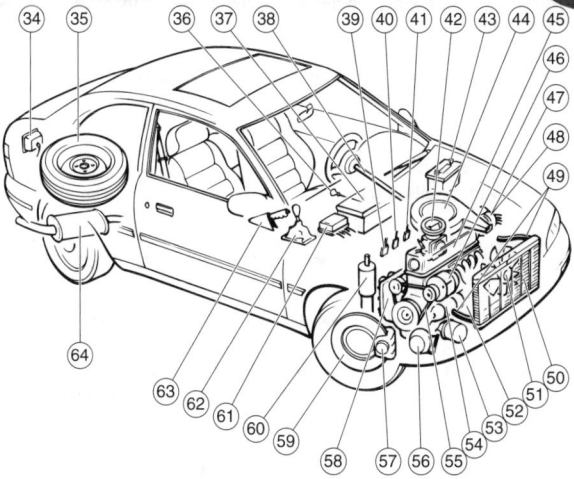

30 warning light **le luci d'emergenza**
31 fuel gauge
l'indicatore della benzina
32 speedometer **l'indicatore di velocità**
33 oil gauge
l'indicatore del livello dell'olio
34 backup lights **le luci di retromarcia**
35 spare tire [wheel] **il pneumatico/ la gomma di ricambio**
36 choke **la valvola d'aria**
37 heater **l'impianto di riscaldamento**
38 steering column il **piantone**
39 accelerator **l'acceleratore**
40 pedal **il pedale**
41 clutch **la frizione**
42 carburetor **il carburatore**
43 battery **la batteria**
44 alternator **l'alternatore**
45 camshaft **l'albero a camme**
46 air filter **il filtro dell'aria**
47 distributor **il distributore**
48 points **le candele**
49 radiator hose (top/bottom)
il tubo del radiatore
50 radiator **il radiatore**
51 fan **il ventilatore**
52 engine **il motore**
53 oil filter **il filtro dell'olio**
54 starter motor **il motorino d'avviamento**
55 fan belt **la cinghia del ventilatore**
56 horn **il claxon**
57 brake pads **la ganascia dei freni**
58 transmission/gearbox
il cambio di velocità
59 brakes **i freni**
60 shock absorbers **gli ammortizzatori**
61 fuses **i fusibili**
62 gear shift **la leva del cambio**
63 handbrake **il freno a mano**
64 muffler **il silenziatore**

Accidents Incidenti

In the event of an accident:

1. put your red warning triangle about 100 meters [metres] behind your car;

2. report the accident to the police (compulsory if there is personal injury); don't leave before they arrive;

3. show your driver's license and green card;

4. give your name, address, insurance company to the other party;

5. report to the appropriate insurance bureaus of the third party and your own company;

6. don't make any written statement without advice of a lawyer or automobile club official;

7. note all relevant details of the other party, any independent witnesses of the accident.

There has been an accident.	**C'è stato un incidente.** *cheh staato oon eencheedayntay*
It's ...	**È ...** *eh*
on the highway [motorway]	**sull'autostrada** *soollowtostraada*
near ...	**vicino a ...** *veecheeno ah*
Where's the nearest telephone?	**Dov'è il telefono più vicino?** *doveh eel taylayfono peeoo veecheeno*
Call ...	**Chiami ...** *keeaamee*
the police	**la polizia/i carabinieri** *la poleetseea/ee karabeeñehree*
an ambulance	**un'ambulanza** *oon amboolantsa*
a doctor	**un medico** *oon maydeeko*
the fire department [brigade]	**i pompieri** *ee pompeeehree*
Help me, please!	**Mi aiuti, per favore!** *mee aeeootee pehr favoray*

Injuries Ferite

There are people injured.	**Ci sono dei feriti.** *chee sono day fayreetee*
No one is hurt.	**Non ci sono feriti.** *non chee sono fayreetee*
He is seriously injured.	**È gravemente ferito.** *eh gravaymayntay fayreeto*
She's unconscious.	**Ha perso conoscenza.** *ah payrso konoshayntsa*

INJURIES/DOCTOR ➤ 162; DIRECTIONS ➤ 94

Legal matters Questioni legali

What's your insurance company? **Qual'è la sua compagnia d'assicurazione?** *kwaleh la sooa kompañeea dasseekooratseeonay*

What's your name and address? **Qual'è il suo nome e il suo indirizzo?** *kwaleh eel soo-o nomay ay eel soo-o eendeereetso*

He ran into me. **Mi ha investito.** *mee ah eenvaysteeto*

She was driving too fast/ too close. **Stava guidando troppo veloce/troppo vicino.** *staava gooeedando troppo vaylochay/ troppo veecheeno*

I had the right of way. **Avevo la precedenza.** *avayvo la praychaydayntsa*

I was only driving ... km/h. **Guidavo solo a ... chilometri all'ora.** *gooeedaavo solo ah ... keelomaytree allora*

I'd like an interpreter. **Vorrei un interprete.** *vorrehee oon eentayrpraytay*

I didn't see the sign. **Non ho visto il segnale.** *non oh veesto eel sayñaalay*

The license plate [registration] number was ... **Il numero di targa era ...** *eel noomayro dee targa ayra*

Mi faccia vedere ... per favore.	Can I see your ... please?
la patente di guida	driver's license/licence
la polizza d'assicurazione	insurance certificate
i documenti del veicolo.	vehicle registration
A che ora è successo?	What time did it happen?
Dove è successo?	Where did it happen?
C'erano altre persone coinvolte?	Was anyone else involved?
Ci sono testimoni?	Are there any witnesses?
Lei stava accelerando.	You were speeding.
Le sue luci non funzionano.	Your lights aren't working.
Deve pagare un'ammenda/ una multa ora.	You'll have to pay a fine (on the spot).
Deve fare una dichiarazione in Commissariato.	You have to make a statement at the station.

POLICE ➤ 152; TIME ➤ 220

Asking directions Chiedere la strada

Excuse me, please.	**Scusi, per favore.** *skoozee pehr favoray*
How do I get to ...?	**Come si arriva a ...?** *komay see arreeva ah*
Where is ...?	**Dov'è ... ?** *doveh*
Can you show me on the map where I am?	**Può indicarmi dove sono sulla carta?** *pwo eendeekaarmee dovay sono soolla karta*
I've lost my way.	**Mi sono perso/smarrito.** *mee sono payrso/ smarreeto*
Can you repeat that, please?	**Può ripetere, per favore?** *pwo reepaytayray pehr favoray*
Thanks for your help.	**Grazie (per il suo aiuto).** *graatseeay (pehr eel soo-o aeeooto)*

Traveling by car Viaggiare in automobile

Is this the right road for ...?	**È questa la strada per ...?** *eh kwaysta la straada pehr*
How far is it to ... from here?	**Quant'è lontano/a ... da qui?** *kwanteh lontaano/a ... da kwee*
Where does this road lead?	**Dove porta questa strada?** *dovay porta kwaysta straada*
How do I get onto the highway [motorway]?	**Come si entra in autostrada?** *komay see ayntra een owtostraada*
What's the next town called?	**Come si chiama la prossima città?** *komay see keeaama la prosseema cheetta*
How long does it take by car?	**Quanto tempo ci vuole in macchina?** *kwanto taympo chee vwolay een makkeena*

– Scusi, per favore. Come si arriva a la stazione?
(Excuse me, please. How do I get to the train station?)
– Prenda la terza svolta a sinistra ed è sempre dritto.
(Take the third left and it's straight ahead.)
– La terza a sinistra. È lontano? (The third left. Is it far?)
– È a dieci minuti ... a piedi. (It's ten minutes ... on foot.)
– Grazie. (Thanks.)
– Prego. (You're welcome.)

È ...	It's ...
(sempre) dritto	straight ahead
a sinistra/a destra	on the left/on the right
dall'altro lato della strada	on the other side of the street
all'angolo	on the corner
dietro l'angolo	around the corner
in direzione di ...	in the direction of ...
di fronte .../dietro...	opposite .../behind ...
vicino a .../dopo ...	next to .../after ...
Scenda ...	Go down the ...
la strada laterale/ la strada principale	side street/main street
Attraversi ...	Cross the ...
la piazza/il ponte	square/bridge
Prenda la terza svolta a destra.	Take the third turn to the right.
Giri a sinistra ...	Turn left ...
dopo il primo semaforo	after the first traffic light
al secondo incrocio	at the second intersection [crossroad]

È ... da qui	It's ... of here.
al nord/al sud	north/south
all'est/all'ovest	east/west
Prenda la strada per ...	Take the road for ...
È sulla strada sbagliata	You're on the wrong road.
Deve ritornare a ...	You'll have to go back to ...
Segua le indicazioni per ...	Follow the signs for ...

È ...	It's ...
vicino/lontano	close/a long way
a cinque minuti a piedi	5 minutes on foot
a dieci minuti in auto	10 minutes by car
a circa dieci chilometri	about 10 km away

TIME ➤ 220; NUMBERS ➤ 216

Road signs La segnaletica

ACCESSO LIMITATO	access only
PERCORSO ALTERNATIVO	alternative route
DEVIAZIONE	detour [diversion]
METTERSI IN CORSIA	get in lane
DARE LA PRECEDENZA	yield [give way]
PONTE BASSO	low bridge
SENSO UNICO	one-way street
STRADA CHIUSA	road closed
SCUOLA	school
ACCENDERE I FARI	use headlights

Town plans Carte della città

aeroporto (m)	*ayroporto*	airport
attraversamento (m) pedonale	*attravayrsamaynto paydonaalay*	pedestrian crossing
campo (m) sportivo	*kampo sporteevo*	playing field [sports ground]
chiesa (f)	*kee-ehza*	church
cinema (m)	*cheenayma*	movie theater [cinema]
città (f) storica	*cheetta storeeka*	old town
commissariato (m)	*kommeessareeaato*	police station
edifici (mpl) pubblici	*aydeefeechee poobbleechee*	public building
fermata (f) d'autobus	*fayrmaata dowtobooss*	bus stop
gabinetti (mpl)	*gabeenayttee*	restrooms [toilets]
lei è qui	*lay eh kwee*	you are here
parcheggio (m)	*paarkaydjo*	parking lot [car park]
parco (m)	*parko*	park
percorso (m) d' autobus	*pehrkoarsoa dowtoabooss*	bus route
posteggio (m) tassì	*postedjo tassee*	taxi stand [rank]
sottopassaggio (m)	*sottopassadjo*	underpass
stadio (m)	*stadeeo*	stadium
stazione (f) (metropolitana)	*statseeonay (maytropoleetana)*	subway [metro] station
ufficio (m) postale	*looffeecho*	post office
via (f) principale	*veea preencheepaalay*	main [high] street
zona (f) pedonale	*dzona paydonaalay*	pedestrian zone

DICTIONARY ➤ 169; SIGHTSEEING ➤ 97–107

Sightseeing

Tourist information	**97**	**Tourist glossary**	**102**
Excursions	**98**	**Who/What/When?**	**104**
Sights	**99**	**Churches**	**105**
Admission	**100**	**In the countryside**	**106**
Impressions	**101**	**Organized walks**	**106**

Tourist information office Ufficio turistico

Tourist information offices are often situated in the town center; look for **Ufficio turistico**.

Where's the tourist office?
Dov'è l'Ufficio turistico?
doveh looffeecho tooreesteeko

What are the main points of interest?
Quali sono i punti principali d'interesse?
kwalay sono ee poontee preencheepaalay deentayraysay

We're here for ...
Siamo qui per ...
seeaamo kwee pehr

only a few hours
solo poche ore
solo pochay oray

a day
un giorno *oon jorno*

a week
una settimana *oona saytteemaana*

Can you recommend ...?
Può suggerire ...?
pwo soodjayreeray

a sightseeing tour
un giro turistico
oon jeero tooreesteeko

an excursion
una escursione
oona ayskoorseeonay

a boat trip
una gita in barca
oona jeeta een baarka

Do you have any information on ...?
Ha informazioni su ...?
a eenformatseeonay soo

Are there any trips to ...?
Ci sono gite a ...?
chee sono jeetay ah

DAYS OF THE WEEK ➤ 218; DIRECTIONS ➤ 94

Excursions Escursiones

How much does the tour cost?
Quanto costa il giro?
kwanto kosta

Is lunch included?
Il pranzo è compreso?
eel prandzo eh komprayzo

Where do we leave from?
Da dove si parte? *da dovay partay*

What time does the tour start?
A che ora comincia la gita?
ah kay ora komeencha la jeeta

What time do we get back?
A che ora si ritorna?
ah kay ora see reetorna

Do we have free time in ...?
C'è del tempo libero a ...?
cheh dayl taympo leebayro ah

Is there an English-speaking guide?
C'è una guida di lingua inglese?
cheh oona gooeeda dee eengglayzay

On tour Durante la gita turistica

Are we going to see ...?
Andiamo a vedere ...?
andeeaamo ah vaydayray

We'd like to have a look at the ...
Vorremmo dare un'occhiata a ...
vorrehmmo daaray oonokeeaata ah

Can we stop here ...?
Possiamo fermarci qui ...?
posseeaamo fayrmaarchee kwee

to take photographs
per prendere fotografie
pehr prayndayray fotografeea

to buy souvenirs
per comprare dei souvenirs
pehr kohmpraaray dayee souvenirs

for the restrooms [toilets]
per la toeletta/il gabinetto
pehr la toaylaytta/eel gabeenaytto

Would you take a photo of us, please?
Le dispiace prendere una fotografia di noi? *lay deespeeachay prayndayray oona fotografeea dee noee*

How long do we have here/in ...?
Quanto tempo abbiamo qui/a ...?
kwanto taympo abbeeaamo kwee/ah

Wait! ... isn't back yet.
Aspetti! ... non è ancora ritornato(-a).
aspayttee non eh ankora reetornaato(-a)

Sights Luoghi d'interesse turistico

Town maps are on display in city centers, train, tram and many bus stations, and at tourist information offices.

Where is the ...?	**Dov'è ...?** *doveh*
abbey	**l'abbazia** *labbatseea*
art gallery	**la galleria d'arte** *la gallayreea dartay*
battleground	**i luoghi della battaglia** *ee looogee daylla battalya*
botanical garden	**il giardino botanico** *eel jardeeno botaneeko*
castle	**il castello** *eel kastayllo*
cathedral	**la cattedrale** *la kattaydraalay*
cemetery	**il cimitero** *eel cheemeetayro*
church	**la chiesa** *la keeayza*
downtown area	**il centro città** *eel chayntro cheeta*
fountain	**la fontana** *la fontaana*
market	**il mercato** *eel mayrkaato*
(war) memorial	**il monumento commemorativo** *eel monoomaynto kommaymorateevo*
monastery	**il monastero** *eel monastayro*
museum	**il museo** *eel moozayo*
old town	**la città vecchia** *la cheetta vaykeea*
opera house	**il teatro dell'opera** *eel teeatro dayllopayra*
palace	**il palazzo** *eel palaatso*
park	**il parco/il giardino** *eel parko/eel jordeeno*
parliament building	**il palazzo del Parlamento** *eel palaatso dayl parlamaynto*
ruins	**le rovine** *lay roveenay*
shopping area	**la zona dei negozi** *la dzona dayee naygotsee*
statue	**la statua** *la statoo-a*
viewpoint	**il punto(m) panoramico** *eel poonto panoraameeko*
Can you show me on the map?	**Può indicarmi sulla carta?** *pwo eendeekahrmee soollah kahrtah*

DIRECTIONS ➤ 94

Admission Ammissione

Check opening times to avoid disappointment: some museums close at 2 p.m. Churches usually close between midday and 4 p.m.

Is the ... open to the public?
... è aperto(-a) al pubblico?
eh apayrto(-a) al poobleeko

Can we look around?
Possiamo dare un'occhiata in giro?
posseeaamo daaray oonokeeaata een jeero

What are the hours?
Qual'è l'orario di apertura?
kwaleh loraareeo dee apayrtoora

When does it close?
A che ora chiude? *ah kay ora keeooday*

Is ... open on Sundays?
... è aperto(-a) la domenica?
eh apayrto(-a) la domayneeka

When's the next guided tour?
Quando è la prossima visita guidata?
kwando eh la prosseema veezeeta gooeedaata

Do you have a guide book (in English)?
C'è una guida (in inglese)?
ah oona gooeeda (een eengglayzay)

Can I take photos?
Posso fare fotografie?
posso faaray fotograafeeay

Is there access for the handicapped?
C'è accesso per disabili?
cheh achaysso pehr deesaabeelee

Is there an audio guide in English?
C'è una guida registrata in inglese?
cheh oona gooeeda rayjeestraata een eengglaysay

Paying/Tickets Pagare/Biglietti d'ingresso

How much is the entrance/entry fee?
Quant'è il biglietto d'ingresso?
kwanteh eel beelyaytto deenggraysso

Are there any discounts for ...?
Ci sono riduzioni/tariffe speciali per ...?
chee sono reedootseeonee/tareeffay spaychaalee pehr

children
bambini *bambeenee*

groups
gruppi *grooppee*

the handicapped
disabili *deesaabeelee*

senior citizens
anziani *antseeaanee*

1 adult and 2 children, please.
Un adulto e due bambini, per piacere.
oon adoolto ay doo-ay bambeenee pehr peeachayray

TIME ➤ 220

– Cinque biglietti, per favore.
Ci sono tariffe speciali?
(Five tickets, please.
Are there any discounts?)

– Sì. Per bambini e anziani fa diecimila Lire.
(Yes, children and senior citizens pay 10,000 L.)

– Due adulti e tre bambini, per favore.
(Two adults and three children, please.)

– Fa ottantamila Lire, per favore.
(That's 80,000 Lire, please.)

INGRESSO GRATUITO	free entry
CHIUSO	closed
ARTICOLI PER REGALO/SOUVENIR	gift shop
L'ULTIMO INGRESSO È ALLE ORE DICIASSETTE.	last entry at 5 p.m.
LA PROSSIMA VISITA ALLE ...	next tour at ...
INGRESSO VIETATO	no entry
VIETATO USARE IL FLASH.	no flash photography
APERTO	open

Impressions Impressioni

It's ...	**È ...** *eh*
amazing	**meraviglioso(-a)** *mayraveeleeoso(-a)*
beautiful	**bello(-a)** *bayllo(-a)*
boring	**noioso(-a)** *noeeozo(-a)*
breathtaking	**sensazionale** *saynsatseeonaalay*
brilliant	**splendido(-a)** *splayndeedo(-a)*
great fun	**molto divertente** *molto deevayrtayntay*
interesting	**interessante** *eentayrayssaantay*
magnificent	**magnifico** *mañeefeeko*
romantic	**romantico(-a)** *romanteeko(-a)*
strange	**strano(-a)** *straano(-a)*
superb	**stupendo(-a)** *stoopayndo(-a)*
terrible	**terribile** *tayrreebeelay*
ugly	**brutto(-a)** *brootto(-a)*
It's a good value.	**Ne vale la spesa.** *nay valay la spayza*
It's a rip-off.	**È una bidonata.** *eh oona beedonaata*
I like it.	**Mi piace.** *mee peeachay*

acquaforte f etching
acquarello m watercolor
affresco m fresco
ala f wing of building
altare m altarpiece
altorilievo m high relief
antichità fpl antiquities
appartamenti mpl **reali** royal apartments
arazzi mpl tapestry
arco m arch
arco m **rampante** buttress
arco m **trionfale** triumphal arch
argenteria f silverware
argento silver
arma f weapon
armeria f armory
artigianato m **d'arte** crafts
atrio m atrium
auriga f charioteer
badia f abbey
basso m **rilievo** bas-relief
biblioteca f library
biga f chariot
campanile m bell tower
camposanto m churchyard
cancello m gate
capolavoro m masterpiece
Cena The Last Supper
ceramica f ceramic
ceramiche fpl pottery
chiesa f church
collezione f collection
completato nel ... completed in
conferenza f lecture
contrafforte f buttress
cornicione m eaves
coro m choirstall
corona f crown
cortile m courtyard
costruito(-a) built in
cupola f dome
d'oro golden
da by person
dagherrotipo m daguerreotype
decorato(-a) da decorated by
decorazione f decoration
dettaglio m detail
dipinto m picture
dipinto(-a) da painted by
disegnato(-a) da designed by
disegno m design, drawing
distrutto(-a) da destroyed by
donato(-a) da donated by
dorato(-a) gilded
duomo m dome
edificio m building
eretto(-a) nel/in erected in
facciata facade
fibula f brooch
finestra f **con vetro colorato** stained-glass window
fondato(-a) nel founded in
fonte f font
foro m forum
fossato m moat
fregio m frieze
frontone m pediment
gargoglia f gargoyle
giardino f **formale** formal garden
gioielli mpl jewelry
guglia f spire
imperatore m emperor
imperatrice f empress
in prestito a on loan to
incisione f carving, engraving
ingresso m foyer

iniziò nel started in
liberto m freedman
maestà Madonna and Child in majesty
marmo m marble
mattone m brick
mobilia f/**mobili** mpl furniture
moneta f coin
morto(-a) nel died in
mostra f display, exhibition
muro m wall
nato(-a) nel ... a ... born in ... (year) in ... (town)
navata f nave
oggetto m **esibito/in mostra** exhibit
orecchini mpl earrings
orologio m clock
padiglione m pavilion
paesaggio m landscape painting
palcoscenico m stage
paliotto m altar frontal
Papato m Papacy
pastello m pastel
piano m plan
pietà f Virgin with crucified Christ
pietra f stone
pietra f **angolare** cornerstone
pietra f **preziosa** gemstone
pietra f **tombale** headstone
pilastro m pillar
pittore m, **pittrice** f painter
pittura f **murale** mural
pitture fpl **a olio** oils
placca f plaque
ponte m bridge
porta f **d'ingresso** doorway
ponte m **levatoio** drawbridge
primo livello m level 1
quadro m painting
rappresenta represents
re m king
regina f queen
regno m reign
restaurato nel restored in
ricostruito nel rebuilt in
ritratto m portrait
rocca m fortress/stronghold
rosone m rose window
rovine f ruins
ruderi fpl ruins
sagrestia sacristy
salone m **per cerimonie** stateroom
scala uno:cento scale 1:100
scala f staircase
scavi mpl excavations
scena f **drammatica** tableau
schiavo m slave
schizzo m sketch
scoperto(-a) nel discovered in
scultore m, **scultrice** f sculptor
scuola f **di** school of
secolo m century
sette colli fpl Seven Hills
spalti mpl battlement
a spina f **de pesce** herringbone
sporgente overhanging
statua f **di cera** waxwork
tapezzerie fpl tapestry
tela f canvas
terme fpl baths
tetto m roof
tomba f grave, tomb
torre f tower
trittico m triptych
vetro m glass
visse lived
volta f vault
zoccolo m molding

What's that building?	**Cos'è quell'edificio?** *koseh kwayllaydeefeecho*
When was it built/painted?	**Quando fu costruito(-a)/dipinto(-a)?** *kwando foo kostreeto(-a)/ deepeento(-a)*
Who was the ...?	**Chi era ...?** *kee ayra*
architect	**l'architetto** *larkeetaytto*
artist	**l'artista** *larteesta*
What style is that?	**Che stile è?** *kay steelay eh*

Roma repubblicana 753–27 b.c.

After periods of Etruscan (**etrusco**) and Greek (**ellenistico**) influence in Italy, Rome was founded in 753 b.c. The Republic was declared in 509 b.c.; the city expanded its empire across the known world (esp. in Punic Wars against the Carthaginians, ca. 2nd b.c.; and the military successes of Julius Caesar). Caesar's assassination (44 b.c.) brought civil war.

Roma imperiale 27 b.c.–467 a.d.

Caesar's adopted son, Octavius (Augustus), became the first emperor. His descendants (Tiberius, Caligula, Claudius, Nero) were followed by the Flavian, Antonine and Severus dynasties. This period of expansion saw great artistic and architectural achievements. In 382 a.d. Christianity was recognized as the state religion. However, decline set in, the Empire split into two and power was moved to Constantinople. Goths and Vandals plundered Rome, which fell to the Ostrogoths.

Età Mediovale 467–1300

Italy remained fractured, featuring powerful families such as the Medicis, independent city states like Venice, and increasing Papal power (with Rome as the capital of Western Christianity) through the Holy Roman Empire (**Santo impero romano**). Foreign involvement (Norman, German, French, Spanish and Austrian) continued in Italy beyond the Middle Ages into the nineteenth century.

il Risorgimento 1815–1870

The reunification of Italy as one kingdom was achieved by Victor Emmanuel II of Piedmont in 1861, with assistance from his minister Cavour and the exploits of Garibaldi. The final piece came when Rome was captured (1870).

Novocento ca. 20th century

Italy fought with the Allies in World War I, but Benito Mussolini allied with Hitler in World War II with devastating consequences. The Democratic Republic was established in 1946, with numerous fragile governments following. Italy was one of the founding members of the European Economic Community in 1957.

Rulers/Government Sovrani/Governi

What period is that? **Che periodo è ...?** *kay payreeodo eh*

Romano(-a) 500 b.c.–467 a.d.

Romans were great builders: ruins remain throughout Italy (esp. Rome) and Western Europe of their forums, basilicas, arenas, theaters, amphitheaters, markets, circuses, libraries, triumphal arches, catacombs, baths, temples, aqueducts, bridges, city walls and mausoleums.

Bizantino 400–1100

Byzantine influence from the Eastern Christian Empire emphasized grandeur and mystery with splendid mosaic-decorated interiors (esp. Ravenna; also later influence in St Mark's in Venice, Sicily and Rome).

Periodo gottico 1300–1400

Gothic style used complex architectural forms, using pointed arches and rib vaults (esp. cathedrals in Genoa and Siena, ornate window openings of Venetian houses, artistic work of Giotto in Padua, Assisi and Florence).

Il Rinascimento 1400–1650

The Renaissance was a hugely significant cultural and artistic movement, with a fascination with antiquity and admiration of beauty, colors, light, stability and poise. It saw stunning artistic creativity in the Quattrocento (ca. 15th cent.) esp. statues of Donatello, paintings of Botticelli; and Cinquecento (ca. 16th cent.) esp. Michelangelo (statues of David and Moses; Sistine Chapel ceiling), Leonardo da Vinci, Raphael, and the Venetian School (Titian, Tintoretto and El Greco).

Mannerismo 1550–1650

Mannerism enjoyed frivolities and exaggerated use of Renaissance features (esp. Tivoli and Bomarzo; artists Caravaggio and Palladio).

Barocco e Rococò 1640–1789

Baroque emphasized movement, using scrolls and ornate embellishments (e.g. Bernini's facade of St Peter's in Rome; artists Canaletto and Bellotto).

Churches Chiese

Predominantly Roman Catholic, Italy is rich in cathedrals and churches. Ask permission before taking photographs; cover bare shoulders before entering.

Catholic/Protestant church	**la chiesa cattolica/protestante** *la kee-ehza katoleeka/protaystantay*
mosque	**la moschea** *la moskeeah*
synagogue	**la sinagoga** *la seenagoga*
What time is ...?	**A che ora è ....?** *ah kay oara eh*
mass/the service	**la messa/il servizio** *la mayssa/eel sayrveetseeo*

In the countryside In campagna

I'd like a map of ... **Vorrei una carta di ...** *vorrehee oona karta dee*

this region **questa regione** *kwaysta rayjonay*

walking routes **percorsi a piedi** *pehrkorsee ah pee-ehdee*

cycle routes **percorsi per ciclisti** *pehrkorsee pehr cheekleestee*

How far is it to ...? **Quanto dista ...?** *kwanto deesta*

Is there a right of way? **C'è diritto di passaggio?** *cheh deereetto dee passadjo*

Is there a trail/scenic route to ...? **C'è un sentiero/una strada panoramica per ...?** *cheh oon saynteeehro/oona straada panorameeka pehr*

Can you show me on the map? **Puo indicarmi sulla carta?** *pwo eendeekaarmee soolla karta*

I'm lost. **Mi sono smarrito(-a).** *mee sono smareeto(-a)*

Organized walks Escursioni organizzate

When does the guided walk start? **A che ora comincia la passeggiata/l'escursione?** *ah kay ora komeencha la passaydjaata/layskoorseeonay*

When will we return? **Quando ritorneremo?** *kwando reetornayrehmo*

What is the walk like? **Com'è la passeggiata?** *komeh la passaydjaata*

gentle/medium/tough **facile/di media difficoltà/difficile** *facheelay/dee maydeea deeffeekolta/deeffeecheelay*

I'm exhausted. **Sono esausto(-a).** *sono aysaoosto(-a)*

What kind of ... is that? **Che tipo di ... è quello?** *kay teepo dee ... eh kwayllo*

animal/bird **animale/uccello** *aneemaalay/oochayllo*

flower/plant/tree **fiore/pianta/albero** *feeoray/peeanta/albayro*

Geographic features Aspetti geografici

bridge	**il ponte** *eel pontay*
cave	**la caverna/la grotta** *la kavayrna/la grotta*
cliff	**la scogliera/la rupe** *la sholee-ehra/ la roopay*
farm	**la fattoria/la cascina** *la fattoreea/ la kasheena*
field	**il campo** *eel kampo*
foot path	**il sentiero pedestre** *eel sayntee-ehro paydaystray*
forest	**la foresta** *la foraysta*
hill	**la collina** *la kolleena*
lake	**il lago** *eel lago*
mountain	**la montagna** *la montaaña*
mountain pass	**il passo di montagna** *eel passo dee montaaña*
mountain range	**la catena di montagne** *la katayna dee montaañay*
nature reserve	**l'oasi naturale** *loazee natooraale*
panorama	**il panorama/la vista** *eel panoraama/ la veesta*
park	**il parco** *eel parko*
peak	**il picco/la cima** *eel peeko/la cheema*
picnic area	**l'area per pic nic** *laraya pehr peekneek*
pond	**lo stagno** *lo staaño*
rapids	**le rapide** *lay rapeeday*
river	**il fiume** *eel feeoomay*
sea	**il mare** *eel maaray*
stream	**il ruscello/il torrente** *eel rooshayllo/ eel torrayntay*
valley	**la valle** *la vallay*
viewpoint	**il punto panoramico** *eel poonto panorameeko*
village	**il paese** *eel pa-ehsay*
winery [vineyard]	**le vigne** *lay veeñay*

Leisure

Events	108	Nightlife	112
Tickets	109	Admission	112
Movies [Cinema]	110	Children	113
Theater	110	Sports	114
Opera/Ballet/Dance	111	At the beach	116
Music/Concerts	111	Skiing	117

Events Spettacoli

Local papers and, in large cities, weekly entertainment guides will tell you what's on.

Do you have a program of events?	**Ha un programma delle manifestazioni?** *ah oon programa dayllay maneefaystatseeonee*
Can you recommend a good ...?	**Può suggerire un(a) buon(a) ...?** *pwo soodjayreeray oon(a) bwon(a)*
Is there a ... somewhere?	**C'è ...?** *cheh*
ballet/concert	**un balletto/un concerto** *oon ballaytto/oon konchayrto*
movie [film]	**un film** *oon film*
opera	**un'opera** *oonopayra*

Tickets for concerts, theater, and other cultural events are on sale at special ticket agencies (e.g. *Anteprima, Prenoticket, Prontobiglietto*) or major music stores (e.g. *Messaggerie Musicali, Ricordi*).

Availability Disponibilità

When does it start?	**A che ora comincia?** *ah kay ora komeencha*
When does it end?	**A che ora finisce?** *ah kay ora feeneeshay*
Are there any seats for tonight?	**Ci sono posti per questa sera?** *chee sono postee pehr kwaysta sayra*
Where can I get tickets?	**Dove si comprano i biglietti?** *dovay see kompraano ee beelyayttee*
There are ... of us.	**Siamo in ...** *see-aamo een*

Tickets Biglietti

How much are the seats?	**Quanto costano i posti?** *kwanto kostano ee postee*
Do you have anything cheaper?	**Ha qualcosa di meno caro?** *ah kwalkosa dee mayno karo*
I'd like to reserve ...	**Vorrei prenotare ...** *vorrehee praynotaaray*
3 for Sunday evening	**tre posti per domenica sera** *tray postee pehr domayneeka sayra*
May I have a program, please?	**Ha un programma, per piacere?** *ah oon programma pehr peeachayray*
Where's the coat room?	**Dov'è il guardaroba?** *doveh eel goo-ardaroba*

Mi dica ... della sua carta di credito?	What's your credit card ...?
il numero	number
il tipo	type
la data di scadenza	expiration date
Ritiri i biglietti ... per favore.	Please pick up the tickets ...
alle ... di sera	by ... p.m.
al banco prenotazioni	at the reservation desk

– Pronto. Teatro Puccini. (Hello, Puccini Theater.)
– Buongiorno. Vorrei due biglietti per la Bohème di questa sera.
(I'd like two tickets for tonight's "La Bohème".)
– Sì, certo. Mi dia il numero della sua carta di credito, per favore.
(Certainly. Your credit card number, please.)
– Sì. È il numero zero cinque zero tre sei cinque sette otto cinque quattro.
(Yes, 050 365 7854.)
– Bene. E qual'è la data di scadenza?
(What's the expiration date?)
– Luglio novantotto. (July ninety-eight.)
– Grazie. Può ritirare i biglietti al botteghino.
(Thank you. Please pick up the tickets at the box office.)

PRENOTAZIONI IN ANTICIPO	Advance bookings
ESAURITO	Sold out
BIGLIETTI PER LO SPETTACOLO DI OGGI	Tickets for today's show

NUMBERS ➤ 216

Movies Al cinema

Foreign films are always dubbed into Italian, but a few movie houses show films in the original version. Italy has a film industry of its own, with famous directors such as Fellini, Antonioni and Visconti, and more recently Bertolucci, the Taviani Brothers, Salvatores and Nanni Moretti. For a view of Italian humor, try a film by Carlo Verdone.

Is there a movie theater [cinema] near here?
C'è un cinema qui vicino?
cheh oon cheenayma kwee veecheeno

What's playing at the movies [What's on at the cinema] tonight?
Cosa danno al cinema questa sera?
kosa danno al cheenayma

Is the film dubbed/subtitled?
Il film è doppiato/ha i sottotitoli?
eel film eh doppeeaato/af ee sottoteetolee

Is the film in the original English?
Il film è in lingua originale inglese?
eel film eh een leengwa oreejeenaalay eengglayzay

A ..., please.
..., per favore. *pehr favoray*

box of popcorn
una scatola del popcorn
oona skatola dayl popcorn

chocolate ice cream [choc-ice]
un pinguino *oon peengweeno*

hot dog
una salciccia calda
oona salcheecha kalda

soft drink/soda
una bibita frizzante
oona beebeeta freetsantay

small/regular/large
piccolo(-a)/medio(-a)/grande
peekolo(a)/maydeeo(-a)/graanday

Theater A teatro

What's playing at the ... Theater?
Cosa danno al Teatro ...?
...kosa danno al teeatro

Who's the playwright?
Chi è il commediografo?
kee eh eel kommaydeeograafo

Do you think I'd enjoy it?
Pensa che mi piacerà?
paynsa kay mee peeachayra

I don't know much Italian.
Non conosco l'italiano molto bene.
non konosko leetaleeaano molto baynay

Opera/Ballet/Dance
All'opera/Balletto/Danza

In addition to the internationally renowned La Scala in Milan, excellent productions are found at the opera houses in Bologna, Florence, Naples, Parma, Rome and Turin. Also look for open-air productions in the summer, often held in Greek and Roman ruins.

Where's the opera house?	**Dov'è il teatro dell'Opera?** *doveh eel teatro dayllopayra*
Who's the composer/soloist?	**Chi è il compositore/il (la) solista?** *kee eh eel komozeetoray/eel (la) soleesta*
Is formal dress required?	**È necessario indossare abiti da sera?** *eh naychayssaareeo eendossaaray abeetee da sayra*
Who's dancing?	**Chi sono i ballerini?** *kee sono ee ballayreenee*
I'm interested in contemporary dance.	**Mi interessa la danza contemporanea.** *mee eentayraysa la dantsa kontaymporaaneha*

Music/Concerts Musica/Concerti

Where's the concert hall?	**Dov'è la sala concerti?** *doveh la sala konchayrtee*
Which orchestra/ band is playing?	**Che orchestra/gruppo sta suonando?** *kay orkaystra/groopo sta soo-onando*
What are they playing?	**Cosa stanno suonando?** *kosa stanno soo-onando*
Who is the conductor/soloist?	**Chi è il direttore d'orchestra/il (la) solista?** *kee eh eel deerayttoray dorkaystra/ eel (la) soleesta*
Who is the support band?	**Chi è il gruppo di supporto?** *kee eh eel grooppo dee soopporto*
I really like ...	**Mi piace molto...** *mee peeachay molto*
country music	**la musica country** *la moozeeka country*
folk music	**la musica folcloristica** *la moozeeka folkloreesteeka*
jazz	**il jazz** *eel djaz*
pop	**la musica pop** *la moozeeka pop*
rock music	**il rock** *eel rock*
soul music	**la musica soul** *la moozeeka soul*

Nightlife Vita notturna

What is there to do in the evenings? **Cosa c'è da fare di sera?** *kosa cheh da faaray dee sayra*

Can you recommend a ...? **Può suggerire ...?** *pwo soodjayreeray*

Is there a ... in town? **C'è ... in città?** *cheh een cheetta*

bar **un bar** *oon bar*

casino **un casinò** *oon kazeeno*

discotheque **una discoteca** *oona deeskotayka*

gay club **un locale gay** *oon lokaalay gay*

nightclub **un nightclub** *oon nightclub*

restaurant **un ristorante** *oon reestorantay*

What type of music do they play? **Che tipo di musica suonano?** *kay teepo dee moozeeka soo-onano*

How do I get there? **Come si arriva?** *komay see arreeva*

Admission Ammissione

What time does the show start? **A che ora comincia lo spettacolo?** *ah kay ora komeencha lo spayttakolo*

Is evening dress required? **È necessario l'abito da sera?** *eh naychayssareeo labeeto da sayra*

Is there a cover charge? **Si deve pagare il coperto?** *see dayvay pagaaray eel kopayrto*

Is a reservation necessary? **Si deve prenotare?** *see dayvay praynotaaray*

Do we need to be members? **È necessario essere soci?** *eh naychayssaareeo ayssayray sochee*

How long will we have to stand in line [queue]? **Per quanto tempo si deve aspettare/fare la coda?** *pehr kwanto taympo see dayvay aspayttaaray/faaray la koda*

I'd like a good table. **Vorrei un buon tavolo.** *vorrehee oon bwon tavolo*

È COMPRESA UNA BIBITA GRATUITA includes 1 complimentary drink

TIME ➤ 220; TAXI ➤ 84

Children Bambini

Can you recommend something for the children?	**Può suggerire qualcosa per i bambini?** *pwo soodjayreeray kwalkosa pehr ee bambeenee*
Are there changing facilities here for infants?	**Dove si possono cambiare i pannolini?** *dovay see possono kambeeaaray ee pannoleenee*
Where are the restrooms [toilets]?	**Dove sono le toelette/i gabinetti?** *dovay sono lay toaylayttay/ ee gabeenayttee*
amusement arcade	**la sala da giochi** *la sala dah jokee*
fairground	**la fiera** *la fee-ehra*
kiddie [paddling] pool	**la piscina per bambini** *la peesheena pehr bambeenee*
playground	**il parco giochi** *eel parko jokee*
playgroup	**un club per bambini/un miniclub** *oon kloob pehr bambeenee/oon meeneekloob*
zoo	**uno zoo** *oono dzoh*

Baby-sitting Servizio di babysitter

Can you recommend a reliable baby-sitter?	**Può raccomandare una buona babysitter?** *pwo rakomandaaray oona bwona babysitter*
Is there constant supervision?	**C'è sorveglianza continua?** *cheh sorvaylyaantsa konteenoo-a*
Are the helpers properly trained?	**Gli assistenti sono tutti addestrati?** *lyee asseestayntee sono toottee addaystraatee*
When can I drop them off?	**Quando posso lasciarli(-le)?** *kwando posso lashaarlee(-lay)*
I'll pick them up at …	**Li (Le) passo a prendere alle …** *lee (lay) passo ah praynday ray allay*
We'll be back by …	**Ritorno alle …** *reetorno allay*
She's 3 and he's 18 months.	**Lei ha tre anni e lui ha diciotto mesi.** *layee ah tray annee ay looee ah deechotto mayzee*

Sports Lo sport

Soccer [football], tennis, boxing, wrestling, windsurfing and bicycle, car and horseracing are the most popular sports.

If you like sailing, fishing, horseback riding, golf, tennis, hiking, cycling, swimming or golf, you'll find plenty of opportunity to satisfy your recreational bent.

il calcio *eel kalcho*

Soccer is the overriding passion in Italy, which boasts probably the best league in the world (Serie A) with teams of the calibre of Juventus (Turin), Inter Milan, AC Milan, Roma and Sampdoria (Florence). The intensity with which fans support their team creates a thrilling atmosphere during matches. In addition, the stadiums in Rome (Stadio Olimpico), Milan (Stadio San Siro) and Naples (Stadio del Vomero) are particularly striking.

Spectator Sports Assistere

Is there a soccer game [football match] this Saturday?	**C'è una partita di calcio questa sera** *cheh oona parteeta dee kalcho kwaysta sayra*
Which teams are playing?	**Quali squadre giocano?** *kwalee skwadray jokano*
Can you get me a ticket?	**Può comprarmi un biglietto?** *pwo komprraaray oon beelyaytto*
What's the admission charge?	**Quanto costa l'entrata?** *kwanto kosta layntraata*
Where's the racetrack [race course]?	**Dov'è l'ippodromo?** *doveh leeppodromo*
Where can I place a bet?	**Dove si scommette?** *dovay see skommayttay*
What are the odds on ...?	**Qual'è il pronostico su ....?** *kwaleh eel pronosteeko soo*
athletics	**l'atletica** *l'atlayteeka*
basketball	**la pallacanestro** *la pallakanaystro*
cycling	**il ciclismo** *eel cheekleesmo*
golf	**il golf** *eel golf*
horseracing	**l'ippica** *leepeeka*
soccer [football]	**il calcio** *eel kalcho*
swimming	**nuoto** *noo-oto*
tennis	**tennis** *tennis*
volleyball	**pallavolo** *pallavollo*

Playing Giocare

Where's the nearest ...?	**Dov'è ... più vicino(-a)?** *doveh peeoo veecheeno(-a)*
golf course	**il campo di golf** *eel kampo dee golf*
sports club	**la palestra sportiva** *la palaystra sporteevo*
Where are the tennis courts?	**Dove sono i campi da tennis?** *dovay sono ee kampee da tennis*
What's the charge per ...?	**Quanto costa per ...?** *kwanto kosta pehr*
day/round/game/hour	**giorno/giro/partita/ora** *jorno/jeero/parteeta/ora*
Do I need to be a member?	**È necessario essere soci?** *eh naychayssaareeo aylssayray sochee*
Where can I rent ...?	**Dove posso noleggiare ...?** *dovay posso nolaydjaaray*
boots	**gli scarponi** *lyee skaarponee*
clubs	**le mazze** *lay matsay*
equipment	**l'attrezzatura** *lattraytsatooray*
a racket	**la racchetta** *la rakaytta*
Can I get lessons?	**Vorrei prendere qualche lezione?** *vorrehee prayndayray kwalkay laytseeonay*
Do you have a fitness room?	**C'è una sala di allenamento?** *cheh oona sala dee allaynamaynto*
Can I join in?	**Posso partecipare?** *posso partaycheepaaray*

Mi dispiace, è tutto prenotato.	I'm sorry, we're booked.
C'è una caparra/un anticipo di ...	There is a deposit of ...
Che taglia/che misura ha ?	What size are you?
Deve avere una fotografia formato passaporto.	You need a passport-size photo.

SPOGLIATOI	Locker rooms
PESCA VIETATA	No fishing
RISERVATO AI DETENTORI DI LICENZA	Permit holders only

At the beach In spiaggia

Italy abounds in beaches and sea resorts, and it is not too difficult to locate near-deserted coves for a quieter time. The most developed resorts offer a full range of facilities for watersports.

Nearly all beaches have private bathing establishments where you can rent cabins, deck chairs and sunbeds. Often the beach boys (**bagnini**) are also lifeguards, distinguished by their red shorts and vests.

A red flag signifies rough sea, a white flag denotes calm sea with safe bathing.

Is the beach ...? pebbly/sandy	**La spiaggia è ...?** *la speeadja eh* **pietrosa/sabbiosa** *peeehtroso/sabbeeosa*
Is there a ... here?	**C'è ... qui?** *cheh ... kwee*
children's pool	**una piscina per bambini** *oona peesheena pehr bambeenee*
swimming pool	**una piscina** *oona peesheena*
indoor/outdoor	**invernale/all'aperto** *eenvayrnaalay/allapayrto*
Is it safe to swim/dive here?	**Si può nuotare tuffare senza pericolo?** *see pwo nootaaray too-fah-ray sayntsa payreekolo*
Is it safe for children?	**È sicuro per i bambini?** *eh seekooro pehr bambeenee*
Is there a lifeguard?	**C'è un bagnino?** *cheh oon bañeeno*
I want to rent a/some...	**Vorrei noleggiare ...** *vorrehee nolaydjaaray*
deck chair	**una sedia a sdraio** *oona saydeea ah sdraeeo*
jet ski	**una moto acquatica** *oona moto akwatika*
motorboat	**una barca a motore** *oona barka ah motoray*
diving equipment	**attrezzature da sub** *attraytsatooray da soob*
umbrella [sunshade]	**un ombrellone** *oon ombrayllonay*
surfboard	**una tavola da surf** *oona tavola da surf*
waterskis	**degli sci d'acqua** *daylyee shee dakwa*
For ... hours.	**Per ... ore.** *pehr ... oray*

Skiing Lo sci

There is excellent skiing for enthusiasts, both beginners and experts, in the Dolomites and the Italian Alps (Valle D'Aosta); further south, the Apennines and the slopes of Etna also offer skiing.

Is there much snow?	**C'è molta neve?** *cheh molta nayvay*
What's the snow like?	**Com'è la neve?** *komeh la nayvay*
heavy / icy	**spessa/ghiacciata** *spayssa/geeachaata*
powdery / wet	**farinosa/bagnata** *fareenosa/bañaata*
I'd like to rent ...	**Vorrei noleggiare ...** *vorrehee nolaydjaaray*
poles	**i bastoncini** *ee bastoncheenee*
skates	**i pattini (da ghiaccio)** *ee patteenee (da geeacho)*
ski boots	**gli scarponi (da sci)** *lyee skarponee (da shee)*
skis	**gli sci** *lyee shee*
These are too ...	**Questi(-e) sono troppo ...** *kwaystee(-ay) sono troppo*
big / small	**grandi/piccoli(e)** *graandee/peekolee(-ay)*
They're uncomfortable.	**sono scomodi(-e).** *sono skomodee(-ay)*
A lift pass for a day / 5 days, please.	**Una tessera per la sciovia per un giorno/cinque giorni, per favore.** *oona tayssayra pehr la sheeoveea pehr oon jorno/cheengkway jornee pehr favoray*
I'd like to join the ski school.	**Vorrei iscrivermi alla scuola sci.** *vorrehee eeskreevayrmee alla skooola shee.*
I'm a beginner.	**Sono un principiante.** *sono oon preencheepeeantay*
I'm experienced.	**Ho esperienza.** *oh ayspayree-ehntsah*

LA FUNIVIA	cable car / gondola	
LA SEGGIOVIA	chair lift	
LA SCIOVIA	tow lift	

Making Friends

Introductions	118	Enjoying your trip?	123
Where are you from?	119	Invitations	124
Who are you with?	120	Encounters	126
What do you do?	121	Telephoning	127

Introductions Presentazioni

Greetings vary according to how well you know someone.
The following is a guide:

It's polite to shake hands, both when you meet and say good-bye.

Begin any formal conversation, whether with a shop assistant or policeman, with a "**Buongiorno**".

Ciao! is an informal, universal expression, meaning both "hello, hi" and "so long, good-bye."

In Italian, there are two forms for "you" (taking different verb forms):
tu (singular) and **voi** (plural) are used when talking to relatives, close friends and children (and between young people);
Lei (singular) and **Loro** (plural) are used in all other cases (with the 3rd person singular/plural of the verb).

Hello, I don't think we've met.	**Buongiorno, non ci conosciamo.** *bwonjorno non chee konosheeaamo*
My name is ...	**Sono ...** *sono*
May I introduce ...?	**Posso presentarle ...?** *posso praysayntaarlay*
Pleased to meet you.	**Piacere/Molto lieto(-a).** *peeachayray/molto leeehto(-a)*
What's your name?	**Come si chiama?** *komay see keeaama*
How are you?	**Come sta?** *komay sta*
Fine, thanks. And you?	**Bene, grazie, e Lei?** *baynay graatseeay ay layee*

– Buongiorno, signora. Come sta?
(Hello, ma'am. How are you?)
– Molto bene, e Lei? (Fine, thanks. And you?)
– Bene, grazie. (Fine, thanks.)

Where are you from? Da dove viene?

Where do you come from?	**Da dove viene?** *da dovay veeaynay*
Where were you born?	**Dove è nato(-a)?** *dovay eh naato(-a)*
I'm from ...	**Vengo ...** *vaynggo*
Australia	**dall'Australia** *dallowstraaleea*
Britain	**dalla Gran Bretagna** *dalla gran braytaña*
Canada	**dal Canada** *dal kanada*
England	**dall'Inghilterra** *dalleenggeeltayrra*
Ireland	**dall'Irlanda** *dalleerlanda*
Scotland	**dalla Scozia** *dalla skotseea*
U.S.	**dagli Stati Uniti** *dalyee staatee ooneetee*
Wales	**dal Galles** *dal gallayss*
Where do you live?	**Dove vive?** *dovay veevay*
What part of ... are you from?	**Da quale parte ... viene?** *da kwalay partay ... vee-ehnay*
Italy	**dell'Italia** *daylleetaaleea*
Sicily	**della Sicilia** *daylla seecheeleea*
Switzerland	**della Svizzera** *daylla sveetsayra*
We come here every year.	**Veniamo ogni anno.** *vayneeaamo oñee anno*
It's my/our first visit.	**È la mia/nostra prima visita.** *eh la meea/nostra preema veezeeta*
Have you ever been to ...?	**È già stato in ...?** *eh ja staato een*
the U.K./the U.S.	**Gran Bretagna/negli Stati Uniti** *gran braytaña/naylyee staatee ooneeteee*
Do you like it here?	**Le piace questo posto?** *lay peeachay kwaysto posto*
What do you think of the ...?	**Cosa pensa di ...?** *kosa paynsa dee*
I love the ... here.	**Mi piace molto ... qui.** *mee peeachay molto ... kwee*
I don't really like the ... here.	**Non mi piace molto ... qui.** *non mee peeachay molto kwee*
food/people	**la cucina/la gente** *la koocheena/la jayntay*

Who are you with? / Family
Con chi è/La famiglia

Who are you with?	**Con chi è?** *kon kee eh*
I'm on my own.	**Sono (da) solo.** *sono (da) solo*
I'm with a friend.	**Sono con un amico/un'amica.** *sono kon oonameeko/oonameeka*
I'm with my ...	**Sono con ...** *sono kon*
wife	**mia moglie** *meea molyeeay*
husband	**mio marito** *meeo mareeto*
family	**la mia famiglia** *la meea fameelya*
children	**i miei figli** *ee meeayee feelyee*
parents	**i miei genitori** *ee meeayee jayneetoree*
boyfriend / girlfriend	**il mio ragazzo/la mia ragazza** *eel meeo ragatso/la meea ragatsa*
my father / son	**mio padre/figlio** *meeo padray/feelyo*
my mother / daughter	**mia madre/figlia** *meea madray/feelya*
my brother / uncle	**mio fratello/mio zio** *meeo fratayllo/meeo dzeeo*
my sister / aunt	**mia sorella/zia** *meea sorraylla/dzeea*
What's your son's / wife's name?	**Come si chiama suo figlio/sua moglie?** *komay see keeama soo-o feelyo/soo molyeeay*
Are you married?	**È sposato(-a)?** *eh sposaato(-a)*
I'm ...	**Sono ...** *sono*
married / single	**sposato(-a)/celibe** *sposaato(-a)/chayleebay*
divorced / separated	**divorziato(-a)/separato(-a)** *deevortseeaato(-a)/saypayraato(-a)*
engaged	**fidanzato(-a)** *feedantsaato(-a)*
We live together.	**Viviamo insieme.** *veeveeaamo eensee-ehmay*
Do you have any children?	**Ha bambini/figli?** *ah bambeenee/feelyee*
2 boys and a girl	**Due ragazzi e una ragazza** *doo-ay ragatsee ay oona ragatsa*
How old are they?	**Quanti anni hanno?** *kwantee annee anno*

What do you do? Che cosa fa?

What do you do?	**Che cosa fa?** *kay kosa fa*
What line are you in?	**Che lavoro fa?** *kay lavooro faa*
What are you studying?	**Che cosa studia?** *kay kosa stoodeea*
I'm studying ...	**Studio ...** *stoodeeo*
I'm in ...	**Mi occupo di ...** *mee okoopo dee*
business	**commercio** *kommayrcho*
engineering	**ingegneria** *eenjayñayreea*
retail	**commercio al dettaglio** *kommayrcho al dayttalyo*
sales	**vendite** *vayndeetay*
Who do you work for?	**Per chi lavora?** *pehr kee lavora*
I work for ...	**Lavoro per ...** *lavoro pehr*
I'm a(n) ...	**Sono ...** *sono*
accountant	**ragioniere(-a)** *rajonee-ehray(-a)*
housewife	**casalinga** *kazaleengga*
student	**studente(ssa)** *stoodayntay(ssa)*
retired	**in pensione** *een paynseeonay*
between jobs	**fra un lavoro e l'altro** *fra oon lavoro ay laltro*
I'm self-employed.	**Lavoro in proprio.** *lavoro een propreeo*
What are your interests/hobbies?	**Quali sono i suoi interessi/hobbies?** *kwalee sono ee sooeee eentayrayssee/hobbies*
I like ...	**Mi piace/piacciono ...** *mee peeachay/peeachono*
music	**la musica** *la moozeeka*
reading	**leggere** *laydjayray*
sports	**lo sport** *lo sport*
I play ...	**Gioco ...** *joko*
Would you like to play ...	**Le piacerebbe giocare ...** *lay peeachayraybbay jokaaray*
cards	**a carte** *ah kartay*
chess	**a scacchi** *ah skaakee*

What weather! Che tempo!

What a lovely day! **Che bella giornata!** *kay baylla jornaata*

What awful weather! **Che tempo orribile!** *kay taympo orreebeelay*

Isn't it cold/hot today! **Che caldo/freddo oggi!** *kay kaldo/frayddo odjee*

Is it usually as warm as this? **È così caldo di solito?** *eh kosee kaldo dee soleeto*

Do you think it's going to ... tomorrow? **Pensa che domani ...?** *paynsa kay domaanee*

be a nice day **sarà una bella giornata** *sara oona baylla jornaata*

rain **pioverà** *peeovayra*

snow **nevicherà** *nayveekayra*

What is the weather forecast? **Che previsioni ci sono?** *kay prayveeseeonay chee sono*

It's ... **È ...** *eh*

cloudy **nuvoloso** *noovoloso*

foggy **nebbioso** *naybbeeoso*

frosty **gelato** *jaylaato*

icy **ghiacciato** *geeachaato*

thundering **temporalesco** *taymporalaysko*

windy **ventoso** *vayntoso*

It's raining. **Piove.** *peeovay*

It's snowing. **Nevica.** *nayveeka*

It's sunny. **C'è il sole.** *chay eel solay*

Has the weather been like this for long? **Il tempo è così da molto tempo?** *eel taympo eh kosee da molto taympo*

What's the pollen count? **Com'è il conteggio del polline?** *komeh eel kontaydjo dayl polleenay*

high/medium/low **alto/medio/basso** *alto/maydeeo/basso*

What's the forecast for skiing? **Che previsioni ci sono per sciare?** *kay prayveeseeonee chee sono pehr sheeaaray*

Enjoying your trip? Si sta divertendo?

È in vacanza?	Are you on vacation?
Come è arrivato qui?	How did you travel here?
Dove alloggia?	Where are you staying?
Da quanto tempo è qui?	How long have you been here?
Quanto tempo si trattiene?	How long are you staying?
Cosa ha fatto finora?	What have you done so far?
Dove andrà dopo?	Where are you going next?
Si sta divertendo?	Are you enjoying your vacation?

I'm here on ...	**Sono qui ...** *sono kwee*
a business trip	**per affari** *pehr affaaree*
vacation [holiday]	**in vacanza** *een vakantsa*
We came by ...	**Siamo venuti(-e) in ...** *seeaamo vaynootee(-ay) een*
train/bus/plane	**treno/pullman/aereo** *trayno/pullman/aayreeo*
car/ferry	**auto/traghetto** *owto/tragaytto*
I have a rental car.	**Ho noleggiato una macchina** *o nolaydjaato oona makeena*
We're staying at ...	**Alloggiamo ...** *allodjaamo*
an apartment	**in un appartamento** *een oon appartamaynto*
a hotel/campsite	**in un albergo/un campeggio** *een oon albayrgo/oon kampaydjo*
with friends	**con amici** *kon ameechee*
Can you suggest ...?	**Può suggerire ...?** *pwo soodjayreeray*
things to do	**cose da fare** *kosay da faaray*
places to eat	**posti per mangiare** *postee pehr manjaaray*
places to visit	**luoghi di interesse** *loo-ogee dee eentayrassay*
We're having a great/ an awful time.	**Ci stiamo divertendo/annoiando.** *chee steeaamo deevayrtayndo/ annoeeando*

Invitations Inviti

Would you like to have dinner with us on ...?
Vuole venire a cena da noi ...? *vwolay vayneeray a chayna da noee*

May I invite you to lunch?
Posso invitarLa a pranzo? *posso eenveetaarla ah prandzo*

Can you come for coffee this evening?
Vuole venire a prendere il caffè da noi questa sera? *vwolay vayneeray ah praynday ray eel kaffeh da noee kwaysta sayra*

We're having a party. Can you come?
Facciamo una festa. Vuole venire? *fachaamo oona faysta. vwolay vayneeray*

May we join you?
Possiamo venire anche noi? *passeeaamo vayneeray ankay noee*

Would you like to join us?
Vuole venire anche Lei? *vwolay vayneeray ankay layee*

Going out Uscire

What are your plans for ...?
Cosa fa ...? *kosa fa*

today/tonight
oggi/questa sera *odjee/kwaysta sayra*

tomorrow
domani *domaanee*

Are you free this evening?
È libero(-a) questa sera? *eh leebayro(-a) kwaysta sayra*

Would you like to ...?
Le piacerebbe ...? *lay pee-achayraybbay*

go dancing
andare a ballare *andaaray ah ballaaray*

go for a drink/meal
andare al bar/al ristorante *andaaray al bar/al reestorantay*

go for a walk
fare una passeggiata *faaray oona passaydjaata*

go shopping
fare acquisti *faaray akweestee*

I'd like to go to ...
Mi piacerebbe andare ... *mee pee-achayraybbay andaaray*

I'd like to see ...
Mi piacerebbe vedere ... *mee pee-achayraybbay vaydayray*

Do you enjoy ...?
Le piace ...? *lay pee-achay*

Accepting or declining
Accettare o declinare

Great. I'd love to.	**Sarebbe magnifico.** *saraybbay mañeefeeko*
Thank you, but I'm busy.	**Grazie, ma ho un'altro impegno.** *graatseeay ma ho oon altro eempayño*
May I bring a friend? *(male/female)*	**Posso portare un amico/una amica?** *posso portaaray oon ameeko(-a)*
Where shall we meet?	**Dove ci incontriamo?** *dovay chee eenkontreeaamo*
I'll meet you ...	**La incontro ...** *la eenkontro*
in front of your hotel	**di fronte al suo albergo** *dee frontay al soo-o albayrgo*
I'll pick you up at 8 p.m.	**La chiamo alle otto/venti.** *la keeaamo allay otto/vayntee*
Could we make it a bit later/earlier?	**Facciamo un po' più tardi/presto?** *fachaamo oon po peeoo tardee/praysto*
How about another day?	**Facciamo un'altro giorno?** *fachaamo oonaltro jorno*
That will be fine.	**Va bene.** *va baynay*

Dining out/in Mangiare al ristorante/a casa

Punctuality varies from region to region in Italy. 15 minutes late may be acceptable in the south, but even 5 minutes would be frowned upon in the north.

Let me buy you a drink.	**Mi permetta di offrirLe una bibita.** *mee payrmeeta dee offreerlay oona beebeeta*
Do you like ...?	**Le piace ...?** *lay peeachay*
What are you going to have?	**Cosa prende?** *kosa praynday*
That was a lovely meal.	**Che pasto squisito!** *kay paasto skweezeeto*

Encounters Incontri

Do you mind if I ...?	**Le dispiace se ...?** *lay deespeeachay say*
sit here/smoke	**mi siedo qui/fumo** *mee see-ehdo kwee/foomo*
Can I get you a drink?	**Posso offrirLe una bibita?** *posso offreerlay oona beebeeta*
I'd love to have some company.	**Mi piacerebbe avere un po' di compagnia.** *me pee-achayraybbay avayray oon po dee kompañeea*
Why are you laughing?	**Perchè ride?** *payrkeh reeday*
Is my Italian that bad?	**Parlo tante male l'italiano?** *parlo tante maale leetaleeaano*
Shall we go somewhere quieter?	**Andiamo in un posto più tranquillo?** *andeeaamo een oon posto peeoo trankweello*
Leave me alone, please!	**Mi lasci in pace!** *mee lashee een pachay*
You look great!	**Sei stupendo(-a)!** *sayee stoopayndo(-a)*
May I kiss you?	**Posso baciarti?** *posso bachaartee*
Would you like to come home with me?	**Vuoi venire da me?** *voo-oee vayneeray da may*
I'm not ready for that.	**Non sono pronto(-a) per questo.** *non sono pronto(-a) pehr kwaysto*
Thanks for the evening.	**Grazie per la serata.** *graatseeay pehr la sayraata*
I'm afraid we've got to leave now.	**Penso che sia ora di partire.** *penso che see-a ora dee parteeray*
Can I see you again tomorrow?	**Posso rivederLa domani?** *posso reevaydayrla domaanee*
See you soon.	**A presto.** *ah praysto*
Can I have your address?	**Posso avere il suo indirizzo?** *posso avayray eel soo-o eendeereetso*

PARTS OF THE BODY ➤ 166; SAFETY ➤ 65

Telephoning Telefonare

Modern payphones take coins (100, 200 and 500 coins) and phonecards (L.5,000 or 10,000). You can also use your telephone credit card for calling home.

Many public cafés and bars have public phones for local calls. You might have to pay after the call or buy a token (**gettone**) to put in the phone.

To phone home from Italy, dial 00 followed by: Australia 61; Canada 1; Ireland 353; New Zealand 64; South Africa 27; UK 44; US 1. Note that you will usually have to omit the initial 0 of the area code.

Can I have your telephone number?	**Mi dà il suo numero di telefono?** *mee da eel soo-o noomayro dee taylayfono*
Here's my number.	**Ecco il mio numero.** *ehko eel meeo noomayro*
Please call me.	**Mi chiami, La prego.** *mee keeaamee la praygo*
I'll give you a call.	**La chiamerò.** *la keeamayro*
Where's the nearest telephone booth?	**Dov'è il telefono pubblico più vicino?** *doveh eel taylayfono poobbleeko peeoo veecheeno*
May I use your phone?	**Posso usare il suo telefono?** *posso oozaaray eel soo-o taylayfono*
It's an emergency.	**È un'emergenza.** *eh oon aymayrjayntsa*
I'd like to call someone in England.	**Vorrei fare una chiamata in Inghilterra.** *vorrehee faaray oona keeamaata een eenggeeltayrra*
What's the area [dialling] code for ...?	**Qual'è il prefisso per ...?** *kwaleh eel prayfeesso pehr*
What's the number for Information [directory Enquiries]?	**Qual'è il numero per Informazione Elenco Abbonati?** *kwaleh eel noomayro pehr eenformatseeony aylaynko abbonaatee*
I'd like the number for ...	**Vorrei il numero per ...** *vorrehee eel noomayro pehr*
I'd like to call collect [reverse the charges].	**Vorrei telefonare a carico del destinatario.** *vorrehee taylayfonaaray ah kareeko dayl daysteenatareeo*

On the phone Telefonare

Hello. This is …	**Pronto. Parla …** *pronto. parla*
I'd like to speak to …	**vorrei parlare a …** *vorrehee parlaaray ah*
Extension …	**Interno …** *eentayrno*
Speak louder/ more slowly, please.	**Parli più forte/più lentamente, per piacere.** *parlee peeoo fortay/peeoo layntamayntay pehr peeachayray*
Could you repeat that, please?	**Può ripetere, per piacere?** *pwo reepaytayray pehr peeachayray*
I'm afraid he/she's not in.	**Mi dispiace, non è qui.** *mee deespeeaachay non eh kwee*
You have the wrong number.	**Ha sbagliato numero.** *ah zbalyaato noomayro*
Just a moment.	**Un momento.** *oon momaynto*
Hold on, please.	**Resti in linea, per piacere.** *een leeneea pehr peeachayray*
When will he/she be back?	**Quando rientra?** *kwando reeayntra*
Will you tell him/her that I called?	**Per favore, gli/le dica che ho chiamato.** *pehr favoray lyee/lay deeka kay o keeamaato*
My name is …	**Mi chiamo …** *mee keeamo*
Would you ask him/her to phone me?	**Può dirgli/dirle di richiamarmi?** *pwo deerlyee/deerlay dee reekeeamaarmee*
I must go now.	**Devo andare ora.** *dayvo andaaray ora*
Nice to speak to you.	**È stato un piacere parlare con lei.** *eh staato oon peeachayray parlaaray kon layee*
I'll be in touch.	**La contatterò.** *la kontattayro*
Bye.	**Arrivederci.** *arreevaydayrchee*

Stores & Services

Stores and services 130
Business hours 132
Services 133
Preferences 134
Decisions 135
Paying 136
Complaints 137
Repairs/Cleaning 137
Banks/ Changing money 138
Pharmacy 140
Toiletries 142
Clothing 143
Color 143
Size 146
Health and beauty 147
Hairdresser 147
Household articles 148
Jeweler 149
Newsstand 150
Photography 151
Police 152
Lost property/ Theft 153
Post office 154
Souvenirs/ Gifts 156
Music 157
Toys and games 157
Antiques 157
Supermarket/ Foodstore 158

ESSENTIAL

I'd like ...	**Vorrei ...** *vorrehee*
Do you have ...?	**Ha ...?** *ah*
How much is that?	**Quanto costa?** *kwanto kosta*
Thank you.	**Grazie.** *graatseeay*

For a view of what Italians are buying, take a look in the big chain stores **La Rinascente**, **Upim** and **Standa**, which have branches in most towns.

Check locally for the location and times of open-air markets, generally held at least once a week in most tourist resorts.

APERTO	open
CHIUSO	closed

Stores and services
Negozi e servizi

Where is ...? Dov'è ...?

Where's the nearest ...? **Dov'è ... più vicino(-a)?**
doveh ... peeoo veecheeno

Where's there a good ...? **Dove c'è un(a) buon(a) ...?**
dovay cheh oon (a) bwon(a)

Where's the main shopping mall [centre]? **Dov'è la zona dei negozi?**
doveh la dzona dayee naygotsee

Is it far from here? **È lontano da qui?** *eh lontaano da kwee*

How do I get there? **Come ci arrivo?** *komay chee arreevo*

Stores Negozi

antiques shop **il negozio di antiquariato**
eel naygotseeo dee anteekwareeaato

bakery **la panetteria** *la panayttayreea*

bank **la banca** *la banka*

bookstore **la libreria** *la leebrayreea*

butcher shop **la macelleria** *la machayllayreea*

camera shop **il negozio di ottica/foto**
eel naygotseeo dee otteeka/foto

pharmacy **la farmacia** *la farmacheea*

clothing store [clothes shop] **il negozio di abbigliamento**
eel naygotseeo dee abbeelyamaynto

delicatessen **la salumeria** *la saloomayreea*

department store **il grande magazzino**
eel granday magatseeno

drugstore [chemist] **la farmacia** *la farmacheea*

fish store [fish monger] **la pescheria** *la payskayreea*

florist **il fioraio** *eel feeoraeeo*

gift shop **il negozio di articoli da regalo**
eel naygotseeo de arteekolee da raygalo

produce store [greengrocer] **il fruttivendolo** *eel frooteevayndolo*

grocery store **la drogheria** *la drogayreea*

health food store [shop] **il negozio di dietetica**
eel naygotseeo dee deeaytayteeka

jewelry store — **la gioielleria** *la joeeayllayreea*

liquor store [off licence] — **la bottiglieria** *la botteelyayreea*

market — **il mercato** *eel mayrkaato*

newsstand — **l'edicola** *laydeekola*

pastry shop — **la pasticceria** *la pasteetchayreea*

record [music] shop — **il negozio di musica** *eel naygotseeo dee moozeeka*

shoe store — **il negozio di scarpe/la calzoleria** *eel naygotseeo dee skarpay/la kaltsolayreea*

shopping mall [centre] — **il centro commerciale** *eel chayntro kommayrchaalay*

souvenir store — **il negozio di ricordi** *eel naygotseeo dee rikordee*

sporting goods store — **il negozio di articoli sportivi** *eel naygotseeo dee arteekolee sporteevee*

supermarket — **il supermercato** *eel soopayrmayrkaato*

cigarette stand — **la tabaccheria** *la tabakkayreea*

toy store — **il negozio di giocattoli** *eel naygotseeo dee jokattolee*

Services Servizi

dentist — **il/la dentista** *eel/la daynteesta*

doctor — **il medico/il dottore(-ressa)** *eel maydeeko/eel dottoray(-rayssa)*

dry cleaner — **la tintoria/la lavanderia a secco** *la teentoreea/la lavandayreea ah saykko*

hairdresser (ladies/men) — **il parrucchiere/la parrucchiera** *eel parrookkeeayray/parrookkeeayra*

hospital — **l'ospedale** *lospaydaalay*

launderette — **la lavanderia a gettone** *la lavandayreea ah jaytonay*

library — **la biblioteca** *la beebleeoatayka*

optician — **l'ottico/il negozio di ottica** *lotteeko/eel naygotseeo dee otteeka*

police station — **il commissariato/la questura** *eel kommeessareeato/la kwaystoora*

Business hours Orario di apertura

In major cities like Rome, Milan, Bologna and Florence, stores usually close on Saturday afternoon during the summer; during the August holidays (**Ferragosto**) you may find very few stores open as most locals have fled to the sea or mountains to escape the humidity.

General times for:	Opening	Closing	Lunch break	Closed
stores (winter)	9	7.30	1–3/4	Sun, one half day
(summer)	9	8	1–4/5	during the week
some shopping areas	10	7	none	Sun, Mon a.m
post office	8.30	6	none	Sat p.m., Sun
banks (main offices)	8.30	4	1–3	weekend

When does the ... open/close? **Quando apre/chiude ...?** *kwando apray/keeooday*

Are you open in the evening? **È aperto la sera?** *eh apayrto la sayra*

Do you close for lunch? **Chiude per pranzo?** *keeooday pehr prandzo*

Where is the ...? **Dov'è ...?** *doveh*

cashier/cash desk **la cassa** *la kassa*

escalator **la scala mobile** *la skala mobeelay*

elevator **l'ascensore** *lashaynsoray*

store directory [guide] **la guida al magazzino** *la gooeeda al magatseeno*

first floor [ground floor] **pianterreno** *peeano tayrra*

second floor [first floor] **primo piano** *preemo peeano*

ORARIO DI APERTURA	business hours
CHIUSO PER LA PAUSA DI MEZZOGIORNO	closed for lunch
APERTO TUTTO IL GIORNO	open all day
L'USCITA	exit
L'INGRESSO	entrance
LA SCALA MOBILE	escalator
L'USCITA D'EMERGENZA	emergency/fire exit
L'ASCENSORE	elevator
LE SCALE	stairs

Services Servizi

Can you help me?	**Può aiutarmi?** *pwo aeeootaarmee*
I'm looking for ...	**Cerco ...** *chayrko*
I'm just browsing.	**Sto solo dando un'occhiata.** *sto solo dando oonokkeeaata*
Do you have any ...?	**Ha ...?** *ah*
I'd like to buy ...	**Vorrei comprare ...** *vorrehee kompraaray*
Could you show me ...?	**Può farmi vedere ...?** *pwo faarmee vaydayray*
How much is this/that?	**Quant'è questo/quello?** *kwanteh kwaysto/kwayllo*
That's all, thanks.	**È tutto, grazie.** *eh tootto graatseeay*

Buongiorno/buonasera, signora/signore.	Good morning/afternoon, madam/sir.
Desidera qualcosa?	Can I help you?
Cosa desidera?	What would you like?
Glielo(-a) controllo subito.	I'll just check that for you.
È tutto?	Is that everything?
Nient'altro?	Anything else?

– Desidera qualcosa? (Can I help you?)
– No grazie. Sto solo dando un'occhiata.
(No, thanks. I'm just browsing.)
– Bene. (Fine.)
– Scusi. (Excuse me.)
– Sì, desidera? (Yes, can I help you?)
– Quanto costa quello? (How much is that?)
– Um, controllo subito ... Costa trentamila Lire.
(Hm, I'll just check that for you ... 30,000 Lire.)

IL SERVIZIO (ASSISTENZA) CLIENTI	customer service
SALDI/LIQUIDAZIONI	sale

Preferences Preferenze

I want something ...	**Voglio qualcosa di ...** *volyo kwalkosa dee*
It must be ...	**Deve essere ...** *dayvay ayssayray*
big/small	**grande/piccolo(-a)** *granday/peekkolo(-a)*
cheap/expensive	**economico(-a)/caro(-a)** *aykonomeeko(-a)/kaaro(-a)*
dark/light	**scuro(-a)/chiaro(-a)** *skooro(-a)/ keearo(-a)*
light/heavy	**leggero(-a)/pesante** *laydjayro(-a) payzantay*
oval/round/square	**ovale/rotondo(-a)/quadrato(-a)** *ovaalay/ rotondo(-a)/kwadraato(-a)*
genuine/imitation	**genuino(-a)/imitazione** *jaynooeeno(-a)/ eemeetatseeonay*
I don't want anything too expensive.	**Non voglio niente di troppo caro.** *non volyo neeayntay dee troppo kaarao*
Around ... lire.	**Sulle ... lire.** *soollay ... leeray*
Do you have anything ...?	**Ha qualcosa di ...?** *ah kwalkosa dee*
larger	**più largo** *peeoo largo*

Che ... desidera/vuole?	What ... would you like?
colore/forma	color/shape
qualità/quantità	quality/quantity
Che tipo preferisce?	What kind would you like?
Su che prezzi vuole rimanere?	What price range are you thinking of?

better quality	**di qualità migliore** *dee kwaleeta meelyoray*
cheaper	**più economico/meno caro** *peeoo aykonomeeko/mayno karo*
smaller	**più piccolo** *peeoo peekkolo*
Can you show me ...?	**Può mostrarmi ...?** *pwo mostraarmee*
that/this one	**quello/questo** *kwayllo/kwaysto*
these/those	**questi/quelli** *kwaystee/kwayllee*

COLORS ➤ 143

Conditions of purchase
Condizioni di vendita

Is there a guarantee? **C'è una garanzia?** *cheh oona garantseea*

Are there any instructions with it? **Ci sono anche delle istruzioni?** *chee sono ankay dayllay eestrootseeonee*

Out of stock Esaurito

Mi dispiace, non ne abbiamo.	I'm sorry, we don't have any.
È esaurito(-a)	We're out of stock.
Posso mostrarLe qualcos'altro/ un tipo diverso?	Can I show you something else/ a different kind?
Glielo(-a) ordino?	Shall we order it for you?

Can you order it for me? **Può ordinarmelo(-a)?** *pwo ordeenaarmaylo(-la)*

How long will it take? **Quanto tempo occorre?** *kwanto taympo okkorray*

Where else could I get ...? **In quale altro negozio posso comprare ...?** *een kwalay altro naygotseeo posso kompraaray*

Decisions Decisioni

That's not quite what I want. **Non è esattamente quello che voglio.** *non eh ayssattamayntay kwayllo kay volyo*

No, I don't like it. **No, non mi piace.** *no non mee peeachay*

That's too expensive. **È troppo caro.** *eh troppo karo*

I'll take it. **Lo (La) prendo.** *lo (la) praynd o*

– Buongiorno, signora. Vorrei una felpa.
(Hello, ma'am. I'd like a sweatshirt.)
– Certo. Che tipo preferisce?
(Certainly. What kind would you like?)
– Arancione, per favore. Deve essere larga.
(Orange, please. And it has to be large.)
– Ecco. Sono duecentomila Lire.
(Here you are. That's 200,000 Lire.)
– Non è esattammento quello che voglio. Grazie comunque.
(That's not quite what I want. Thanks anyway.)

Paying Pagare

Most stores, restaurants and hotels, and some highway service stations accept major credit cards, traveler's checks and Eurocheques–look for the signs on the door.

Tax can be reclaimed on larger purchases when returning home (outside the EU).

Where do I pay?	**Dove si paga?** *dovay see paga*
How much is that?	**Quant'è/Quanto costa?** *kwanteh/kwanto kosta*
Could you write it down, please?	**Può scrivermelo, per favore?** *pwo skreevayrmaylo pehr favoray*
Do you accept traveler's checks?	**Accetta assegni turistici?** *atchaytta assayñee tooreesteechee*
I'll pay ...	**Pago ...** *pago*
by cash	**in contanti** *een kontantee*
by credit card	**con carta di credito** *kon karta dee kraydeeto*
I don't have any small change.	**Non ho spiccioli.** *non o speecholee*
Sorry, I don't have enough money.	**Mi dispiace, non ho abbastanza soldi.** *mee deespeeachay non o abbastantsa soldee*
Could I have a receipt, please?	**Mi dà la ricevuta, per favore?** *mee da la reechayvoota pehr favoray*
I think you've given me the wrong change.	**Credo che si sia sbagliato(-a) nel darmi il resto.** *kraydo kay see see-a zbalyeeaato(-a) nayl daarmee eel raysto*

Come paga?	How are you paying?
Questa operazione non è stata approvata/accettata.	This transaction has not been approved/accepted.
Questa carta non è valida.	This card is not valid.
Può mostrarmi un altro documento d'identità?	May I have further identification?
Ha spiccioli?	Have you got any small change?

CASSA	cashier
I TACCHEGGIATORI SARANNO PUNITI A NORMA DI LEGGE	shoplifters will be prosecuted

Complaints Reclami

This doesn't work.	**Questo è difettoso(-a).** *kwaysto eh deefayttoso(-a)*
Can you exchange this, please?	**Può cambiare questo, per favore?** *pwo kambeeaaray kwaysto pehr favoray*
I'd like a refund.	**Vorrei un rimborso.** *vorrehee oon reemborso*
Here's the receipt.	**Ecco la ricevuta.** *eko la reechayvoota*
I don't have the receipt.	**Non ho la ricevuta.** *non o la reechayvoota*
I'd like to see the manager.	**Vorrei parlare con il gestore.** *vorrehee parlaaray kon eel jaystoray*

Repairs/Cleaning Riparazioni/Pulitura

This is broken. Can you repair it?	**Questo è rotto(-a). Può ripararlo(-a)?** *kwaysto eh rotto(-a) pwo reeparaarlo(-la)*
Do you have ... for this?	**Ha ... per questo?** *ah ... pehr kwaysto*
a battery	**una pila** *oona peela*
replacement parts	**dei pezzi di ricambio** *dayee paytsee dee reekambeeo*
There's something wrong with ...	**C'è qualcosa che non va con ...** *cheh kwalkosa kay non va kon*
Can you ... this ...?	**Può ... questo(-a) ...?** *pwo ... kwaysto(-a)*
clean	**pulire** *pooleeray*
press	**stirare** *steeraaray*
mend	**riparare** *reeparaaray*
Can you alter this?	**Può aggiustarmi questo(-a)?** *pwo ajeeoostaarmee kwaysto(-a)*
When will it be ready?	**Quando sarà pronto(-a)?** *kwando sara pronto(-a)*
This isn't mine.	**Questo non è mio.** *kwaysto non eh meeo*
... is missing.	**Manca ...** *manka*

Bank/Currency Exhange
Banca/Ufficio Cambio

At some banks, cash can be obtained from ATMs [cash machines] with Visa, Eurocard, American Express and many other international cards. Instructions are often given in English.

You can also change money at most hotels, but the rate will not be as good. Main railway stations and airports also have currency exchange offices.

Remember your passport when you want to change money.

Where's the nearest ...?	**Dov'è ... più vicino(-a)?** *doveh ... peeoo veecheeno(-a)*
bank	**la banca** *la banka*
currency exchange	**l'ufficio cambio** *looffeecho kambeeo*

TUTTE LE OPERAZIONI	all transactions
SPINGERE/TIRARE/PREMERE	push/pull/press
APERTO/CHIUSO	open/closed
CASSA	cashiers

Changing money Cambiare la valuta

Can I exchange foreign currency here?	**Si può cambiare la valuta straniera qui?** *see pwo kambeeaaray la valoota strañehray kooee*
I'd like to change some dollars/pounds into lire.	**Vorrei cambiare alcuni dollari/sterline in lire.** *vorrehee kambeeaaray alkoonee dollaree/stayrleenay een leeray*
I want to cash some traveler's checks [cheques].	**Voglio incassare dei traveller's cheques/ Eurocheques.** *volyo eenkassaaray travellers cheques/eurocheques*
What's the exchange rate?	**Quant'è il cambio?** *kwanteh eel kambeeo*
How much commission do you charge?	**Quanto prende di commissione?** *kwanto praynday dee kommeesseeonay*
Could I have some small change, please?	**Posso avere delle banconote di taglio più piccolo/spiccioli?** *posso avayray dayllay bankonotay dee talyo peekkolo/speetcholee*
I've lost my traveler's checks. These are the numbers.	**Ho perso i miei traveller's cheques. Ecco i numeri.** *oa payrso ee meeayee travellers cheques. eko ee noomayree*

Security Misure di sicurezza

Posso vedere ...?	Could I see ...?
il suo passaporto	your passport
un documento d'identità	some identification
la sua carta bancaria	your bank card
Qual'è il suo indirizzo?	What's your address?
Dove alloggia?	Where are you staying?
Compili/riempia questo modulo, per favore.	Fill out this form, please.
Per favore firmi qui.	Please sign here.

ATMs [Cash machines] Bancomat/Cassa automatica

Can I withdraw money on my credit card here?	**Posso fare un prelievo con la mia carta di credito qui?** *posso faaray oon prayleeayvo kon la meea karta dee kraydeeto kwee*
Where are the ATMs [cash machines]?	**Dove sono i Bancomat/le casse automatiche?** *dovay sono ee bankomat/lay kassay owtomateekay*
Can I use my ... card in the ATM [cash machine]?	**Posso usare la mia carta ... nel Bancomat?** *posso oozaaray la meea karta ... nayl bankomat*
The ATM [cash machine] has eaten my card.	**Il Bancomat ha mangiato la mia carta.** *eel bankomat ah manjaato la meea karta*

BANCOMAT/ CASSA AUTOMATICA	automated teller [cash machine]

Currency	Lira (plural lire); abbreviation L. or Lit.; Switzerland: 100 centesimi = 1 franco
Italy	*Coins:* 50, 100, 200, 500 lire *Notes:* 1,000, 2,000, 5,000, 10,000, 50,000, 100,000 lire
Switzerland	*Coins:* 5, 10, 20, 50 ct.; 1/2, 1, 2, 5 Fr. *Notes:* 10, 20, 50, 100, 500, 1000 Fr.

Pharmacy La farmacia

Pharmacies are easily recognized by their sign: a green cross, usually lit up. If you are looking for a pharmacy at night, on Sundays or holidays, you'll find the address of emergency pharmacies (**farmacia di turno**) listed in the newspaper or displayed in all pharmacy windows.

Where's the nearest (all-night) pharmacy?
Dov'è la farmacia (notturna) più vicina?
doveh la farmacheea (nottoorna) peeoo veecheena

What time does the pharmacy open/close?
A che ora apre/chiude la farmacia?
ah kay ora apray/keeooday la farmacheea

Can you make up this prescription for me?
Può farmi questa ricetta?
pwo faarmee kwaysta reechaytta

Shall I wait?
Devo aspettare?
dayvo aspayttaaray

I'll come back for it.
Passerò a ritirarla.
passayro ah reeteeraarla

Dosage instructions Dosi e uso

How much should I take?
Quanto devo prenderne?
kwanto dayvo praynday rnay

How often should I take it?
Con quale frequenza devo prenderlo(-la)?
kon kwalay fraykwehntsa dayvo_ praynday rlo(-la)

Is it suitable for children?
È adatto per bambini?
eh adatto pehr bambeenee

Prenda ... pastiglie/cucchiaini ...	Take ... tablets/teaspoons ...
prima/dopo i pasti	before/after meals
con acqua	with water
intero(-a)	whole
la mattina/la sera	in the morning/at night
per ... giorni	for ... days

SOLO PER USO ESTERNO for external use only
NON PER USO INTERNO not to be taken internally

Asking advice Chiedere consiglio

What would you recommend for ...?	**Che cosa consiglia per ...?** *kay kosa konseelya pehr*
a cold	**un raffreddore** *oon raffraydoray*
a cough	**la tosse** *la tossay*
diarrhea	**la diarrea** *la deearraya*
a hangover	**i postumi di una sbornia** *ee postoomee dee oona zborneea*
hayfever	**la febbre del fieno** *la faybbray dayl fee-ayno*
insect bites	**le punture d'insetto** *lay poontooray deensaytto*
a sore throat	**il mal di gola** *eel mal dee gola*
sunburn	**una scottatura solare** *oona skottatoora solaaray*
motion [travel] sickness	**la cinetosi** *la cheenaytozee*
an upset stomach	**mal di stomaco** *mal dee stomako*
Can I get it without a prescription?	**Si può comprare senza ricetta?** *see pwo kompraaray sayntsa reechaytta*

Over-the-counter treatment Trattamento senza ricetta

Can I have ...?	**Ha ...?** *ah*
antiseptic cream	**della pomata antisettica** *dayllay pomaata anteesaytteeka*
(soluble) aspirin	**dell'aspirina (solubile)** *dayllaspeereena (sooobeelay)*
bandage	**delle bende** *dayllay baynday*
condoms	**dei profilattici** *dayee profeelatteechee*
cotton	**del cotone idrofilo** *dayl kotonay eedrofeelo*
insect repellent/spray	**della pomata contro gli insetti/dello spray insetticida** *daylla pomaata kontro lyee eensayttee/dayllo spray eensaytteecheeda*
pain killer	**dell'antinevralgico** *dayllanteenayvraljeeko*
vitamin pills	**delle vitamine** *dayllay veetameenay*

Toiletries Articoli da toeletta

I'd like ...	**Vorrei ...** vorrehee
aftershave	**un dopobarba** *oon dopobarba*
after-sun lotion	**una lozione doposole** *oona lotseeonay doposolay*
deodorant	**un deodorante** *oon deeodorantay*
moisturizing cream	**una crema idratante** *oona krayma eedratantay*
razor blades	**delle lamette da barba** *dayllay lamayttay da barba*
sanitary napkins [towels]	**degli assorbenti** *daylyee assorbayntee*
soap	**del sapone** *dayl saponay*
sun block	**un blocco antisolare** *oon block anteesolaaray*
suntan lotion	**una crema/una lozione abbronzante** *oona krayma/oona lotseeonay abbrondzantay*
factor ...	**fattore ...** *fattoray*
tampons	**dei tamponi** *dayee tamponee*
tissues	**dei fazzoletti di carta** *dayee fatsolayttee dee karta*
toilet paper	**della carta igienica** *daylla karta eejayneeka*
toothpaste	**un dentifricio** *oon daynteefreecho*

Haircare Prodotti per i capelli

comb	**un pettine** *oon paytteenay*
conditioner	**del balsamo** *dayl balsamo*
hair mousse	**della schiuma volumizzante** *daylla skeeooma voloomeedzantay*
hair spray	**della lacca per capelli** *daylla lakka pehr kapayllee*
shampoo	**dello shampoo** *dayllo shampoo*

For the baby Per il neonato

baby food	**degli alimenti per neonati** *daylyee aleemayntee pehr neonaatee*
baby wipes	**dei fazzolettini/delle salviette per neonati** *dayee fatzolayteenee/dayllee salveeayttee pehr neeonaatee*
diapers [nappies]	**dei pannolini** *dayee pannoleenee*

Clothing Abbigliamento

The fashion capital of Italy is Milan, where many of the great designers, such as **Armani**, **Versace**, **Trussardi**, **Ferré**, **Moschino** and **Krizia** have salons.

You'll find that airport boutiques offering tax-free shopping may have cheaper prices but less selection.

General Generale

I'd like ...	**Vorrei ...** *vorrehee*
Do you have any ...?	**Avete ....?** *avaytay*

ABBIGLIAMENTO PER DONNA	ladies wear
ABBIGLIAMENTO PER UOMO	menswear
ABBIGLIAMENTO PER BAMBINI	children's wear

Color Colore

I'm looking for something in ...	**Cerco qualcosa in ...** *chayrko kwalkosa een*
beige	**beige** *beige*
black	**nero** *nayro*
blue	**blu** *bloo*
brown	**marrone** *marronay*
green	**verde** *vayrday*
gray	**grigio** *greejo*
orange	**arancione** *aranchonay*
pink	**rosa** *rosa*
purple	**viola** *veeola*
red	**rosso** *rosso*
white	**bianco** *beeanko*
yellow	**giallo** *jallo*
light ...	**chiaro** *keeaaro*
dark ...	**... scuro** *... skooro*
I want a darker/lighter shade.	**Vorrei una tonalità più scura/chiara.** *vorrehee oona tonaleeta peeoo skoora/keeaara*
Do you have the same in ...?	**Ce l'ha anche in ...?** *chay la ankay een*

Clothes and accessories
Capi di abbigliamento e accessori

belt	**la cintura** *la cheentoora*
bikini	**il bikini** *eel beekeenee*
blouse	**la camicetta** *la kameechaytta*
bra	**il reggiseno** *eel raydjeesayno*
briefs	**le mutandine** *lay mootandeenay*
cap	**il berretto** *eel bayrraytto*
coat	**il cappotto** *eel kappotto*
dress	**il vestito** *eel vaysteeto*
handbag	**la borsetta** *la borsaytta*
hat	**il cappello** *eel kapayllo*
jacket	**la giacca** *la jakka*
jeans	**i jeans** *ee jeans*
jumper	**la maglia** *la malya*
leggings	**i fuseaux** *ee fooso*
pants	**i pantaloni** *ee pantalonee*
pullover	**il maglione** *eel malyonay*
raincoat	**l'impermeabile** *leempayrmeeabeelay*
scarf	**la sciarpa/il foulard** *la sharpa/eel foolar*
shirt	**la camicia** *la kameecha*
shorts	**gli shorts** *lyee shorts*
skirt	**la gonna** *la gonna*
socks	**i calzini** *ee kaltseenee*
stocking	**le calze** *lay kaltsay*
suit	**il completo** *eel komplayto*
sweatshirt	**la felpa** *la faylpa*
swimming trunks	**i calzoncini da bagno** *ee kaltsoncheenee da baño*
swimsuit	**il costume da bagno** *eel kostoomay da baño*
T-shirt	**la T-shirt/la maglietta** *la tee shirt/la malyaytta*
tie	**la cravatta** *la kravatta*
tights	**il collant** *eel kollant*
tracksuit	**la tuta da ginnastica** *la toota da jeennasteeka*
underpants	**le mutande** *lay mootanday*

Shoes Scarpe

A pair of ...	**un paio di** *oon pa-yo dee*
boots	**gli scarponi** *lyee skarponay*
flip-flops	**le ciabatte** *lay cheeabattay*
sandals	**i sandali** *ee sandalee*
shoes	**le scarpe** *lay skarpay*
slippers	**le pantofole** *lay pantofolay*
running shoes [trainers]	**le scarpe da ginnastica** *lay skarpay da jeennasteeka*

Walking/hiking gear Abbigliamento escursionismo

windbreaker	**la giacca a vento** *la jakka ah vaynto*
knapsack	**lo zaino** *lo dza-eeno*
walking boots	**gli scarponi** *lyee skarponee*
waterproof jacket	**la giacca a vento** *la jakka ah vaynto*

Fabric Stoffe

I want something in ...	**Vorrei qualcosa in ...** *vorrehee kwalkosa een*
cotton	**cotone** *kotonay*
denim	**tela jeans** *tayla "jeans"*
lace	**pizzo** *peetso*
leather	**pelle** *payllay*
linen	**lino** *leeno*
wool	**lana** *lana*
Is this ...?	**È ...?** *eh*
pure cotton	**in puro cotone** *een pooro kotonay*
synthetic	**in fibra sintetica** *een feebra seentayteeka*
Is it hand washable/ machine washable?	**Si può lavare a mano/in lavatrice?** *see pwo lavaaray ah maano/ een lavatreechay*

LAVARE A SECCO	dry clean only
LAVARE A MANO	handwash only
NON STIRARE	do not iron
COLORI SOLIDI	colorfast

Does it fit? Come le va?

Can I try this on?	**Me lo/la posso provare?** *may lo/la posso provaaray*
Where's the fitting room?	**Dov'è la cabina di prova?** *doveh la kabeena dee prova*
It fits well. I'll take it.	**Mi va bene. Lo/La prendo.** *mee va baynay. lo/la praynd o*
It doesn't fit.	**Non mi va bene.** *non mee va baynay*
It's too...	**È troppo ...** *eh troppo*
short/long	**corto(-a)/lungo(-a)** *korto(-a)/loonggo(-a)*
tight/loose	**stretto(-a)/largo(-a)** *straytto(-a)/largo(-a)*
Do you have this in size ...?	**Ha questo nella taglia/misura ...?** *ah kwaysto naylla talya/meesoora*
What size is this?	**Che taglia è?** *kay talya eh*
Could you measure me, please?	**Può misurarmi, per piacere?** *pwo meesooraarmee pehr peeachayray*
What size do you take?	**Cha taglia/misura prende?** *kay talya/meesoora praynday*
I don't know Italian sizes.	**Non conosco le misure italiane.** *non konosko lay meesooray eetaleeaanay*

Size Misure

	Dresses/Suits						Women's shoes			
American	8	10	12	14	16	18	6	7	8	9
British	10	12	14	16	18	20	4 1/2	5 1/2	6 1/2	7 1/2
Continental	36	38	40	42	44	46	37	38	40	41

	Shirts				Men's shoes								
American / British	15	16	17	18	5	6	7	8	8 1/2	9	9 1/2	10	11
Continental	38	41	43	45	38	39	41	42	43	43	44	44	45

EXTRA GRANDE	extra large (XL)
GRANDE	large (L)
MEDIA	medium (M)
PICCOLA	small (S)

1 centimeter (cm.) = 0.39 in.
1 meter (m.) = 39.37 in.
10 meters = 32.81 ft.

1 inch = 2.54 cm.
1 foot = 30.5 cm.
1 yard = 0.91 m.

Health and beauty
Salute e bellezza

I'd like a …	**Vorrei …** *vorrehee*
facial	**un trattamento per il viso** *oon trattamaynto pehr eel veezo*
manicure	**una manicure** *oona maneekooray*
massage	**un massaggio** *oon massadjo*
waxing	**una ceretta** *oona chayraytta*

Hairdresser Parrucchiere

Tipping: up to 15% is normal.

I'd like to make an appointment for …	**Vorrei un appuntamento per …** *vorrehee oon appoontamaynto pehr*
Can you make it a bit earlier/later?	**Può un po' più presto/tardi?** *pwo oon po peeoo praysto/tardee*
I'd like a …	**Vorrei …** *vorrehee*
cut and blow-dry	**un taglio e asciugatura con fon** *oon talyo ay ashoogatoora kon fon*
shampoo and set	**uno shampoo e messa in piega** *oono shampoo ay mayssa een peeayga*
trim	**una spuntatina** *oona spoontateena*
I'd like my hair …	**Vorrei …** *vorrehee*
colored/tinted	**fare il colore** *faaray eel koloray*
permed	**una permanente** *oona payrmanayntay*
Don't cut it too short.	**Non li tagli troppo corti.** *non lee talyee troppo kortee*
A little more off the …	**Tagli ancora un po' …** *talyee ankora oon po*
back/front	**dietro/davanti** *deeaytro/davantee*
neck/sides	**al collo/ai lati** *al kollo/lattee*
top	**in cima** *een cheema*
That's fine, thanks.	**Va bene, grazie.** *va baynay graatseeay*

Household articles
Articoli casalinghi

I'd like a(n)/some ... **Vorrei ...** *vorrehee*

adapter **una presa multipla** *oona praysa moolteepla*

aluminum foil **della carta stagnola** *daylla karta stañolay*

bottle opener **un apribottiglie** *oon apreebotteelyay*

candles **delle candele** *dayllay kandaylay*

clothespins [pegs] **delle mollette da bucato** *dayllay mollayttay da bookaato*

plastic wrap [cling film] **della pellicola** *daylla paylleekola*

corkscrew **un cavatappi** *oon kavatappee*

lightbulb **una lampadina** *oona lampadeena*

matches **dei fiammiferi** *dayee feeammeefayree*

paper napkins **dei tovaglioli di carta** *dayee tovalyolee dee karta*

plug *(electrical)* **una spina elettrica** *oona spee na aylayttreeka*

scissors **un paio di forbici** *oon paeeo dee forbeechee*

screwdriver **un cacciavite** *oon katchaveetay*

can [tin] opener **un apriscatole** *oon apreeskatolay*

Cleaning items Articoli di pulizia

bleach **della candeggina** *daylla kandaydjeena*

dish cloth [tea towel] **uno strofinaccio per i piatti** *oono strofeenatcho pehr ee peeattee*

detergent [washing powder] **un detersivo per lavatrice** *oon daytayrseevo pehr lavatreechay*

dishwashing [washing-up] detergent **un detersivo per lavastoviglie** *oon daytayrseevo pehr lavastoveelyay*

dishwashing [washing-up] liquid **un detersivo per i piatti** *oon daytayrseevo pehr ee peeattee*

garbage [refuse] bags **dei sacchetti per i rifiuti** *dayee sakkayttee pehr ee reeffeeootee*

Dishes/Utensils [Crockery/Cutlery] Stoviglie e posate

cups **delle tazze** *dayllay tatsay*

forks **delle forchette** *dayllay forkayttay*

glasses **dei bicchieri** *dayee beekkeeehree*

knives **dei coltelli** *dayee koltayllee*

mugs **dei boccali** *dayee bokkaalee*

Jeweler In gioielleria

Even if you can't afford the wares of **Bulgari** and **Buccellati**, Italy's most famous jewelers, you will find the jewelry is generally beautifully crafted and 18-carat gold is a good buy.

Could I see ...?	**Vorrei vedere ...?** *vorrehee vaydayray*
this/that	**questo/quello** *kwehsto/kwehllo*
It's in the window/ display case.	**È in vetrina/nell'armadietto vetrina.** *eh een vaytreena/nayllarmadeeaytto vaytreena*
I'd like a(n)/some ...	**Vorrei ...** *vorrehee*
alarm clock	**un orologio sveglia** *oon orolojo zvaylya*
bracelet	**un braccialetto** *oon bratcheealaytto*
brooch	**una spilla** *oona speella*
chain	**una catenina** *oona katayneena*
clock	**un orologio** *oon orolojo*
earrings	**degli orecchini** *daylyee oraykkeenee*
necklace	**una collana** *oona kollana*
ring	**un anello** *oon anayllo*
watch	**un orologio da polso** *oon orolojo da polso*
watch battery	**una pila per orologi** *oona peela pehr orolojee*

Materials Materiali

Is this real silver/gold?	**È argento/oro vero?** *eh arjaynto/oro vayro*
Is there a certificate for it?	**C'è un certificato di garanzia?** *cheh oon chayrteefeekaato dee garantseea*
Do you have anything in ...?	**Ha qualcosa ...?** *ah kwalkosa*
copper	**in rame** *een ramay*
crystal (quartz)	**in cristallo** *een kreestallo*
cut glass	**in vetro tagliato** *een vaytro talyaato*
diamond	**con diamante** *kon deeamantay*
enamel	**in smalto** *een smalto*
gold	**in oro** *een oro*
gold-plated	**placcato d'oro** *plakaato doro*
pearl	**con perle** *kon payrlay*
pewter	**in peltro** *een paylro*
platinum	**in platino** *een plateeno*
silver	**in argento** *een arjaynto*

Newsstand Il giornalaio

Foreign newspapers can usually be found at rail stations or airports, or on newsstands in major cities.

Tobacco is a state monopoly in Italy. Licensed tobacconists are marked by a large white "**T**" on a black background. Cigarettes are also sold in some cafés and bars with a tobacco license.

Do you sell English-language books/newspapers?	**Ha libri/giornali inglese?** *ah leebree/jornaalee eengglayzay*
I'd like a(n)/some ...	**Vorrei ...** *vorraiee*
book	**un libro** *oon leebro*
candy [sweets]	**dei dolci** *dayee dolchee*
chewing gum	**della gomma da masticare** *daylla gomma da masteekaaray*
chocolate bar	**una tavoletta di cioccolata** *oona tavolaytta dee chokkolaata*
pack of cigarettes	**un pacchetto di sigarette** *oon pakkaytto dee seegarayttay*
cigars	**dei sigari** *dayee seegaaray*
dictionary	**un dizionario** *oon deetseeonaareeo*
Italian-English	**Italiano-Inglese** *eetaleeano eengglayzay*
envelopes	**delle buste** *dayllay boostay*
guidebook for ...	**una guida di ...** *oona gooeeda dee*
lighter	**un accendino** *oon atchayndeeno*
magazine	**una rivista** *oona reeveesta*
road map of ...	**una carta stradale di ...** *oona karta stradaalay*
matches	**dei fiammiferi** *dayee feeaammeefayree*
newspaper	**un giornale** *oon jornaalay*
American/English	**americano/inglese** *amayreekaano/eengglayzay*
paper	**della carta** *daylla karta*
pen	**una penna** *oona paynna*
pencil	**una matita** *oona mateeta*
postcard	**una cartolina** *oona kartoleena*
stamps	**dei francobolli** *dayee frankobollee*
tobacco	**del tabacco** *dayl tabako*

Photography La fotografia

I'm looking for a(n) … camera.	**Cerco una macchina fotografica …** *chayrko oona makkeena fotografeeka*
automatic	**automatica** *owtomateeka*
compact	**compact** *kompakt*
disposable	**usa-e-getta** *ooza ay jaytta*
SLR	**SLR** *ayssay ayllay ayrray*
I'd like a/an …	**Vorrei …** *vorrehee*
battery	**la pila** *la peela*
camera case	**la custodia per macchina fotografica** *la koostodeea pehr makkeena fotografeeka*
(electronic) flash	**il flash (elettronico)** *eel flash (aylayttroneeko)*
filter	**il filtro** *eel feeltro*
lens	**l'obiettivo** *lobeeaytteevo*
lens cap	**il cappuccio per l'obiettivo** *eel kappootcho pehr lobyaytteevo*

Film/Processing Pellicole/Sviluppo

I'd like a … film for this camera.	**Vorrei una pellicola … per questa macchina (fotografica).** *vorrehee oona paylleekola … pehr kwaysta makkeena (fotografeeka)*
black and white	**in bianco e nero** *een beeanko ay nayro*
color	**a colori** *ah koloree*
24/36 exposures	**da 24/36 pose** *da vaynteekwatro/trayntasay pozay*
I'd like this film developed, please.	**Vorrei fare sviluppare questo film.** *vorrehee faaray zveeloopaaray kwehsto film*
Would you enlarge this, please?	**Può ingrandire questa, per favore?** *pwo eenggrandeeray kwaysta pehr favoreh*
How much do … exposures cost?	**Quanto costa lo sviluppo …?** *kwanto kosta lo zveelooppo*
When will the photos be ready?	**Quando saranno pronte le foto?** *kwando saranno prontay lay foto*
I'd like to pick up my photos. Here's the receipt.	**Vorrei ritirare le mie foto. Ecco la ricevuta.** *vorrehee reeteeraaray lay meeay foto. eko la reechayvoota*

Police Polizia

In Italy, dial ☎ 113 for all emergency services and ☎ 118 for fire. Dial ☎ 7 for the police in Switzerland.

Beware of pickpockets, particularly in crowded places. Report all thefts to the local police within 24 hours for your own insurance purposes.

Where's the nearest ...?	**Dov'è ... più vicino(-a)?** *doveh ... peeoo veecheeno(-a)*
police station	**il Commissariato/la Questura** *eel kommeessareeaato/la kwehstoora*
Does anyone here speak English?	**C'è qualcuno che parla inglese?** *cheh kwalkoono kay parla eengglayzay*
I want to report a(n) ...	**Voglio denunciare ...** *volyo daynoonchaaray*
accident/attack	**un incidente/un'aggressione** *oon eencheedayntay/oonaggraysseeonay*
mugging/rape	**un'aggressione per rapina/uno stupro.** *oonaggraysseeonay pehr rapeena/oono stoopro*
My child is missing.	**Il/La mio(-a) bambino(-a) è scomparso(-a).** *eel/la meeo(-a) bambeeno(-a) eh skompaarso(-a)*
Here's a photo of him/her.	**Ecco la sua foto.** *ehko la soo-a foto*
Someone's following me.	**Qualcuno mi sta seguendo.** *kwalkoono mee sta saygoo-ayndo*
I've seen a suspicious package.	**Ho visto un pacco sospetto.** *o veesto oon pakko sospaytto*
I need an English-speaking lawyer.	**Vorrei un avvocato che parla l'inglese.** *vorrehee oon avokaato kay parla leengglayzay*
I need to make a phone call.	**Devo fare una telefonata.** *dayvo faaray oona taylayfonaata*
I need to contact the ... Consulate.	**Devo contattare il Consolato ...** *dayvo kontataaray eel konsolaato*
American	**americano** *ahmayreekaanoa*

Lo/la può descrivere?	Can you describe him/her?
uomo/donna	male/female
biondo(-a)/bruno(-a)	blonde/brunette
con capelli rossi/grigi	red-headed/gray
con capelli lunghi/corti/stempiato	long/short hair/balding
altezza approssimativa ...	approximate height ...
di (circa) ... anni	aged (approximately) ...
indossava ...	He/She was wearing ...

CLOTHES ➤ 144; COLORS ➤ 143

Lost property / Theft Oggetti smarriti/Furti

I want to report a theft / break-in.	**Voglio denunciare un furto/una rapina.** *volyo daynoonchaaray oon foorto/oona rapeena*
I've been mugged / robbed.	**Sono stato aggredito/derubato.** *sono staato aggraydeto/dayroobaato*
I've lost my …	**Ho perso …** *o payrso*
My … has been stolen.	**Mi hanno rubato …** *mee anno roobaato*
bicycle	**la bicicletta** *la beecheeklaytta*
camera	**la macchina fotografica** *la makeena fotografeeka*
(rental) car	**l'auto (noleggiata)** *lowto (nolaydjaata)*
credit cards	**le carte di credito** *lay kartay dee kraydeeto*
handbag	**la borsetta** *la borsaytta*
money	**i soldi** *ee soldee*
passport	**il passaporto** *eel passaporto*
purse	**il portamonete** *eel poartamonaytay*
ticket	**il biglietto** *eel beelyaytto*
wallet	**il portafoglio** *eel portafolyo*
watch	**l'orologio** *lorolojo*
What shall I do?	**Cosa faccio?** *kosa fatcho*
I need a police report for my insurance claim.	**Devo avere una copia della mia denuncia per la mia assicurazione.** *dayvo avayray oona kopeea daylla meea daynooncha pehr la meea asseekooratseeonay*

Cosa manca?	What's missing?
Quando è successo?	When did it happen?
Dove alloggia?	Where are you staying?
Da dove è stato(-a) preso(-a)?	Where was it taken from?
Dov'era lei in quel momento?	Where were you at the time?
Le abbiamo chiamato un interprete.	We're getting an interpreter for you.
Ci occuperemo della faccenda.	We'll look into the matter.
Compili questo modulo, per favore.	Please fill out this form.

Post office L'Ufficio Postale

Italian post offices bear the sign PT. Mail boxes are red in Italy, though some post offices have yellow boxes for express mail.

In major towns, the main post offices are normally open from 8.30 a.m. through to 6 p.m., while smaller branches close at 2 p.m. Stamps can be bought from tobacconists **(tabaccaio),** some hotel desks, as well as from the Post Office.

General queries Informazioni generali

Where is the main post office?	**Dov'è l'ufficio postale principale?** *dovai looffeecho postaalay preencheepaalay*
What time does the post office open/close?	**A che ora apre/chiude l'ufficio postale?** *ah kay oray apray/keeooday looffeecho postaalay*
Does it close for lunch?	**Chiude per pranzo?** *keeooday pehr prandzo*
Where's the mailbox [postbox]?	**Dov'è la cassetta delle lettere?** *doveh la kassaytta dayllay layttayray*
Where's the general delivery?	**Dov'è il Fermo Posta?** *doveh eel fayrmo posta*
Is there any mail for me? My name is ...	**C'è posta per me? Mi chiamo ...** *cheh posta pehr may. mee keeaamo*

Buying stamps Comprare francobolli

A stamp for this postcard, please.	**Un francobollo per questa cartolina, per favore.** *oon frankobollo pehr kwaysta kartoleena pehr favoray*
A ...-lire stamp, please.	**Un francobollo da ... lire, per favore.** *oon frankobollo da ... leeray pehr favoray*
What's the postage for a letter to ...?	**Quanto costa spedire una lettera a ...?** *kwanto kosta spaydeeray oona layttayra ah*

– Buongiorno, vorrei spedire queste cartoline negli Stati Uniti, per piacere.
(Hello. I'd like to send these postcards to the U.S, please.)
– *Quante? (How many?)*
– Dieci, per favore. (Ten, please.)
– *Fa settecentocinquanta Lire per dieci.*
(That's 750 Lire for ten.)

Sending packages Mandare pacchi

I want to send this package [parcel] by ...	**Voglio spedire questo pacco ...** *volyo spaydeeray kwaysto pahkko*
airmail	**per via aerea** *pehr veea aayreea*
express/special delivery	**per espresso** *pehr ayspraysso*
It contains ...	**Contiene ...** *konteeaynay*

Telecommunicazioni Telecomunicazioni

Deve compilare il modulo per la dogana.	Please fill out the customs declaration form.
Che valore ha?	What is the value?
Cosa c'è dentro?/Cosa contiene?	What's inside?

I'd like a phonecard, please.	**Vorrei una carta telefonica, per favore.** *vorraiee oonah kahrtah taylayfoneekah pair fahvoray*
5000/10,000 lire.	**Da cinquemila/diecimila lire.** *da cheenkwaymeela/deeaycheemeela leeray*
Do you have a photocopier?	**Ha un servizio fotocopie?** *ah oon sayrveetseeo fotokopeeay*
I'd like ... copies.	**Vorrei ... copie.** *vorrehee ... kopee-eh*
I'd like to send a message ...	**Vorrei trasmettere un messaggio ...** *vorrehee trasmayttayray oon mayssajeeo*
by E-mail/fax	**per posta elettronica/fax.** *pehr posta aylaytroneeka/fax*
What's your E-mail address?	**Qual'è il suo indirizzo di e-mail?** *kwalay eel soo-o eendeereetso dee e-mail*
Can I access the Internet here?	**Posso accedere all'internet da qui?** *posso achaydayray aleentaynet da kwee*
What are your charges per hour?	**Quanto si paga all'ora?** *kwanto see paaga allora*
How do I log on?	**Come ci si collega?** *komay chee see kollayga*

Souvenirs Ricordi

Italy is a shopping wonderland and you'll find no shortage of souvenirs and gifts to take home.

Italian designer clothes for men, women and children are internationally renowned, as well as shoes, accessories and other leather goods (handbags, beauty cases, luggage). You'll also find knitwear, cloth (silk, linen) and lace; or jewelry, including gold and silverware.

Regional crafts include pottery, ceramics, olivewood, glass and crystal work, straw and raffia goods. If you're still stuck for a souvenir, try a bottle of fine Italian wine, liqueur or aperitif or an art book or reproduction.

antiques	**gli oggetti di antiquariato** *lyee ojayttee dee anteekwareeaato*
ceramics	**la ceramica** *la chayraameeka*
doll	**la bambola** *la bambola*
glassware	**gli articoli di vetro** *lyee arteekolee dee vehtro*
jewelry	**i gioielli** *ee joeeehllee*
knitware	**la maglieria** *la malyayreea*
needlework	**il ricamo** *eel reekaamo*
silk	**la seta** *la sehta*
woodwork	**il lavoro in legno** *eel lavoro een lehño*

Gifts Regali

bottle of wine	**una bottiglia di vino** *oona botteelya dee veeno*
box of chocolates	**una scatola di cioccolatini** *oona skatola dee chokkolaateenee*
calendar	**un calendario** *oon kalayndaareeo*
key ring	**un portachiavi** *oon portakeeavee*
postcard	**una cartolina** *oona kartoleena*
souvenir guide	**una guida-ricordo** *oona gooeeda reekordo*
ceramic plate	**un piatto in ceramica** *oon peeatto*
T-shirt	**una maglietta** *oona malyaytta*

Music Musica

I'd like a ... **Vorrei ...** *vorrehee*

cassette **un nastro/una cassetta** *oon nastro/oona kassaytta*

compact disc **un compact/un CD** *oon compact/oon cheedee*

record **un disco** *oon deesko*

videocassette **una videocassetta** *oona veedeeokassaytta*

Who are the popular Italian singers/bands? **Chi sono i cantanti/gruppi italiani più famosi?** *chee sono ee kantantee/grooppee eetaleeaanee peeoo famozee*

Toys and games Giocattoli e giochi

I'd like a toy/game ... **Vorrei un giocattolo/un gioco ...** *vorrehee oon jokattolo/oon joko*

for a boy **per un bambino** *pehr oon bambeena*

for a 5-year-old girl **per una bambina di cinque anni** *pehr oona bambeena dee cheenkway annee*

pail and shovel [bucket and spade] **un secchiello e una paletta** *oon saykeeayllo ay oona palaytto*

chess set **un gioco degli scacchi** *oon joko daylyee skakee*

doll **una bambola** *oona bambola*

electronic game **un gioco elettronico** *oon joko aylayttroneeko*

teddy bear **un orsacchiotto** *oon orsakkeeotto*

Antiques Oggetti di antiquariato

How old is this? **Quanti anni ha questo(-a)?** *kwantee annee a kwehsto(-a)*

Do you have anything from the ... era? **Ha qualcosa del periodo ...?** *ah kwalkosa dayl payreeodo*

Can you send it to me? **Può spedirmelo(-la)?** *pwo spaydeermeelo(-la)*

Will I have problems with customs? **Avrò problemi con la dogana?** *avro problaymee kon la dogaana*

Is there a certificate of authenticity? **C'è un certificato di autenticità?** *cheh oon chayrteefeekato dee owtaynteecheeta*

Supermarket / Foodstore
Il supermercato/Il negozio di alimentari

Supermarkets and convenience stores are found in most tourist resorts and all towns; however, Italy is still rich in markets, smaller stores and delicatessens (**salumeria**), where it can be more fun to shop.

At the supermarket Al supermercato

Excuse me. Where can I find ...?	**Scusi. Dove posso trovare ...?** *skoozee. dovay posso trovaaray*
Do I pay for this here or at the checkout?	**Pago qui o alla cassa?** *pago kwee o alla kassa*
Where are the baskets/ shopping carts [trolleys]?	**Dove sono i cestelli/carrelli?** *dovay sono ee karrayllee/chestayllee*
Is there a ... here?	**C'è ... qui?** *cheh ... kwee*
delicatessen	**una salumeria** *oona saloomayreea*
pharmacy	**farmacia** *farmacheea*

PANE E DOLCI	bread and cakes
PRODOTTI DI PULIZIA	cleaning products
LATTICINI	dairy products
PESCE FRESCO	fresh fish
CARNI FRESCHE	fresh meat
PRODOTTI FRESCHI	fresh produce
PRODOTTI SURGELATI	frozen foods
ARTICOLI CASALINGHI	household goods
POLLAMI	poultry
FRUTTA E VERDURA	fruit and vegetables
VINI E LIQUORI	wines and spirits

Weights and measures

- **1 kilogram** or **kilo** (**kg.**) = **1000 grams** (**g.**); **100 g.** = 3.5 oz.; **1 kg.** = 2.2 lb [1 oz. = **28.35 g.**; 1 lb. = **453.60 g.**]
- **1 liter** (**l.**) = 0.88 imp. quart or 1.06 U.S. quart [1 imp. quart = **1.14 l.** 1 U.S. quart = **0.951 l.** 1 imp. gallon = **4.55 l.** 1 U.S. gallon = **3.8 l.**]

Food hygiene Igiene alimentare

CONSUMARE ENTRO ... DAL GIORNO DI APERTURA.	eat within ... days of opening
TENERE IN FRIGORIFERO	keep refrigerated
ADATTO(-A) ALLA COTTURA NEL FORNO A MICROONDE	microwaveable
DATA DI SCADENZA ...	sell by ...
PER VEGETARIANI	for vegetarians

At the convenience store Al negozio di alimentazione

I'd like some of that/these.	**Vorrei un pò di quello/questo.** *vorrehee oon po dee kwayllo/kwaysto*
This one/those	**Questo/quelli** *kwaysto/kwayllee*
To the left/right	**A sinistra/destra** *ah seeneestra/daystra*
Over there/Here	**Lì/qui** *lee/kwee*
Which one/ones?	**Quale/quali** *kwalay/kwalee*
That's all, thanks.	**È tutto, grazie.** *eh tootto graatseeay*
I'd like a(n) ...	**Vorrei ...** *vorrehee*
kilo of apples	**un chilo di mele** *oon keelo dee maylay*
half-kilo of tomatoes	**mezzo chilo di pomodori** *maytso keelo dee pomodoree*
100 grams of cheese	**100 grammi di formaggio** *chaynto grammee dee formadjo*
liter of milk	**un litro di latte** *oon leetro dee lattay*
half-dozen eggs	**mezza dozzina di uova** *maytsa dotseena dee ooova*
... slices of ham	**... fette del prosciutto affettato** ... *fehttay dayl proshootto affayttaato*
piece of cake	**un pezzo di torta** *oon paytso de torta*
box of chocolates	**una scatola di cioccolatini** *oona skatola dee chokkolateenee*
bottle of wine	**una bottiglia di vino** *oona botteelya dee veeno*
carton of milk	**una scatola di latte** *oona skatola dee lattay*
jar of jam	**un vasetto di marmellata** *oon vasaytto dee marmayllaata*

- Vorrei mezzo chilo
di quel formaggio, per favore.
(I'd like half a kilo of that cheese, please.)
- Questo? (This one?)
- Sì, il gorgonzola, per piacere.
(Yes, the "Gorgonzola", please.)
- Certo ... E' tutto?
(Certainly. Anything else?)
- E trecento grammi di quel prosciutto
a sinistra, per favore.
(And 300 grams of that ham on the left, please.)

Provisions/Picnic Provviste/Picnic

beer	**birra** *beerra*
butter	**burro** *boorro*
cheese	**formaggio** *formadjo*
cookies [biscuits]	**biscotti** *beeskottee*
chips	**patatine** *patateenay*
eggs	**uova** *oo-ova*
grapes	**uva** *oova*
ice cream	**gelato** *jaylaato*
instant coffee	**caffè solubile** *kaffeh soloobeelee*
loaf of bread	**pagnotta di pane** *pañotta dee panay*
milk	**latte** *lattay*
rolls *(bread)*	**i panini** *ee paneenee*
sausages	**salciccie** *salcheechay*
soft drink/soda	**bibita analcolica** *beebeeta analkoleeka*
tea bags	**bustine di tè** *boosteenay dee teh*
bottle of wine	**bottiglia di vino** *botteelyay dee veeno*

del pane *dayl paanay*
Bread; look for **pane all'olio** (olive oil white bread), **pane al latte** (milk bread), **panettone** (Christmas bread enriched with butter and candied fruit, sultanas and raisins), **pandoro** (a large sponge cake topped with powdered vanilla), **pangiallo** and **panforte** (firm nut and honey cake), **panpepato** (spicy nut cake) and **veneziana** (sweet holiday bread with whole almonds).

focaccia *fokatcha*
Savory flatbread; which may be flavored ~ **alla salvia** (sage bread), ~ **alla salsiccia** (sausage bread) or ~ **alle noci** (walnut bread).

Health

Doctor (general)	**161**	**Gynecologist**	**167**
Accident and injury	**162**	**Hospital**	**167**
Symptoms	**163**	**Optician**	**167**
Doctor's inquiries	**164**	**Dentist**	**168**
Parts of the body	**166**	**Payment/Insurance**	**168**

Insurance and payment (➤ 168 for phrases)

Before you leave, make sure your health insurance policy covers any illness or accident while on vacation [holiday]. If not, ask your insurance representative, automobile association or travel agent for details of special health insurance. In Italy, EU citizens with a Form E111 are eligible for free medical treatment from the Italian national health system.

Hospital emergency departments (**Pronto Soccorso**) will treat all emergencies. However, it you are a non-EU citizen or without an E111 form, you will later have to sign a declaration that either you or your consulate will pay.

Doctor (general) Dottore (espressioni generali)

Where can I find a doctor/dentist?	**Dove posso trovare un medico/un dentista?** *dovay posso trovaaray oon maydeeko/oon daynteesta*
Where's there a doctor who speaks English?	**C'è un medico che parla inglese?** *cheh oon maydeeko kay paarla eengglayzay*
What are the office hours?	**Quando apre l'ambulatorio?** *kwando apray lamboolatoreeo*
Could the doctor come to see me here?	**Posso avere una visita domiciliare?** *posso avayray oona veeseeta domeecheelyaaray*
Can I make an appointment ...?	**Vorrei (fissare) un appuntamento ...?** *vorrehee (feessaaray) oon appoontamaynto*
for tomorrow	**per domani** *pehr domaanee*
for as soon as possible	**al più presto** *al peeoo praysto*
It's urgent.	**È urgente.** *eh oorjayntay*
I've got an appointment with Doctor ...	**Ho un appuntamento con il dottor/la dottoressa ...** *oh oon apoontamaynto kon eel dottor/dottorayssa*

– Vorrei un appuntamento al più presto possibile.
(I'd like an appointment for as soon as possible.)
– Oggi è tutto prenotato. È urgente?
(Today is fully booked. Is it urgent?)
– Sì. (Yes.)
– Beh, possiamo farla passare
alle 10.15 domani con i doctor Rossi.
(You can see Dr. Rossi at 10:15 tomorrow.)
– Dieci e un quarto. Molto grazie.
(Ten-fifteen. Thank you.)

Accident and injury Incidenti e lesioni

My ... is hurt/injured.
... si è fatto(-a) male/è ferito(-a).
see eh fatto(-a) malay/eh fayreeto(-a)

husband/wife
Mio marito/Mia moglie
meeo mareeto/meea molyeeay

son/daughter
Mio figlio/Mia figlia *meeo feelyo/meea feelya*

friend (m./f.)
Il mio amico/La mia amica
eel meeo ameeko/la meea ameeka

He/She is unconscious.
Ha perso conoscenza.
ah payrso konoshayntsa

He/She is bleeding (heavily).
Perde (molto) sangue.
payrday (molto) sanggway

He/She is (seriously) injured.
È ferito(-a) (gravemente).
eh fayreeto(-a) gravamayntay

I've got a/an ...
Ho ... *o*

blister
una vescica *oona vaysheeka*

bruise
una contusione *oona kontooseeonay*

burn
una scottatura *oona skottatoora*

cut
un taglio *oon talyo*

scratch [graze]
un'escoriazione *oonayskoreeatseeonay*

insect bite
una puntura d'insetto
oona poontoora deensaytto

lump
un bernoccolo *oon bayrnokkolo*

rash
un'eruzione della pelle *oonayrootseeonay dayllay payllay*

swelling
un gonfiore *oon gonfeeoray*

My ... hurts.
Mi fa male ... *mee fa malay*

PARTS OF THE BODY ➤ 166

Short-term symptoms Sintomi recenti

I've been feeling sick [ill] for … days.	**Mi sento male da … giorni.** *mee saynto malay da … jornee*
I feel faint.	**Mi sento svenire.** *mee saynto svayneeray*
I feel feverish.	**Mi sento la febbre.** *mee saynto la faybbray*
I've been vomiting.	**Ho vomitato.** *o vomeetaatao*
I have diarrhea.	**Ho la diarrea.** *o la deeaarraya*
I have a/an…	**Ho …** *o*
backache	**male alla schiena** *malay allay sheeayna*
cold	**il raffreddore** *eel raffrayddoray*
cramps	**i crampi** *ee krampee*
earache	**male alle orecchie** *malay allay orraykkeeay*
headache	**mal di testa** *mal dee taysta*
sore throat	**mal di gola** *mal dee gola*
stiff neck	**il collo rigido** *eel kollo reejeedo*
stomachache	**mal di stomaco** *mal dee stomako*
sunstroke	**un colpo di sole** *oon kolpo dee solay*

Health conditions Stato di salute

I have arthritis.	**Ho l'artrite** *o lartreetay*
I have asthma.	**Ho l'asma** *o lasma*
I am …	**Sono …** *sono*
deaf	**sordo(-a)** *sordo(-a)*
diabetic	**diabetico(-a)** *deeabayteeko(-a)*
epileptic	**epilettico(-a)** *aypeelaytteeko(-a)*
handicapped	**disabile** *deesabeelay*
(… months) pregnant	**incinta di … mesi** *eencheenta dee … maysee*
I have a heart condition.	**Ho disturbi cardiaci.** *o deestoorbee kardeeachee*
I have high blood pressure.	**Ho la pressione alta.** *o la praysseeonay alta*
I had a heart attack … years ago.	**Ho avuto un infarto … anni fa.** *o avooto oon eenfaarto … annee fa*

Doctor's inquiries Domande del dottore

Da quanto tempo si sente così?	How long have you been feeling like this?
È la prima volta che ha avuto questo?	Is this the first time you've had this?
Prende altre medicine?	Are you taking any other medicines?
È allergico(-a) a qualcosa?	Are you allergic to anything?
È vaccinato(-a) contro il tetano?	Have you been vaccinated against tetanus?
Ha perso l'appetito?	Have you lost your appetite?

Examination La visita medica

Le prendo la temperatura/ la pressione del sangue.	I'll take your temperature/ blood pressure.
Arrotoli/tiri sù la manica, per favore.	Roll up your sleeve, please.
Si spogli fino alla vita, per favore.	Please undress to the waist.
Si sdrai, per favore.	Please lie down.
Apra la bocca.	Open your mouth.
Respiri profondamente.	Breathe deeply.
Tossisca, per favore.	Cough please.
Dove le fa male?	Where does it hurt?
Fa male qui?	Does it hurt here?

Diagnosis Diagnosi

Deve fare una radiografia.	I want you to have an x-ray.
Voglio un campione di sangue/feci/urina.	I want a specimen of your blood/stool/urine.
Deve farsi visitare da uno specialista.	I want you to see a specialist.
Deve andare in ospedale.	I want you to go to the hospital.
È rotto(-a)/slogato(-a).	It's broken/sprained.
È dislocato(-a)/strappato(-a).	It's dislocated/torn.

Ha ...	You've got (a/an) ...
l'appendicite	appendicitis
la cistite	cystitis
l'influenza	flu
l'avvelenamento alimentare	food poisoning
una frattura	fracture
la gastrite	gastritis
l'ernia	hernia
un'infiammazione di	inflammation of ...
il morbillo	measles
la polmonite	pneumonia
la sciatica	sciatica
la tonsillite	tonsilitis
un tumore	tumor
una malattia venerea	venereal disease
È infetto(-a).	It's infected.
È contagioso(-a)	It's contagious.

Treatment Cura

Le do ...	I'll give you ...
un antisettico	an antiseptic
un analgesico	a pain killer
Le prescrivo ...	I'm going to prescribe ...
una cura di antibiotici	a course of antibiotics
delle supposte	some suppositories
È allergico(-a) a qualche medicina?	Are you allergic to any medicines?
Prenda una pillola ...	Take one pill ...
ogni ... ore/... volte al giorno	every ... hours/... times a day
prima/dopo dei pasti	before/after meals
in caso di dolore	if there is any pain
per ... giorni	for ... days
Ritorni fra ... giorni.	I'd like you to come back in ... days.
Consulti un medico quando ritorna a casa.	Consult a doctor when you get home.

Parts of the body Parti del corpo

appendix	**l'appendice** *lappayndeechay*
arm	**il braccio** *eel bratcho*
back	**il dorso/la schiena** *eel dorso/la skeeehna*
bladder	**la vescica** *la vaysheeka*
bone	**l'osso** *losso*
breast	**il petto/il seno** *eel paytto/eel sayno*
chest	**il torace** *eel toraachay*
ear	**l'orecchio** *loraykkeeo*
eye	**l'occhio** *lokkeeo*
face	**la faccia/il viso** *la fatcha/eel veezo*
finger	**il dito** *eel deeto*
foot	**il piede** *eel peeehday*
gland	**la ghiandola** *la geeandola*
hand	**la mano** *la mano*
head	**la testa** *la taysta*
heart	**il cuore** *eel kooray*
jaw	**la mascella** *la mashehlla*
joint	**l'articolazione** *larteekolatseeonay*
kidney	**il rene** *eel raynay*
knee	**il ginocchio** *eel jeenokkeeo*
leg	**la gamba** *la gamba*
lip	**il labbro** *eel labbro*
liver	**il fegato** *eel faygato*
mouth	**la bocca** *la bokka*
muscle	**il muscolo** *eel mooskolo*
neck	**il collo** *eel kollo*
nose	**il naso** *eel naaso*
rib	**la costola** *la kostola*
shoulder	**la spalla** *la spalla*
skin	**la pelle** *la payllay*
stomach	**lo stomaco** *lo stomako*
thigh	**la coscia** *la kosha*
throat	**la gola** *la gola*
thumb	**il pollice** *eel polleechay*
toe	**il dito del piede** *eel deeto dayl peeehday*
tongue	**la lingua** *la leenggooy*
tonsils	**le tonsille** *lay tonseellay*
vein	**la vena** *la vayna*

Gynecologist Dal ginecologo

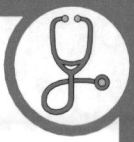

I have …	**Ho …** *o*
abdominal pains	**dolori addominali** *dolo<u>r</u>ee addomee<u>na</u>alee*
period pains	**mestruazioni dolorose** *maystrooatsee<u>o</u>nay dolo<u>ro</u>say*
a vaginal infection	**un'infezione vaginale** *ooneenfaytsee<u>o</u>nay vajee<u>na</u>alay*
I haven't had my period for … months.	**Non ho le mestruazioni da … mesi.** *non o lay maystrootsee<u>o</u>nay da … <u>may</u>see*
I'm on the Pill.	**Prendo la pillola (anticoncezionale).** *<u>prayn</u>do la <u>pee</u>llola (anteekonchaytseeo<u>na</u>alay)*

Hospital Ospedale

Please notify my family.	**Per favore informi la mia famiglia.** *pehr fa<u>vo</u>ray eenf<u>or</u>mee la <u>mee</u>a fa<u>mee</u>lya*
I'm in pain.	**Ho dolori.** *o dolo<u>r</u>ee*
I can't eat/sleep.	**Non posso mangiare/dormire.** *non <u>po</u>sso man<u>jaa</u>ray/dor<u>mee</u>ray*
When will the doctor come?	**Quando verrà il dottore?** *<u>kwan</u>do vayr<u>ra</u> eel dot<u>to</u>ray*
Which section [ward] is … in?	**In che reparto/corsia è …?** *een kay ray<u>paar</u>to/kor<u>see</u>a eh*
I'm visiting …	**Visito …** *<u>vee</u>seeto*

Optician Ottico

I'm nearsighted/farsighted [shortsighted/longsighted].	**Sono miope/presbite.** *<u>so</u>no mee<u>o</u>pay/<u>prays</u>beetay*
I've lost …	**Ho perso …** *o <u>pay</u>rso*
one of my contact lenses	**una delle mie lenti a contatto** *<u>oo</u>na <u>day</u>llay <u>mee</u>ay <u>layn</u>tee ah kon<u>tat</u>to*
my glasses	**i miei occhiali** *ee mee<u>ay</u>ee okee<u>aa</u>lee*
a lens	**una lente** *<u>oo</u>na <u>layn</u>tay*
Could you give me a replacement?	**Può sostituirmelo(-la)?** *pwo sosteetoo<u>eer</u>maylo(-la)*

Dentist Dentista

If you need to see a dentist, you'll probably have to pay the bill on the spot; save all receipts for reimbursement.

I have a toothache.	**Ho mal di denti.** *o mal dee dayntee*
This tooth hurts.	**Questo dente mi fa male.** *kwaysto dayntay mee fa malay*
I don't want it extracted.	**Non voglio un'estrazione.** *non volyo oon aystratseeonay*
I've lost a filling/a tooth.	**Ho perso un'otturazione/un dente.** *o pehrso oonottooratseeonay/oon dayntay*
Can you repair this denture?	**Può riparare questa dentiera?** *pwo reeparaaray kwaysta dayntee-ehra*

Le faccio un'iniezione/ un'anestesia locale.	I'm going to give you an injection/ a local anesthetic.
Ci vuole un'otturazione/ una capsula/una corona.	You need a filling/cap [crown].
Devo fare un'estrazione.	I'll have to take it out.
Posso fissarlo solo temporaneamente.	I can only fix it temporarily.
Non mangi niente per ... ore.	Don't eat anything for ... hours.

Payment and insurance
Pagamento e assicurazione

How much do I owe you?	**Quanto Le devo?** *kwanto lay dayvo*
I have insurance.	**Sono assicurato.** *sono asseekooraato*
Can I have a receipt for my health insurance?	**Vorrei una ricevuta per la mia assicurazione medica.** *vorrehee oona reechayvoota pehr la meea asseekooratseeonay maydeeka*
Would you fill out this health insurance form, please?	**Compili questo modulo di assicurazione medica, per favore.** *koampeelee kwehsto modoolo dee asseekooratseetseeonay maydeeka pehr favoray*
Do you have... ?	**Ha ...?** *ha*
Form E111/health insurance	**il modulo E111/l'assicurazione medica** *eel modoolo ay-chento-oondeechee/ lasseekooratseeonay*

MAKING APPOINTMENTS ➤ 161

Dictionary
English ➤ Italian

A-Z

To enable correct usage, most terms in this dictionary are either followed by an expression or are cross-referenced to pages where the word appears in a full phrase. The notes below provide some basic grammar guidelines.

Nouns

Nouns in Italian are classed as either masculine (m) or feminine (f). Nouns ending in **-o** are generally masculine (to form their plural, change **-o** to **-i**). Nouns ending in **-a** are usually feminine (to form their plural, change **-a** to **-e**). Nouns ending in **-e** can be either gender (to form their plural, change **-e** to **-i**). The articles they take depend on their gender:

	definite article *(the)*		**indefinite article** *(a)*	**partitive** *(some, any)*	
	singular	plural		singular	plural
masc. beginning with:					
a vowel	**l'amico**	**gli amici**	**un amico**	**dell'amico**	**degli amici**
z or **s**+consonant	**lo studio**	**gli studi**	**uno studio**	**dello studio**	**degli studi**
all other consonants	**il treno**	**i treni**	**un treno**	**del treno**	**dei treni**
fem. beginning with:					
a vowel	**l'ora**	**le ore**	**un'ora**	**dell'ora**	**delle ore**
a consonant	**la casa**	**le case**	**una casa**	**della casa**	**delle case**

Adjectives

Adjectives agree in gender and number with the noun they are describing. In this dictionary the feminine form (where it differs from the masculine) is shown in brackets, e.g.

leggero(-a) – light (in weight) **feminine form:** **leggera**

If the masculine form ends in **-e** or with a consonant, the feminine generally keeps the same form:

il museo/la casa grande the large museum/house

Most adjectives form their plurals in the same way as nouns:

il museo italiano – i musei italiani **la cattedrale interessante – le cattedrali interessanti**

Verbs

Verbs are generally shown in the infinitive (to say, to eat, etc.) Here are three of the main categories of regular verbs in the present tense:

	amare (to love) ends in **-are**	**vendere** (to sell) ends in **-ere**	**partire** (to leave) ends in **-ire**
io (I)	**amo**	**vendo**	**parto**
tu (you)	**ami**	**vendi**	**parti**
lui, lei (he, she, it)	**ama**	**vende**	**parte**
noi (we)	**amiamo**	**vendiamo**	**partiamo**
voi (you)	**amate**	**vendete**	**partite**
essi/esse (they)	**amano**	**vendono**	**partono**

Note that the subject pronouns are generally omitted, except for emphasis. Negatives are generally formed by putting **non** before the verb: **Non vado a Roma.** I am not going to Rome.

A-Z

A

a few alcuni(e) 15
a little un poco 15
a lot molto(-a) 15
a.m. di mattina
abbey abbazia f 99
able, to be potere
about *(approximately)* circa
above *(place)* sopra
abroad all'estero
abscess ascesso
accept, to accettare 136
access accesso m 100
accessories accessori mpl 144
accident incidente 152; *(road)* incidente stradale m 92
accidentally accidentalmente 28
accommodations sistemazione f
accompaniments condimenti mpl, salse f 38
accompany, to accompagnare 65
accountant ragioniere (a) m/f
ace *(cards)* asso m
activities le attività fpl
acne acne f
across attraverso
action film film m d'azione
actor/actress attore m/attrice f
adaptor presa f multipla 148
address indirizzo m 84, 93
adhesive bandage bende fpl adesive
adjoining room camera f adiacente 22
admission charge prezzo m d'entrata 114
adult adulti mpl 100
advance, in in anticipo 21
aerial *(car/tv)* antenna f
aerobics aerobica f
after *(time)* dopo 13; *(place)* 95
aftershave dopobarba m 142
after-sun lotion lozione f doposole
afternoon, in the nel pomeriggio 221
age: what age? età: quanti anni?
aged, to be avere ... anni
ago fa 13
agree: I agree sono d'accordo
air conditioning aria f condizionata 22
air mattress materasso m di gomma 31
air pump pompa f per l'aria 87
air-freshener deodorante m per ambienti
airline linea f aerea
airmail via f aerea 155
airplane aeroplano m
airport aeroporto m
air steward/hostess assistente m/f di volo
aisle seat posto m nel corridoio 69
alarm clock orologio m sveglia 149
alcoholic *(drink)* alcolico(-a)
all tutto(-a)
all-night bar bar m aperto tutta la notte
all-night pharmacy farmacia f notturna 140
allergic, to be essere allergico(-a) a 164
allergy allergia f
allowed: is it allowed? è permesso?
almost quasi
alone solo(-a) 120
alphabet alfabeto m 9
already già
also anche
alter, to ritoccare
aluminum foil carta f stagnola 148
always sempre 13
am: I am sono
amazing meraviglioso(-a) 101
ambassador ambasciatore m
amber ambra f
ambulance ambulanza f 92
American *(person/adj)* americano(-a) m/f 150, 152
American football calcio m americano
amethyst ametista m
amount ammontare m, cifra (f) 42
and e 19
anesthetic anestetico m
angling pesca m con lenza
animal animale m 106
announcement: what was that announcement? cos'era quell'annuncio?
another un altro/un'altra 21
another time un'altra volta 125
antacid antiacido m
antibiotics antibiotici mpl 165
antifreeze antigelo m
antique oggetti mpl di antiquariato 157
antiques shop negozio m di antiquariato 130

antiseptic antisettico m 165; **~ cream** pomata f antisettica
any qualsiasi
anyone: does anyone speak English? c'è qualcuno che parla inglese?
anyone else altre persone 93
anything cheaper qualcosa di più economico 21
anything else? nient'altro?
apartment appartamento 28
apologies scuse fpl 10
apologize: I apologize chiedo scusa
appendicitis appendicite f 165
apples mele fpl 160
appointment appuntamento m 161
approximately circa/approssimativamente
architect architetto m 104
architecture architettura f
area regione f 97; **~ code** codice m, prefisso m
arm braccio m 166
armbands *(swimming)* bracciali mpl salvagente
around *(place)* attorno, intorno ; *(time)* circa
arrange: can you arrange it? può organizzarlo(-a)?
arrest, to be under essere in arresto
arrive, to arrivare 68, 70, 71, 76
art arte f
art gallery galleria d'arte f, pinacoteca f 99
artery arteria f 166
arthritic, to be essere artritico(-a) 163
artificial sweetener zucchero m dietetico 38
artist artista m/f 104
ashtray posacenere m 39
asked for ... ho ordinato ... 41
asking the way chiedere la strada 94
asleep, to be essere addormentato(-a)
aspirin aspirina f 114, 140
asthmatic, to be essere asmatico(-a) 163
astringent astringente m
at *(place)* a 12; *(time)* a/alle 13
at least almeno, minimo 23
ATM *(cash machine)* Bancomat m 139
attack *(crime)* aggressione f 152; *(medical)* attacco m
attendant guardiano m
attractive attraente m/f
aunt zia f 120
Australian *(n)* australiano(-a) m/f
Austrian *(person)* austriaco(-a) m/f
authentic: is it ? è autentico(-a)?
automatic *(car)* auto f con cambio automatico 86
automatic camera macchina f fotografica automatica 151
autumn autunno m 219
avalanche valanga f
away via 12
awful orribile

B

baby bambino m/bambina f 162; neonato(-a) m/f 113
baby food alimenti per neonati 142
baby seat sedile m per bambini
baby wipes fazzolettini mpl/salviette fpl per neonati 142
baby's bottle biberon f
babysitter babysitter f
back dorso m, schiena f 166
backache mal m di schiena 163
backpack zaino m 31
backpacking girare il mondo con lo zaino
bad cattivo(-a) 14
baked al forno
bakery panetteria f 130
ball palla f
ballet balletto m 108
ballroom sala f da ballo
bandage bende fpl
bank banca f 130, 138
bank account conto m bancario
bank card carta bancaria f 139
bank loan prestito m bancario
bar *(hotel)* bar m 26
barber shop barbiere m
barge *(long boat)* lancia f
basic expressions espressioni comuni 10
basin bacino m
basket cestello m 158
basketball pallacanestro f 114
bath towel asciugamano m 27
bath: to take a fare il bagno

bathroom bagno m 29; sala f da bagno
battery batteria f 88; pila f 137, 151
be able, to potere 18
be, to essere
beach spiaggia f 116
beard barba f
beautiful bello(-a) 14, 101; stupendo(-a)
because perchè
because of a causa di
bed letto m 21
bed and breakfast pernottamento m e colazione f 24
bed: I'm going to vado a letto
bedding biancheria f da letto 29
bee ape f
beer birra f 49
before *(time)* prima di 13, 221
begin, to *(see also to start)* iniziare
beginner principiante m/f 117
beginning inizio m
belong: this belongs to me questo è mio
below 15°C sotto i 15ºC
belt cintura f 144
beneath sotto
berth cuccetta f 74, 77
best il migliore
better migliore 14
between fra, tra
bib bavaglino m
bicycle bicicletta f 83, 153
bicycle parts 82
bicycle rental noleggio (m biciclette) 83
big grande 14, 117, 134
bill conto m 32, 42; **put it on the ~** lo metta sul conto
bin liner sacco m di plastica per bidoni di spazzatura
binoculars binocolo m
bird uccello m 106
birthday compleanno m 219
biscuits biscotti m 160
bite *(insect)* puntura f
bitten: I've been bitten by a dog sono stato morsicato da un cane
bitter amaro(-a) 41
bizarre bizzarro(-a)
black nero(-a) 143
black and white film *(camera)* bianco e nero 151
black coffee *(weak)* caffè m lungo
bladder vescica f 166
blanket coperta f 27
bleach candeggina f 148
bleeding, to be perdere sangue 162
blind tapparella f 25
blister vescica f 162
blocked bloccato(-a) 25; **the drain is ~** le fognature sono bloccate; **the road is ~** la strada è bloccata
blood sangue m 164
blood group gruppo m sanguigno
blood pressure pressione f (del sangue) 163, 164
blouse camicetta f 144
blow-dry asciugatura f a fon 147
blue blu 143
blush *(rouge)* rosso m per guance
board, on a bordo
boarding pass carta f d'imbarco 69, 70
body: parts of the body parti fpl del corpo 166
boiled bollito
bone osso m 166
book libro m 150
book of tickets blocchetto m di biglietti 79
book, to prenotare 21, 74, 109
booked up, to be essere prenotato(-a) 115
booking prenotazione f 22, 36
booking office ufficio m prenotazioni
bookstore libreria f 130
boots stivali mpl 145; *(for sport)* scarponi mpl 115
border *(country)* frontiera f
boring noioso(-a) 101
born: I was born in sono nato a/nel
borrow: may I borrow your ...? posso prendere in prestito il suo...?
bottle bottiglia f 159
bottle-opener apribottiglie m 148
bowel intestino m 166
box of chocolates scatola f di cioccolatini 156
box office biglietteria f
boxing pugilato m

boy bambino m 157; ragazzo m 120
boyfriend ragazzo m 120
bra reggiseno m 144
bracelet braccialetto m 149
brass ottone m
bread pane m 38
break, to rompere 28; **~ the journey** interrompere il viaggio 75
break-in rapina f 153
breakage rottura f
breakdown guasto m 88
breakfast (prima) colazione f 26, 27
breast petto m, seno m 166
breathe, to respirare 164
breathtaking sensazionale 101
bridge ponte m 107; *(cards)* bridge m
briefcase valigetta f portadocumenti
briefs mutandine fpl 144
brilliant splendido(-a) 101
bring, to portare 37
Britain Gran Bretagna f 119
British *(person/adj)* britannico(-a) m/f
brochure opuscolo m
broken rotto(-a) 25, 137, 164
bronchitis bronchite f
bronze *(adj)* bronzeo(-a)
brooch spilla f 149
broom scopa f
brother fratello m 120
brown marrone 143
browse, to dare un'occhiata 133
bruise contusione f 162
brush spazzola f
bubble bath schiuma f per bagno
bucket secchiello m 157
buffet car vagone m ristorante
build, to costruire 104
building edificio m
built costruito(-a) 104
buoy boa f
burger hamburger m 40
burger stand chiosco m per hamburger 35
burn scottatura f 162
burn: it's burned è bruciato(-a)
bus autobus m 70, 78, 79
bus route percorso m d' autobus 96
bus station stazione f autobus 78
bus stop fermata f d'autobus 65, 96
business trip viaggio m d'affari 123
business, on per lavoro 66
businessman uomo m d'affari
businesswoman donna f d'affari
busy, to be *(occupied)* occupato(-a) 125
but ma 19
butane gas campingaz m 30, 31
butcher shop macelleria f 130
butter burro m 38, 160
button bottone m
buy, to comprare 67, 80
bye! arrivederci
bypass circonvallazione f

cabaret cabaret m
cable car funivia f
café bar m 35, 40
cake torta f 40
cake shop pasticceria f
calendar calendario m 156
call, to chiamare 92, 128; *(phone)* telefonare 127; **~ call the police!** chiami la polizia! 92
camcorder videocamera f
camera macchina f fotografica 151
camera case custodia f per macchina fotografica 151
camera store [shop] negozio m di ottica/foto 130
campbed lettino m da campeggio 31
camping campeggio m 30
camping equipment 31
campsite campeggio m 30
can I posso 18
can opener apriscatole m
cancel, to annullare 68
cancer *(disease)* cancro m
candles candele fpl 148
candy caramella f 150
cap berretto m 144
cap *(dental)* capsula f corona f 168
capital city capitale f
car auto(mobile) f, macchina f 86–9, 153; **by ~** in auto/macchina 95
car alarm antifurto m per auto

car rental noleggio auto m, autonoleggio m 70, 86
car parts 90-1
car pound deposito auto m 87
car repairs 89
car wash lavaggio auto m
cardphone telefono m a scheda
cards carte 121
careful: be careful! faccia attenzione!
carpet *(fitted)* moquette f; *(rug)* tappeto m
carrier bag sacchetto m 136
carry-cot portabebe m
carton scatola f (di cartone) 159; ~ **of milk** cartone m di latte
cartoon cartoni mpl animati
cash contanti mpl, soldi mpl 136
cash card carta f bancaria 139
cash desk cassa f 132
cash machine Bancomat m 139
cash, to incassare 138
cassette cassetta f, nastro m 157
castle castello m 99
cat gatto m
catch, to *(bus)* prendere (l'autobus)
cathedral cattedrale f 99
cave caverna m, grotta f 107
CD compact m, il CD m
CD-player lettore m per compact
cemetery cimitero m 99
central heating impianto m di riscaldamento
center of town centro m città 21
ceramics ceramica f
certificate certificato m 157
certification certificato m 149
chain catenina f 149
chair sedia f
chair-lift seggiovia f 117
change *(coins)* moneta f 87; resto m, spiccioli mpl
change lanes, to cambiare corsìa
change, to cambiare
change, to *(bus, train)* cambiare 78, 79, 84; *(money)* 136; *(reservation)* 68
change: keep the change tenga il resto
chapel cappella f
charcoal carbone m 31
charter flight volo m charter
cheap a buon prezzo 14, economico 134
cheaper più economico(-a) 21, 24; meno caro(-a) 109
check conto m 42
check in, to registrare 68
check out, to *(hotel)* saldare il conto
checkbook libretto m degli assegni
checkers *(draughts)* gioco m della dama
checkout cassa f 158
check guarantee card carta f bancaria
cheers! alla salute!
cheese formaggio m 48; 160
chemist farmacia f
checkbook libretto m degli assegni
chess scacchi 121
chess set gioco m degli scacchi 157
chest torace m 166
chewing gum gomma f da masticare 150
chickenpox varicella f
child bambino m/bambina f 152; figlio m/figlia f
child seat *(in car)* sedile per bambini m
children bambini mpl 24, 39, 66, 74, 100, 113; figli mpl 120
children's meals piatti mpl per bambini 39
Chinese (cuisine) (cucina) Cinese 35
chips patatine fpl 160
choc-ice pinguino m 110
chocolate cioccolata f 40, 160; **box of ~** scatola f di cioccolatini
chocolate bar tavoletta f di cioccolata 150
chop *(meat)* braciola f
Christian *(adj)* cristiano(-a)
Christmas Natale m 219
church chiesa f 96, 99, 105
cigarette machine distributore m automatico di sigarette
cigarettes, pack of sigarette fpl 150
clamps (car) i ceppi bloccaruote fpl 87
class: first class prima classe f 68
clean *(adj)* pulito(-a) 14, 39, 41
clean, to pulire 137
cleaning person cameriera f 28
cliff scogliera f/rupe f 107
cling film pellicola f trasparente 148
cloakroom guardaroba m 109
clock orologio m 149
close *(near)* vicino(-a) 95

close, to chiudere 100, 132, 140
clothes abbigliamento m 144
clothes dryer asciugatore m elettrico
clothes line corda f per il bucato
clothing store *(clothing store)* negozio m di abbigliamento 130
cloudy, to be essere nuvoloso 122
clown clown, pagliaccio m
clubs *(golf)* mazze fpl
coach corriera f, pullman m 78; *(train compartment)* carrozza f 75
coat cappotto m 144
code *(area/dialling)* codice m telefonico
coffee caffè m 40
coin moneta f
cold freddo(-a) 14; 41, 122
cold *(flu)* raffreddore m 141, 163
cold meats affettati mpl
collapse: he's collapsed ha avuto un collasso
collect, to ritirare 151
color colore m 134, 143; *(film)* a colori 151
comb pettine m 142
come back , to *(return)* ritornare 36, 165; *(for collection)* passare a ritirare 140
communication difficulties difficoltà di comunicazione 11
compact camera macchina f compact 151
company *(business)* azienda f; *(companionship)* compagnia f 126
compartment *(train)* scompartimento m
complaints reclami mpl 25, 41; **to make a ~** fare un reclamo 137
computer computer m, l'ordinatore m
concert hall sala f concerti
concession tariffa f speciale
concussion, to have a avere la commozione cerebrale
condoms profilattici mpl
conductor direttore m d'orchestra
conference conferenza f
confirm, to *(reservation)* confermare 22, 68
confirmation conferma f 22
congratulations! congratulazioni!
connection *(transport)* coincidenza f
conscious, to be *(medical)* riprendere conoscenza
Consulate consolato m 152
consult, to consultare 165
consultant *(medical)* specialista m/f
contact lens lenti fpl a contatto 167
contact, to contattare 28
contact lens fluid fluido m per lenti a contatto 167
contagious, to be essere contagioso(-a)
contain, to contenere 39, 69, 155
contraceptive contraccettivo m
convenience store nepozio m di alimentari 158
convenient conveniente
conversion charts 85, 145, 158
convertible *(car)* auto f decappottabile
cook cuoco m, cuoca f
cook, to cucinare
cooker cucina f a gas/elettrica
cookies biscotti mpl 160
cooking *(cuisine)* cucina *f*
copper rame m 149
copy copia f 155
corkscrew cavatappi m 148
corn pad callifugo m
corner angolo m 95
correct *(also right)* giusto
cosmetics cosmetici mpl
cottage la villa f 28, il rustico m
cotton cotone m
cotton wool *(absorbent cotton)* cotone m idrofilo 114, 142
cough tosse f 141
cough syrup sciroppo m per la tosse 114
cough, to tossire 164
counter *(shop)* banco m *(post office, bank)* sportello m
country *(nation)* paese m
countryside campagna f 119
couple *(pair)* paio m
courier *(guide)* guida m/f, l'accompagnatore m
course *(meal)* portata f
courthouse palazzo m di giustizia
cousin cugino m, la cugina f
cover *(lid)* coperchio m
cover charge coperto m 112
craft shop negozio m di artigianato
cramps crampi mpl 163
crash: I've had a crash ho avuto un incidente d'auto

creche asilo-nido m
credit card carta f di credito 42, 136,
credit status posizione f finanziaria
credit credito m
crib culla f 22
crisps chips fpl 160
crockery stoviglie fpl 148
cross, to *(road)* attraversare 95
cross-country skiing trail pista f per sci di fondo
crossroads incrocio m 95
crowded affollato(-a)
crown *(dental)* corona f 168
cruise crociera f
crutches stampelle f
cup tazza f 39, 148
cupboard credenza f, l'armadio m
currency valuta f 67, 138
currency exchange office ufficio m cambio 70, 73, 138
curtains tende fpl
cushion cuscino m
customs dogana f 67, 157
customs declaration dichiarazione f doganale 155
cut taglio m 162
cut and blow-dry taglio m e asciugatura a fon
cutlery posate fpl 148
cycle helmet casco m per ciclista
cycle path pista f ciclabile
cycling ciclismo m 114
cyclist ciclista m/f
cystitis cistite f 165

D

daily giornalmente 13
damaged, to be essere danneggiato(-a) 28, 71
damp *(n)* umidità f; *(adj)* umido(-a)
dance *(performance)* danza f 111
dancing, to go andare a ballare 124
dangerous pericoloso(-a)
dark scuro(-a) 14, 134, 143; buio(-a) 24
daughter figlia f 120, 162
day giorno m 97; *(ticket)* giornaliero 79
day trip gita f di un giorno
dead morto(-a); *(battery)* scarico(-a) 88
deaf, to be essere sordo(-a) 163
dear *(greeting)* caro(-a)
decide: we haven't decided yet non abbiamo ancora deciso
deck *(ship)* ponte m
deck chair sedia f a sdraio 116
declare, to dichiarare 67
deduct, to *(money)* detrarre
deep profondo(-a)
deep frozen surgelato(-a)
defrost, to scongelare
degrees *(temperature)* gradi mpl
delay ritardo m 70
delicatessen salumeria f 130, 158
delicious *(food)* squisito(-a) 125; delizioso(-a) 14
deliver, to consegnare
dental floss filo m per denti
dentist dentista m/f 131, 168
dentures dentiera fsing 168
deodorant deodorante m 142
depart, to (*train, bus*) partire
department store grande magazzino m 130
departure *(train)* partenza f 76
departure lounge sala f partenze
depend: it depends on dipende da
deposit caparra f 83; anticipo m 24, 115
describe, to descrivere 152
design *(dress)* disegno m
designer stilista m/f
dessert dolci mpl 150
destination destinazione f
details dettagli mpl
detergent detersivo m
develop, to *(photos)* sviluppare 151
diabetes diabete m
diabetic diabetico(-a)
dialing *(area)* **code** codice m, prefisso m
diamond diamante m 149; *(cards)* quadri mpl
diapers pannolini mpl 142
diarrhea diarrea f 141; **to have ~** avere la diarrea
dice dadi mpl
dictionary dizionario m 150
diesel diesel m 87
diet: I'm on a diet sono a dieta
difficult difficile 14
digital digitale 149
dine, to mangiare
dining car carrozza ristorante f 75, 77

dining room sala f da pranzo 26
dinner jacket smoking m
dinner, to have cenare 124
direct diretto 75
direct, to indicare la via 18
direct-dial telephone telefono m a linea diretta
direction direzione f 80, 94; **in the ~ of** in direzione 95;
director *(of company)* direttore m; *(film)* regista m/f
directory *(telephone)* elenco m abbonati
Directory Inquiries Informazioni Elenco Abbonati 127
dirty sporco(-a) 14, 28
disabled disabili m/fpl 22, 100
discount sconto m; **can you offer me a ~?** può farmi uno sconto?
disgusting disgustoso(-a)
dish *(meal)* piatto m 37
dish cloth strofinaccio m per i piatti 148
dishes posate fpl 148
dishwashing detergent detersivo m per lavastoviglie 148
dislocated, to be essere dislocato(-a) 164
display cabinet armadietto m vetrina 149
display case astuccio m 134
disposable camera macchina f usa-e-getta 151
distilled water acqua f distillata
district zona f
disturb: don't non disturbare
dive, to tuffarsi 116
diversion deviazione f
divorced, to be essere divorziato(-a) 120
dizzy, to feel avere il capogiro 163
do: things to do cose fpl da fare 123
doctor dottore(ssa) m/f, medico m 131, 161, 165, 224
dog cane m
doll bambola f
door porta f 25, 29
dosage dose f
double bed letto m matrimoniale 21
double room camera f doppia 21
down giù
downstairs al piano inferiore 12
downtown area centro m città 99
dozen dozzina f 159, 217
drain fognatura f
draught *(wind)* corrente f d'aria
dress vestito m 144
drink bibita f 124, 125, 126
drinking water acqua f potabile 30
drinks bevande f
drip: the faucet [tap] drips il rubinetto perde
drive, to guidare 93
driver conducente m; *(bus, etc)* autista m/f
driver's [driving] license patente di guida f
drop someone off, to fare scendere 83
drowning: someone is ~ qualcuno sta annegando
drugstore farmacia f
drunk ubriaco(-a)
dry-clean, to lavare a secco
dry cleaner lavanderia f a secco 131
dry clothes, to asciugare i vestiti
dubbed, to be essere doppiato 110
during durante
dusty polveroso(-a)
duty: to pay duty pagare il dazio
duvet piumone m

E

each: how much each? quant'è ciascuno?
ear orecchio m 166; **~ache** mal d'orecchia m 163; **~drops** le gocce fpl per orecchie; **~rings** orecchini mpl
earlier più presto 125
early di buon'ora
east est m 95
Easter Pasqua f
easy facile 14
eat, to mangiare 41, 167; **places ~** posti mpl per mangiare 123
eaten: have you ~? ha già mangiato?; **we've already ~** abbiamo già mangiato
economical economico(-a)
economy class in classe turistica 68
eggs uova fpl
either ... or ... o ... o ...
elastic *(adj)* elastico(-a)
electric: ~ meter contatore m dell'elettricità 28; **~ shaver** rasoio m elettrico

electrical items articoli mpl elettrici
electrician elettricista m
electricity elettricità f
electronic: ~ flash flash m elettronico 151; **~ game** gioco m elettronico 157
elevator ascensore m 26, 132
else: something ~ qualcos'altro
embark, to *(boat)* imbarcarsi
embassy ambasciata f
emerald smeraldo m
emergency emergenza f 127; **it's an ~** è un'emergenza; **~ room** pronto soccorso m
emergency exit uscita f d'emergenza
empty vuoto(-a) 14
enamel smalto m 149
end, to finire
end: at the end in fondo
engaged, to be essere fidanzato(-a) 120
engine motore m
engineer ingegnere m/f
England Inghilterra f 119
English *(language)* inglese m 11, 67, 110, 150, 152, 161
enjoy, to piacere 110, 124
enlarge, to *(photos)* ingrandire 151
enough abbastanza 15, 42
entertainment: what ~ is there? cosa c'è come divertimenti/spettacoli?
entertainment guide guida f spettacoli
entirely completamente
entrance fee tariffa f d'ingresso 100
entry visa visto m d'entrata
envelope busta f
epileptic epilettico(-a); **to be ~** essere epilettico(-a) 163
equally equamente 17
equipment *(sports)* attrezzatura f
error errore m
escalator scala mobile f 132
essential essenziali 89
estate agent agente m/f immobiliare
EU Unione f Europea
evening dress abito m da sera 112
events manifestazioni fpl 108
every day tutti i giorni
every week ogni settimana 13
examination *(medical)* visita f medica
example, for per esempio
excellent *(adj)* eccellente
except eccetto
excess baggage eccedenza bagaglio f 69
exchange rate tasso m di cambio 138
exchange, to cambiare 138
excluding meals pasti m esclusi 24
excursion escursione f 97
excuse me *(apology. attention)* scusi 10
exhausted, to be essere esausto(-a) 106
exhibition mostra f
exit uscita f 70; **at the ~** all'uscita
expensive caro(-a) 14, 134
expiration date data f di scadenza 109
expire, to: when does it expire? quando scade?
exposure *(photos)* posa f 151
expressway autostrada f
extension interno 128
extension cord prolunga f
extra *(additional)* supplementare
extracted, to be *(tooth)* avere un'estrazione 168
extremely estremamente 17
eye occhio m 166

F

fabric *(material)* stoffa f
face faccia f, viso m 166
facial trattamento per il viso m
facilities servizi mpl 22, 30; attrezzature f
factor *(sun protection)* fattore
factory outlet vendita diretta in fabbrica
faint, to feel sentirsi svenire 163
fall *(season)* autunno m 219
fall: he's had a fall è caduto
family famiglia f 66, 74, 120, 167
famous famoso(-a)
fan *(air)* ventaglio m 25
far lontano(-a) 12; **how ~ is it?** quanto dista? 73; **is it ~?** è lontano?
farsighted presbite 167
fare tariffa f
fashionable, to be essere alla moda
fast-food restaurant tavola calda f, self-service m
fast, to be *(clock)* anticipare
fat grasso m
father padre m 120

fault: it's my/your fault è colpa mia/sua
faulty difettoso(-a)
faulty, to be essere difettoso(-a)
favorite favorito(-a)
fax facilities servizio m fax
fax, to spedire un fax 155
feeding bottle biberon m
feel ill, to sentirsi male 163
feel sick, to sentirsi male/vomitare
female donna f; femmina f 152
festival festival m
fetch help! chiami aiuto! 92
feverish, to feel sentirsi la febbre 163
few pochi (e) 15
fiancé(e) fidanzato(-a) m/f
field campo m 107
fight *(brawl)* rissa f
fill out, to compilare/riempire 155
filling *(dental)* otturazione f 168; *(in sandwich)* ripieno m
filling station stazione f di servizio
film *(camera)* pellicola f 151; film m 108
film speed velocità f della pellicola
filter filtro m 151; **~ paper** *(for coffee)* filtro m per il caffè
find out: could you find that out? può informarsi?
fine *(penalty)* multa f 93; *(well)* bene 118
finger dito m 166
fire alarm allarme m antincendio
fire department pompieri (pl) 92
fire escape uscita f di sicurezza
fire extinguisher estintore m
fire: there's a fire! c'è un incendio!
fireplace caminetto m
first primo(-a) 68, 75, 81
first class in prima classe 68; di prima classe 74
first course primo (piatto) m
first floor *(UK)* primo piano m
first floor *(US)* pianterreno
first name nome m
first-aid kit astuccio m pronto soccorso
fish store pescheria f
fishing rod canna f da pesca
fishing, to go andare a pesca
fit, to *(clothes)* andare bene 146
fitting room cabina di prova f 146
fix, to: can you fix it? può ripararlo(-a)?
flag bandiera f
flash *(photography)* flash m elettronico 151
flashlight *(torch)* pila 31
flat *(tire)* pneumatico m scoppiato
flavor: what flavors do you have? che gusti ha?
flea pulce f
flea market mercato m delle pulci
flight volo m 70; **~ number** numero m del volo 68; **~ attendant** assistente m/f di volo
flip-flops ciabatte fpl 145
flood inondazione f
floor *(level)* piano m 132
floor mop Vileda (trademark)
floor show spettacolo m di varietà
florist fiorista m 130
flour farina f
flower fiore m 106
flu influenza f 165
fluent: to speak fluent Italian parlare italiano correntemente
fly *(insect)* mosca f
fly, to volare
foggy, to be essere nebbioso(-a) 122
folding chair/table sedia/tavola f pieghevole
folk art arte f popolare
folk music musica f folcloristica
follow, to seguire 95
food poisoning avvelenamento m alimentare 165
foot piede m 166
football *(soccer)* calcio m 114
footpath sentiero m pedestre 107
for a week per una settimana 86
forecast previsioni f 122
foreign straniero(-a)
foreign currency valuta f straniera 138
forest foresta f 107
forget, to dimenticare 42
fork forchetta f 39, 41, 148; *(in the road)* incrocio m
form modulo m 153, 168
formal dress tenuta f da sera 111
forms moduli mpl 23
fortunately fortunatamente 19
forward: please forward my mail per favore faccia proseguire la mia posta

foundation *(make-up)* crema f base
fountain fontana f 99
four-door car auto f a quattro porte
four-wheel drive auto fuoristrada f
foyer *(hotel/theater)* atrio m
frame *(glasses)* cornice f per occhiali
France Francia f
free *(available, not busy)* libero(-a) 36, 77, 124; *(of charge)* gratuito(-a) 69
French *(cuisine)* (cucina) Francese
French *(language)* francese m
frequent: how frequent? che frequenza? 76
frequently frequentemente
fresh fresco(-a) 41
freshly squeezed fruit juice spremuta f di frutta
fridge frigorifero m
fried fritto(-a)
friend amico m/amica f 162
friendly amichevole, simpatico(-a)
fries patate f fritte 38, 40
frightened, to be essere spaventato(-a)
fringe frangia f
from da 12; **~ ... to** *(time)* da ... a 13
front door porta f d'ingresso; **~ key** chiave f della porta d' ingresso
frosty, to be *(weather)* essere gelato(-a) 122
frozen congelato(-a)
fruit juice succo m di frutta 40
fuel *(gasoline/petrol)* carburante (benzina) m 86
full pieno(-a) 14
full board *(A.P.)* pensione f completa 24
full insurance una polizza f di assicurazione completa 86
fun, to have divertirsi
funny *(amusing/odd)* buffo/divertente
furniture i mobili mpl
fuse fusibile m
fuse box fusibili mpl 28
fuse wire filo m a piombo

G

gallon gallone m
gambling giocare d'azzardo
game *(toy)* gioco m 157
garage garage m, autorimessa f 26
garden giardino m
gardener giardiniere m
gardening giardinaggio m
gas bottle bombola f del gas 28
gas: I smell gas! c'è odore di gas!
gasoline benzina f 87
gastritis gastrite f 165
gate *(airport)* uscita f 70
gay club locale m gay 112
generous: that's very ... è molto generoso
genuine autentico(-a) 134
get, to *(find)* cercare
get by: may I get by? permesso?
get off, to *(transport)* scendere 79
get out, to *(of vehicle)* scendere
get to, to arrivare a 77; **how do I get to ...?** come si arriva a ...? 73, 94
gift regalo m 67, 156
gift shop negozio m di articoli da regalo 130
girl ragazza f 120; bambina f 157
girlfriend ragazza f 120
give way, to *(on the road)* dare la precedenza 93
give, to dare
glacier ghiacciaio m
gland ghiandola f 166
glass bicchiere m 37, 39
glasses *(optical)* occhiali mpl 167
gliding volare con il deltapiano
gloomy tetro(-a)
glossy finish *(photos)* smaltato(-a)
glove guanto m
go, to andare; **let's go!** andiamo!; **where does this bus go?** dove va questo autobus?
go away! vada via!
go back, to *(turn around)* ritornare
go for a walk, to fare una passeggiata 124
go out, to *(in evening)* uscire
go shopping, to fare acquisti 124
goggles occhialini per nuoto
gold oro m 149
goldplate placcato d'oro
good buono(-a) 14
good afternoon buonasera *(from 1pm)* 10
good evening buonasera 10
good morning buongiorno 10

good night buonanotte 10
good-bye arrivederci 10
gorge gola f
got: have you got any ...? ha del....?
grade *(fuel)* grado del carburante m
gram grammo m 159
grandparents nonni mpl
grapes uva f 160
grass erba f
gratuity mancia f
gray grigio 143
graze escoriazione f 162
greasy *(hair)* grasso(-a)
great fun molto divertente 101
Greek (cuisine) (cucina) Greca
green verde 143
greengrocer fruttivendolo m 130
greetings saluti 10
greyhound racing corsa f di levrieri
grilled alla griglia
grocer *(grocery)* drogheria f
ground: camping ~ terreno m del campeggio 30
ground floor pianterreno
groundsheet telo m per il terreno 31
group gruppo m 66, 100
guarantee garanzia f 135
guarantee: is it guaranteed? è garantito(-a)?
guide *(tour)* guida m/f 98
guidebook guida f/m turistica 100, 150
guided tour visita f guidata 100
guitar chitarra f
gum *(mouth)* gengiva f
gynecologist ginecologo m 167

hair capelli mpl 147
hair brush spazzola f per capelli
hair dryer asciugacapelli m, il fon m
hair gel gel m per i capelli
hair spray lacca f per capelli 142
haircare prodotti per i capelli 142
haircut taglio di capelli m
hairdresser's parrucchiera f, parrucchiere m 131, 147
half, a mezzo 217
half board *(M.A.P.)* mezza pensione f 24
half fare metà prezzo
half past e mezza/... e trenta 220
hammer martello m 31
hand mano f 166
hand cream crema f per mani
hand luggage bagaglioa mano m 69
hand towel asciugamano m
hand washable lavaggio a mano
handbag borsetta f 144, 153
handicapped, to be essere disabile 163
handicrafts artigianato m
handkerchief fazzoletto m
handle maniglia f
hang-gliding fare il deltapiano
hanger gruccia f portabiti 27
hangover postumi mpl della sbornia 141
happen: what happened? che cosa è successo?
happy: I'm not happy with the service non sono soddisfatto(-a) del servizio
harbor porto m
hard shoulder *(road)* corsia f d'emergenza
hardware store negozio m di ferramenta
hat cappello m 144
hatchback auto f a cinque porte
have, to avere
have to, to *(must)* dovere 79
hayfever febbre f del fieno 141
head testa f 166
head waiter capocameriere m
headache mal di testa m 163
heading, to be *(in a direction)* andare in direzione di 83
health food store [shop] negozio *m* di dietetica
health insurance assicurazione *f* medica 168
hear, to sentire
hearing aid protesi *f* per udito
heart cuore *m* 166
heart attack infarto *m* 163
heart condition condizione *f* del cuore, disturbi cardiaci 163
hearts *(cards)* cuori *mpl*
heating riscaldamento m 25
heavy pesante 134

height altezza f 152
helicopter elicottero m
hello buongiorno 118; salve 10
help aiuto m 94
help, to aiutare 18; **help me!** mi aiuti! 92
helper assistente m/f
hemorrhoids emorroidi fpl
her lei 16; suo(-a) 16
here qui 12
hernia ernia f 165
hers suo(-a) 16
hi! ciao! 10
high alto(-a)
high/main street via principale f 96
high tide alta marea f
hike *(walk)* escursione f a piedi 106
hiking fare escursioni a piedi
hill collina f 107
him lui 16
hire out, to *(rent out, to)* noleggiare 29
hire, for libero
hire, to noleggiare 83, 86
his suo(-a) 16
history storia f
hitchhike, to fare l'autostop
HIV-positive sieropositivo(-a)
hobby *(pastime)* hobby 121
hockey field campo m di hockey
hold, to *(contain)* contenere
hold on, to restare in linea 128
hole *(in clothes)* buco m
holiday resort posto m di villeggiatura
holiday, on per/in vacanza 66, 123
home casa f; **to go ~** rientrare
homeopathic remedy rimedio m omeopatico
homosexual *(adj)* omosessuale
honeymoon, to be on essere in luna di miele
hopefully con (la) speranza di 19
horse cavallo m
horseracing ippica 114
horseback trip escursione f a cavallo
hospital ospedale m , policlinico m 131, 164, 167
hot caldo(-a) 14, 24; *(weather)* caldissimo(-a)
hot chocolate cioccolata f calda
hot dog salciccia f calda 110
hot spring sorgente f calda
hot water acqua f calda 25; **~ bottle** bottiglia f dell'acqua calda
hotel albergo m 21
hour ora f 97; **in an ~** fra un'ora 84
hours *(opening)* orario m di apertura
house casa f
household articles articoli casalinghi 148
housewife casalinga f 121
how? come? 17
how are you? come sta? 118
how far? quanto dista? 106
how long? quanto (tempo)? 23, 75, 76, 78, 135
how many? quanti? 15
how much? quanto? 15, 21, 69, 84; quanto costa? 109
how often? con che frequenza? 140; ogni quanto?
how old? quanti anni? 120
however comunque 19
hungry, to be avere fame
hurry, to be in a avere fretta
hurt, to be essere ferito(-a) 92; farsi male 162; **it hurts** fa male 162
husband marito m 120, 162

I

I'd like vorrei 18, 36, 40, 74
I'll have prendo 37
I've lost ho perso 153
ice ghiaccio m 38
ice cream gelato m 40
ice cream parlor gelateria f 35
ice dispenser distributore m di ghiaccio
ice lolly ghiacciolo m
ice pack borsa f da ghiaccio
ice rink pista f di pattinaggio su ghiaccio, il palazzo m del ghiaccio
ice-hockey hockey m su ghiaccio
icy, to be essere ghiacciato(-a) 122
identification documento m d'identità 136
ill, to be stare male 152
illegal, to be essere illegale
illness malattia f
imitation imitazione 134
immediately immediatamente
impressive di grande effetto
in *(place)* in 12; *(time)* fra 13

in-law: father/mother-in-law suocero(-a)
included: is it included? è incluso/compreso? 86, 98
inconvenient scomodo(-a)
Indian (cuisine) (cucina) indiana
indicate, to indicare
indigestion indigestione f
indoor all'interno
indoor pool piscina f invernale 116
inexpensive economico(-a)
infection infezione f 167
inflammation infiammazione f 165
informal *(dress)* abbigliamento m casuale
information informazione f 97
information desk banco m informazioni 73
information office ufficio m informazioni 96
injection iniezione f 168
injured, to be essere ferito(-a) 92, 162
innocent innocente
inquiry desk banco m informazioni
insect insetto m 25
insect bite puntura f d'insetto 141, 162
insect repellent [spray] pomata f contro gli insetti/ dello spray insetticida 141
inside dentro 12
inside lane corsia f interna
insist: I insist insisto
insomnia insonnia f
instant coffee caffè m solubile
instead of invece di
instructions istruzioni fpl 135
instructor istruttore m
insulin insulina f
insurance assicurazione f 86, 89, 93, 168
insurance certificate polizza f d'assicurazione 93
insurance claim richiesta f di rimborso assicurazione 153
insurance company compagnia f d'assicurazione 93
interest *(hobby)* gli interessi 121
interest rate tasso m d'interesse
interesting interessante 101
international internazionale
International Student Card Carta f Internazionale Studenti 29
interpreter interprete m/f 93, 153
intersection intersezione f 95
interval intervallo m
into dentro, in
introduce oneself, to presentarsi 118
introductions presentazioni 118
invitation invito m
invite, to invitare
involved, to be essere coinvolto(-a) 93
iodine iodio m
Ireland Irlanda f 119
Irish *(n)* irlandese m/f
iron *(for clothing)* ferro m da stiro
iron, to stirare
is there ...? c'è...? 17
island isola f
it is è 17
Italian *(language)* italiano m 11, 126; *(person)* italiano(-a) m/f
itch: it itches prude
itemized bill conto m dettagliato 32

jack *(cards)* fante m
jacket giacca f 144
jam marmellata f/conserva f di frutta
jammed: it's jammed è bloccato(-a) 25
jar vasetto m
jaw mascella f 166
jellyfish medusa f
jet lag: I have soffro il cambiamento di fuso orario
jewelry store/jeweler's gioielleria f 149
Jewish *(adj)* ebreo(-a)
job: what's your job? che lavoro fa?
join: may we join you possiamo venire anche noi 124
joint *(body)* articolazione f 166; *(meat)* pezzo m (di carne)
joke scherzo m la barzelletta f
joker *(cards)* matta f, il jolly m
journalist giornalista m/f
journey viaggio m 76, 78, 123
jug *(of water)* brocca f
jumper maglia f 144
junction *(exit)* uscita f autostrada; *(intersection)* intersezione f autostrada

K

kerosene cherosene m
ketchup ketchup m
kettle bollitore m
key chiave f 27, 28, 88
key ring portachiavi m 156
kidney rene m 166
kilo(gram) chilo(grammo) m 159
kilometer chilometro m
kind *(pleasant)* gentile
kind: what kind of ...? che tipo di ...?
king *(cards, chess)* re m
kiosk chiosco m
kiss, to baciare 126
kitchen paper carta f assorbente uso cucina
kitchenette zona cottura f
knee ginocchio m 166
knife coltello m 39, 41, 148
knight *(chess)* cavallo m
knocked down, to be essere buttato a terra
know: I don't know non so
kosher puro(-a)

L

label etichetta f
lace pizzo m
ladder scala f
ladies room *(toilet)* toeletta f signore
lake lago m 107
lamp lampada f 25
land, to atterrare
landing *(house)* pianerottolo m
landlord/landlady locatore m, la locatrice f
lane corsìa f
language course corso m di lingua
large grande 40, 110
last ultimo(-a) 14, 68, 75, 80
last, to *(time)* durare
late *(delayed)* in ritardo 70, 221; tardi 221
later più tardi 125, 147
laugh, to ridere 126
launderette lavanderia f a gettone 131
lavatory gabinetto m
lawn prato m coltivato
lawyer avvocato m
laxative lassativo m
lead, to *(road)* portare
lead-free *(gas/petrol)* benzina verde f 87
leader *(of group)* capogruppo m/f
leaflet opuscolo m
leak, to *(roof/pipe)* perdere; *(car)*
learn, to *(language/sport)* imparare
learner studente m, la studentessa f
least expensive il meno caro m, la meno cara f
leather pelle f
leave, to *(exit)* partire 32, 70, 73, 78, 86, 98; *(abandon)* lasciare 71, 73, 86; **leave me alone!** mi lasci in pace! 126
lecturer docente, insegnante m/f
left-hand side dal lato sinistro
left, on the a sinistra 76, 95
left-handed mancino(-a)
left-luggage office *(baggage check)* deposito m bagagli 71, 73
leg gamba f 166
legal matters *(car accident)* 93
legal, to be essere legale
lemon limone m 38
lemonade limonata f
lend: could you lend me ...? può imprestarmi ...?
length lunghezza f
lens obiettivo m 151; lenti fpl 167
lens cap cappuccio m per obiettivo 151
lesbian club club m per lesbiche
less (di) meno 15
lesson lezione f
letter lettera f 154; **by ~** per lettera 22
letterbox cassetta f per lettere
level *(ground)* livellato
library biblioteca f
license plate number numero di targa m 88, 93
lie down, to sdraiarsi
lifebelt cintura f di salvataggio
lifeboat scialuppa f di salvataggio
lifeguard bagnino m 116
lifejacket giubba f di salvataggio
lift pass tessera f per la sciovia 117
light *(color)* chiaro(-a) 14; *(weight)* leggero(-a) 134
light bulb lampadina f 148
lighter accendino m 150
lighthouse faro m
lightning fulmine m

like, to piacere; **I'd like ...** vorrei ...; **I don't like it** non mi piace
like this *(similar)* simile a questo(-a)
limousine berlina f
line *(subway [metro])* linea f 80; *(profession)* professione f, lavoro m
line: an outside line, please una linea esterna, per favore
linen lino m
lip(s) labbro m, labbra fpl 166
lipsalve balsamo m per le labbra
lipstick rossetto m
liqueur liquore m
liter/litre litro m 87, 159
little piccolo(-a)
live, to vivere 104; **~ together** abitare insieme 120
liver fegato m 166
loaf of bread pagnotta f di pane 160
lobby *(theater/hotel)* atrio m
local della regione, regionale
local anesthetic anestesia f locale 168
local road strada f comunale
lock *(key)* serratura f; *(canal)* chiusa f
lock oneself out, to chiudersi fuori 27
locked, to be essere chiuso(-a) 26; **it's locked** è chiuso a chiave
locker armadietto m
locker rooms spogliatoi mpl
lollipop leccalecca m
long *(clothing)* lungo(-a) 146
long *(time)* molto 36; **how long?** quanto tempo? 164; **how much longer?** per quanto tempo? 41
long-distance call telefonata f interurbana
look: I'm just looking sto solo guardando
look for, to cercare 18
loose *(clothing)* largo(-a) 146
lose, to perdere 28, 153; **I've lost ...** ho smarrito ...; ho perdito
lost, to be essere smarrito
lost-and-found/lost property office ufficio m oggetti smarriti 73
lotion lozione f
lots molti (e)
loud, it's too è troppo rumoroso(-a)
louder più forte 128
love: I love Italian food amo la cucina italiana; **I love you** ti amo
low-fat con grasso minimo
lower berth cuccetta inferiore f 74
lubricant lubrificante m
luck: good luck buona fortuna 219
luggage *(baggage)* bagaglio m 32, 67
luggage allowance peso m consentito
luggage locker deposito m bagagli automatico 73
luggage tag etichetta f per bagaglio
luggage ticket biglietto m per i bagagli 71
luggage carts *(trolleys)* carrelli mpl portabagagli
lumpy *(mattress)* pieno di protuberanze
lunch pranzo m 98
lung polmone m

machine washable lavaggio a macchina 145
madam signora
made: what is it made of? di che cosa è fatto(-a)?
magazine rivista f 150
magician mago m
magnetic north nord m magnetico
magnificent magnifico 101
maid cameriera f 27
maiden name nome m da nubile
mail, to imbucare
mail *(post)* posta f
mailbox cassetta f postale
main principale 130
main course secondo (piatto) m 37
main train station stazione f ferroviaria principale 73
main street via f principale 96
mains conduttura f principale
make *(brand)* marca f
makeup cosmetici mpl trucco m
male uomo, maschio m 152
mallet maglio m 31
man uomo m
manager direttore m, direttrice f 25; gestore m/f 41, 137
manicure manicure f
manual *(car)* manuale m
many molti (e) 15

map carta f 94, 106, 150
margarine margarina f
market mercato m 99; **~ day** giorno m di mercato
married, to be essere sposato(-a) 120
mascara mascara m
mask *(diving)* maschera f subacquea
mass messa f 105
massage massaggio m 147
match *(game)* partita f 114
matches fiammiferi mpl 31, 150
material *(fabric)* stoffa f
matinée spettacolo m del pomeriggio 109
matter: what's the matter? cosa succede?; **it doesn't matter** non importa
mattress materasso m 31
may I ...? posso ... ? 18, 37
maybe forse
me me 16
meal pasto m 38; 125
mean, to significare 11
measles morbillo m 165
measure, to misurare 146
measurement le misure fpl
meat carne f 41
medical certificate certificato m medico 168
medicine medicina f 164, 165
medium *(regular)* regolare 40; *(steak)* cottura media
meet, to incontrare 125; **pleased to meet you** piacere/molto lieto(-a) 118
meeting place luogo m d'incontro
member *(of club)* socio m 115
memorial monumento m commemorativo
men *(toilets)* gabinetti mpl, signori
mend, to riparare 137
mention: don't mention it prego 10
menu menu m
message messaggio m 128
metal metallo m
meter *(taxi)* tassametro m 84
methylated spirits alcol denaturato
microwave *(oven)* forno m a microonde
midday mezzogiorno
midnight mezzanotte
migraine emicrania f
mileage chilometraggio m
milk latte m 160; **with ~** con latte
milk of magnesia latte m di magnesia
million un milione 216
mince carne f tritata
mine mio(-a) 16
mineral water acqua f minerale
minibar minibar m
minibus minibus m
minimum *(n)* minimo m
minister ministro m
minor road strada f secondaria
minute minuto m 221
mirror specchio m
miss, to passare, mancare; **have I missed the bus to ...?** ho perso l'autobus per ...?
missing, to be mancare 137; scomparire 152
mistake errore m 32, 41, 42
misunderstanding: there's been a ~ c'è stato un malinteso
mittens guantoni mpl
mobile home camper m
modern art arte f moderna
moisturizing cream crema f idratante
monastery monastero m 99
money soldi mpl 139, 153
money order vaglia m postale
money-belt cintura f portasoldi
month mese m 218
monthly *(ticket)* mensile 79
monument monumento m 99
moped motorino m
more (di) più 15; **I'd like some more ...** vorrei ancora un po' di ... 39
morning, in the al mattino; di mattina 221
moslem *(adj)* mussulmano(-a)
mosquito zanzara f
mosquito bite puntura f di zanzara
mother madre f 120
motorbike motocicletta f 83
motorboat barca f a motore
motorcycle motocicletta f 83
motorcycle parts 82
motorway autostrada f 94
mountain montagna f 107
mountain pass passo m di montagna 107
mountaineering alpinismo m

mousetrap trappola f per topi
moustache baffi mpl
mouth bocca f 166
move, to cambiare 25; *(car)* spostare la macchina; *(house)* traslocare; **don't move him!** non lo muova! 92
Mr. signor m
Mrs. signora f
much molto 15
mugged, to be essere aggredito(-a)
mugging aggressione per rapina f
mugs boccali mpl
multiple trip *(ticket)* biglietto m multiplo 79
mumps gli orecchioni mpl
muscle muscolo m 166
museum museo m 99
music musica f
music box carillon m
musician musicista m/f
must: I must devo
mustard senape f 38
my mio 16
myself: I'll do it myself lo farò io

N

nail polish lo smalto m per unghie
nail scissors le forbicine f da unghie
name cognome m
name *(first name)* nome m 36, 93, 118; **what's your name?** come si chiama? 118
napkin tovagliolo m 39
narrow stretto(-a) 14
national health servizio m sanitario
nationality nazionalità f
natural history storia f naturale
nature reserve oasi f naturalistica 107
nature trail percorso m naturalistico 107
nausea nausea f
navy blue blu m marino
near vicino 12
nearsighted miope 167
nearest più vicino(-a) 88, 92, 130
neck collo m 166; *(clothes)* 144
necklace collana f 149
need: I need to ... ho bisogno di ... 18
needle ago m
negative *(photo)* negativa f
neighbor vicino(-a) m/f
nephew nipote m
nerve nervo m 166
nervous system sistema m nervoso
never mai 13
never mind non importa 10
new nuovo(-a) 14
New Year Anno m Nuovo 219
New Zealand Nuova Zelanda f
newsagent giornalaio m 150
newsdealer giornalaio m 150
newspaper giornale m 150
newsstand edicola f 73, 150
next prossimo(-a) 14, 68, 75, 80, 87; **next stop!** la prossima fermata! 79
next to accanto(-a) a 12; vicino(-a) a 95
niece nipote f
night, at di notte 221; **per night** per notte
night porter portiere m di notte
nightdress camicia f da notte
nobody else nessun altro
noisy rumoroso(-a) 14, 24
non-alcoholic non-alcolico(-a)
non-smoking area zona non fumatori f 36
none nessuno(-a) 16
noon mezzogiorno 220
no one nessuno(-a) 16
normal normale 67
north nord m 95
Northern Ireland Irlanda f del nord
nose naso m 166
nosebleed emoraggia nasale f
not yet non ancora 13
note banconota f
notebook taccuino m 150
nothing else nient'altro 15
nothing to declare nulla da dichiarare
notice board bacheca f 26
notify, to informare 167
now subito 84; ora, adesso 13
nudist beach spiaggia f per nudisti
number numero m 109; *(telephone)* numero (di telefono) m 84
number plate *(registration plate)* numero di targa m
nurse infermiere m
nut *(for bolt)* dado m per bullone
nylon nylon m

O

o'clock, it's ... è .../sono le ... 220
observatory osservatorio m
occasionally occasionalmente
occupations 121
occupied occupato(-a) 14
of di, da
of course naturalmente, certamente 19
off-peak bassa stagione f
office ufficio m
often sovente/spesso 13
oil olio m
oil lamp lampada f a olio
oily *(hair)* grasso(-a)
okay d'accordo./va bene 10
old vecchio(-a) 14
old town città f vecchia 99; città f storica 96
old-fashioned antiquato(-a) 14
olive oil olio m d'oliva
omelet frittata f 40
on *(day, date)* il 13
on *(place)* in
on the left a sinistra 12
on the other side all'altro lato 95
on the right a destra 12
on/off switch interruttore m
once una volta 217; **~ a week** una volta alla settimana
open aperto(-a) 14; **~ to the public** aperto(-a) al pubblico **~ to traffic** aperto(-a) al traffico
open, to aprire 132, 140
opening hours orario m d'apertura
opera house teatro m dell'opera 99, 111
operation operazione f
operator operatore m
opposite di fronte 12
optician ottico m 131, 167; negozio m di ottica
or o/oppure 19
orange arancione
oranges arance fpl
orchestra orchestra f
order, to ordinare 37, 41; *(taxi)* chiamare 32
our nostro 16
out: he's out è fuori
outdoor all'esterno; **~ pool** piscina f all'aperto 116
outside fuori 12, 36
outside lane corsia f di sorpasso
oval ovale 134
oven forno m
over sopra
over there laggiù 76
overcharged: I've been il prezzo è eccesivo
overdone *(adj)* troppo cotto(-a) 41
overdraft scoperto m
overdrawn, to be avere uno scoperto bancario
overheat, to surriscaldare
overnight una notte f
overnight service servizio m ventiquattro ore
owe: how much do I owe you? quanto le devo?
own: on my own da solo(-a) 65
owner proprietario

P

pacifier tettarella f
pack, to fare i bagagli 69
pack of cards mazzo m di carte
pack of cigarettes pacchetto m di sigarette
package pacco m
packed lunch pranzo m al sacco
pack [packet] pacco m, pacchetto m
padlock lucchetto m
pail secchiello m
pain, to be in avere male 167
painkillers antinevralgico m; analgesico m, antidolorifico m 165
paint, to dipingere
painted dipinto(-a)
painter pittore m, pittrice f 104
painting quadro m
pair of, a un paio di 217
pajamas pigiama m
palace palazzo m 99
palpitations palpitazioni fpl
panorama panorama m/vista f 107
pantomime pantomima f
pants pantaloni mpl
pantyhose collant m 144
paper carta f 150
paper napkins tovaglioli mpl di carta 148

paraffin paraffina f
paralysis paralisi f
parcel *(package)* pacco m 155
pardon? prego? 11
parents genitori mpl 120
park parco m, giardini mpl 96, 99, 107
park ranger guardia f forestale
park, to parcheggiare
parking parcheggio m 87
parking disk disco m orario
parking lot parcheggio m 26
parking meter parchimetro m 87
parliament building palazzo m del Parlamento 99
partner *(boyfriend/girlfriend)* compagno m, compagna f
parts *(components)* pezzi mpl di ricambio 89
party *(social)* festa f 124
pass passo m 107
pass, to passare 77
passenger passeggero m, passeggera f
passport passaporto m 66, 69, 153
passport control controllo m passaporti 66
pastry shop pasticceria f
patch, to rattoppare
path sentiero m 107
patient paziente m/f
pavement, on the sul marciapiede m
pay, to pagare 32, 42, 136; **~ a fine** pagare un'ammenda/una multa 93; **~ by credit card** pagare con carta di credito
pay phone telefono m a gettone/a scheda
payment pagamento m
peak picco m/cima f
pebbly *(beach)* pietroso(-a) 116
pedalo pedalo m
pedestrian crossing attraversamento m pedonale 96
pedestrian zone/precinct isola f/zona f pedonale 96
pedicure pedicure f
pen penna f 150
pencil matita f 150
penicillin penicillina f
penknife coltellino m
penpal il, corrispondente m/f
people gente f 119
people carrier *(minivan)* furgoncino m
pepper *(condiment)* pepe m 38; *(vegetable)* peperone m
per day al giorno 83, 86, 87; per giorno 30, 115
per hour all'ora 87; per ora 115
per night per notte 21
per week alla settimana 83, 86
performance spettacolo m
perhaps forse 19
period periodo m ; *(menstrual)* mestruazioni fpl 167
period pains dolori mpl mestruali 167
perm *(hair)* permanente f
perm, to fare la permanente 147
permit permesso m, licenza f
personal stereo stereo m personale
pet *(animal)* animale m domestico
pharmacy reparto m di farmacia 158
phone telefono m
phone call telefonata f 152
phonecard carta f telefonica 127
photo, to take a fare una fotografia
photo: passport-size photo fotografia f formato passaporto 115
photocopy fotocopia f
photographer fotografo m/negozio m di ottica
photography fotografia f 151
phrase frase f 11
phrase book frasario m 11
piano pianoforte m
pick up, to passare a prendere 28, 113; *(ticket)* ritirare
pick-up truck autocarro m
picnic picnic m, scampagnata f; **~ area** area f per pic nic 107
piece articolo di bagaglio m; pezzo m 159; **a ~ of ...** un pezzo di ...
Pill *(contraceptive)*, **to take the** prendere la pillola (contraccettiva) 167
pillow cuscino m 27
pillowcase federa f per cuscino
pilot light luce f-spia
pink rosa 143
pint pinta f
pipe *(smoking)* pipa f
pipe cleaners puliscipipa m

pipe tobacco tabacco m da pipa
piste map carta f delle piste
pitch *(for camping)* posto m tenda
pity: it's a pity è un peccato
place *(space)* posto m
place a bet, to scommettere
plain pianura f; *(not patterned)* in tinta unita
plane volo m 68
plans, to have fare 124
plant pianta f
plastic bags sacchetti mpl di plastica
plate piatto m 39,148
platform binario m 73, 76, 77
platinum platino m
play, to *(drama)* rappresentare *(music)* suonare
playground parco m giochi 113
playgroup club m per bambini 113
playing cards carte fpl da gioco
playing field campo m da gioco 96
pleasant gradevole 14
please per piacere./per favore 10
pliers le pinze fpl
plug *(bath)* presa f; *(electric)* spina f elettrica
plumber idraulico m
p.m. di pomeriggio, di sera
pneumonia polmonite f 165
point of interest luoghi mpl d'interesse
point to, to indicare 11
poison veleno m
poisonous velenoso(-a)
police polizia f, carabinieri (pl) 92, 152
police report denuncia f 153
police station commissariato m, questura f 96, 131, 152
pollen count conteggio m del polline 122
polyclinic policlinico m
pond stagno m
pony ride passeggiata f in pony
pop music musica f pop
popcorn popcorn m
port *(harbor)* porto m
porter portiere m; facchino m 71
portion porzione f 39, 41
possible: as soon as possible appena possibile
possibly possibilmente
post, to *(mail, to)* imbucare
post *(mail)* posta f
post office ufficio m postale 96, 131, 154
postbox *(mailbox)* cassetta f delle lettere
postcard cartolina f 150, 154, 156
poster manifesto m
postman postino m
potato patate f 38
pottery ceramica f
pound *(sterling)* lira f sterlina 138
power failure interruzione f della corrente
power point presa f di corrente
practice: to practice speaking Italian praticare l'italiano parlato
pregnant, to be esser incinta 163
prescribe, to prescrivere 165
prescription ricetta f 140, 141
present *(gift)* regalo m
press, to stirare 137
pretty carino(-a)
priest prete m
primus stove fornello m da campeggio
prison carcere m
private bathroom bagno f privato
probably probabilmente
program programma m 109; **~ of events** programma m delle manifestazioni 108
prohibited: is it prohibited? è proibito?
promenade deck ponte m di coperta
pronounce, to pronunciare 11
properly correttamente
Protestant protestante
pub osteria f
public building edifici pubblici mpl 96
public holidays giorni mpl festivi 219
pullover maglione m
pump *(gas/petrol)* pompa f
puncture *(flat)* foratura f 88
pure *(material)* puro(-a)
purple viola 143
purpose motivo m 66
purse portamonete m 153
push-chair passeggino m
put: where can I put ...? dove posso mettere ..?

put aside, to *(in shop)* mettere da parte
put up: can you put me up for the night? può ospitarmi per una notte?
putting course terreno m da golf

Q

quality qualità f 134
quantity quantità f 134
quarantine quarantina f
quarter, a un quarto 217
quarter past *(after)* e un quarto 220
quarter to *(before)* meno un quarto 220
quay molo m
queen *(cards, chess)* regina f
question domanda f
quick veloce 14
quickest: what's the quickest way to ... qual'è la via più breve per ...?
quickly presto! 17
quiet silenzioso(-a) 14
quieter più tranquillo(-a) 24, 126

R

rabbi rabbino m
race *(cars)* gara f automobilistica; *(horses)* corsa f di cavalli
racetrack ippodromo m
racing bike bicicletta f da corsa
racket *(tennis, squash)* racchetta f 115
rail station stazione f ferroviaria
railroad ferrovia f
rain, to piovere 122
raincoat impermeabile m 144
rape stupro m 152
rapids rapide fpl 107
rare *(unusual)* raro(-a); *(steak)* poco cotta
rarely raramente 13
rash eruzione f della pelle 162
rather piuttosto; **~ noisy** piuttosto rumoroso(-a)
ravine burrone m
razor rasoio m
razor blades lamette fpl da barba 142
re-enter, to rientrare
reading *(interest)* lettura f
reading glasses gli occhiali mpl per lettura
ready, to be essere pronto(-a) 89, 137, 151; **are you ready?** è pronto(-a)?
real *(genuine)* vero/autentico 149
real estate agent agente m/f immobiliare
receipt ricevuta f 32, 89, 136, 137, 151
reception *(desk)* ricezione f
receptionist ricezionista m/f 27
reclaim tag talloncino m 71
reclaim, to ottenere il rimborso m
recommend, to consigliare 35, 141; raccomandare 21; **can you recommend?** può suggerire? 97
record *(lp)* (disco) microsolco m
red rosso(-a) 143
red wine vino m rosso 40
reduction sconto m, riduzione f 24, 68, 74, 100
refreshments rinfreschi (pl)
refrigerator frigorifero m
refund rimborso m
regards to ... saluti a ... 219
region regione f 106
register receipt ricevuta f di cassa
registered mail posta f raccomandata
registration form modulo m di registrazione 23
registration number numero di targa m 88, 93
regular *(gas/petrol)* normale 87; *(size of drink)* medio(-a) 110
regulations: I didn't know the regulations non conoscevo il regolamento
religion religione f
remember: I don't remember non ricordo
removed, to be essere rimossa
rent, to noleggiare 115, 116, 117
rent: for rent affittasi
rental car auto f noleggiata 153
repair, to riparare 89, 137, 168
repairs riparazioni fpl 89, 137
repeat, to ripetere 94, 128; **please repeat that** per piacere può ripetere 11
replacement *(n)* sostituzione f
replacement part pezzo di ricambio m 137
report, to denunciare
representative rappresentante m/f 27
required necessario(-a) 111, 112
reservation prenotazione f 22, 68

reservation desk botteghino m 109
reserve, to prenotare 36, 109
rest, to riposare
retired, to be essere in pensione 121
return ticket biglietto di andata e ritorno m 68, 74; biglietto circolare m 79
return, to *(travel)* ritornare 75; *(surrender)* restituire
reverse the charges, to *(call collect, to)* telefonare a carico del destinatario 127
revolting disgustoso(-a) 14
rheumatism reumatismo m
rib costola f 166
right *(correct)* giusto(-a) 14
right, on the a destra 76, 95
right of way diritto m di passaggio; precedenza f 93
right-handed che usa la mano destra
ring anello m
rip-off bidonata f 101
river fiume m 107
road strada f 94, 95
road accident incidente m stradale
road assistance soccorso m stradale
road map carta f stradale 150
road signs segnaletica f, lindicazioni fpl stradali
roasted arrosto(-a)
robbed, to be essere derubato(-a) 153
robbery rapina f
rock climbing alpinismo m di roccia
rock concert concerto m rock
rocks rocce fpl
roller blades roller blades mpl
rolls panini mpl 160
romance *(film/play)* romanzo m
romantic romantico(-a) 101
roof *(house/car)* tetto m
roof-rack portabagagli m esterno
rook *(chess)* torre f
room camera f 21
room service servizio m camera 26
rope corda f
round *(shape)* rotondo(-a) 134; *(of golf)* giro m; **it's my ~** è il mio turno
roundabout rotatoria f
roundtrip ticket biglietto di andata e ritorno m 68, 74; biglietto circolare m 79
route strada f, percorso m 106
row, to remare
rowboat barca f a remi
rude, to be essere maleducato(-a)
rugby rugby m
ruins rovine fpl 99
run into, to *(crash)* venire addosso 93
run out, to *(fuel)* finire 88
run over, to *(people)* investire
rush hour ora f di punta

S

safe *(lock-up)* cassaforte f 27
safe *(not dangerous)* sicuro(-a) 116; **to feel ~** sentirsi sicuro(-a)
safety sicurezza f 65
safety pins spille fpl di sicurezza
sailboat barca f a vela
salad insalata f
sales rep agente m/f di vendita
salt sale m 38, 39
same day lo stesso giorno
same: the same again please stesso, per favore
sand sabbia f
sandals sandali mpl
sandwich panino m 40
sandwich bar paninoteca f
sandy sabbioso(-a) 116
sanitary napkins assorbenti mpl 142
satellite TV televisione f via satellite
satisfied: I'm not satisfied with this non sono soddisfatto(-a) di
sauce salsa f 38
saucepan pentola f
sausages salcicce fpl 160
saw *(tool)* sega f
say: how do you say ...? come si dice ..?; **what did he say?** cosa ha detto?
scarf sciarpa f 144
scenic route strada f panoramica
scheduled flight volo m di linea
school scuola f
sciatica sciatica f 165
scientist scienziato m, scienziata f
scissors un paio di forbici fpl 148
scooter motoretta f
Scotland Scozia f
Scottish *(person/adj.)* scozzese m/f
screw vite f
screwdriver cacciavite m 148
scrub brush spazzola f dura

sculptor scultore m, scultrice f
sea mare m 107
seafront passeggiata f a mare
seasick, I feel ho il mal di mare
season ticket tessera f
seasoning condimenti mpl 38
seat posto m 77
second secondo(-a) 217
second class di seconda classe 74
second floor *(US)* primo piano m
secondhand di seconda mano
secretary segretaria f
security guard guardia f di sicurezza
sedative sedativo m
see, to *(inspect, witness)* vedere 24, 93; **~ someone again** rivedere 126
self-catering in affitto
sell, to vendere
send, to mandare 88, 155; spedire
senior citizens anziani (pl) 74
separated, to be essere separato(-a)
separately *(adv)* separatamente
septic tank fognatura f
serious serio
served, to be *(meal)* essere servito; sevire
service servizio m 105, 142; **~ charge** servizio m; **is service included?** è compreso il servizio? 42
service station stazione f di servizio
serviette tovagliolo m
set menu menù m fisso
sex *(act)* sesso m
shade sfumatura f
shady ombreggiato
shallow basso(-a)
shampoo shampoo m
shampoo and set shampoo e messa in piega
shampoo for dry/oily hair shampoo m per capelli secchi/grassi
shape forma f 134
sharp tagliente
shatter, to *(glass)* rompere
shaver rasoio m elettrico
shaver socket presa f per rasoio
shaving brush spazzola f per barba
shaving cream crema f per barba
she lei
sheet *(bedding)* le lenzuola fpl 28
shelf scaffale m
ship nave f
shirt camicia f 144
shiver, to sentirsi i brividi
shock *(electric)* scossa f elettrica
shoelaces lacci mpl delle scarpe
shoepolish lucido m per scarpe
shoe repair riparatura f delle scarpe
shoe-cleaning service servizio m pulizia scarpe
shoemaker calzolaio m, calzoleria f
shoes scarpe fpl 145
shop *(store)* grande magazzino m 130
shop assistant commesso(-a) m/f
shop/storekeeper negoziante m/f
shopping area zona f dei negozi, centro m commerciale
shopping basket *(bag)* cesto f della spesa; cestello m
shopping mall [centre] centro m commerciale 130
shopping list lista f della spesa
shopping cart [trolley] carrello m
shopping, to go *(food)* andare a fare la spesa; *(other items)* andare a fare acquisti
shore *(sea/lake)* riva f del mare/lago
short corto(-a) 146
shorts shorts mpl 144
shoulder spalla f 166
show spettacolo m
show, to indicare, mostrare 18, 133; **can you show me?** può indicarmi? 94, 106
shower gel gel m per doccia
shower room sala f docce (pl)
showers docce f 30
shutter persiana f
shy timido(-a)
sick, to feel sentirsi male; **I'm going to be ~** sto per vomitare
side *(of road)* lato m 95
side order contorno m 37, 38
side street strada f laterale 95
sidewalk sul marciapiede m
sights luoghi mpl d'interesse
sightseeing tour giro m turistico 97
sightseeing, to go visitare luoghi d'interesse

sign *(road)* segnali (pl), indicazioni stradali fpl 93, 95
signpost indicatore m stradale
silk seta f
silver argento m 149
silverplate placcato d'argento
similar, to be essere simile a
since *(time)* da
singer cantante m/f
single, to be essere celibe 120
single *(one-way)* **ticket** biglietto di andata m 68, 74; biglietto di corsa semplice m 79
single room camera f singola
sink lavandino m
sister sorella f 120
sit, to sedersi 36, 77; sedere 126
sit down, please si accomodi, prego
six-pack of beer confezione f di sei lattine di birra
size misura f, taglia f 146
skates pattini mpl da ghiaccio
skating rink palazzo m del ghiaccio
ski bindings gli attacchi mpl per sci
ski boots scarponi mpl da sci 117
ski instructor istruttore m di sci
ski lift sciovia f
ski pants pantaloni mpl da sci
ski poles bastoncini mpl da sci 117
ski school scuola f di sci 117
ski suit tuta f per sci
ski wax cera f per sci
skid: we skidded abbiamo slittato
skiing sci m
skin pelle f, epidermide f 166
skin-diving equipment attrezzatura f per l'immersione subacquea
skirt gonna f 144
skis sci mpl 117
sledge slitta f
sledge run pista f per slitte
sleep, to dormire 167
sleeping bag sacco m a pelo
sleeping car vagone m letto 77
sleeping pill sonnifero m in pillola
sleeve manica f
slice fetta f 159
slide film le diapositive fpl
slip *(undergarment)* sottoveste f
slippers pantofole fpl 145
slope *(ski)* discesa f
slow lento(-a) 14
slow down! rallenti!
slow, to be *(clock)* ritardare 221
slowly lentamente 11, 17, 94, 128
small piccolo(-a) 14, 24, 40, 110, 117; basso(-a)
small change moneta f; spiccioli mpl
small spoon cucchiaino m
smell: there's a bad smell c'è un cattivo odore
smoke, to fumare
smoke: I don't smoke non fumo
smoking area zona fumatori f
snacks spuntini mpl
sneakers scarpe fpl da tennis
snorkel maschera f da subacqueo
snow neve f
snow, to nevicare 122
snowed in, to be essere bloccato dalla neve
snowplow spazzaneve m
soaking solution *(contact lenses)* soluzione f per pulire lenti a contatto
soap sapone m 142
soap powder detersivo m in polvere
socket presa f
socks calzini mpl 144
sofa divano m
sofa-bed divano-letto m
soft drink *(soda)* bibita f frizzante 110; bibita f analcolica 160
sold out esaurito(-a)
sole *(shoes)* suola f
soluble aspirin aspirina f solubile 141
some alcuni, del/dei/dell'/della/delle
someone qualcuno 16
sometimes qualche volta 13
son figlio m 120, 162
soon presto 13; **as ~ as possible** al più presto 161
sore throat mal m di gola 163
sore: it's sore fa male
sorry! sono spiacente 10
sort tipo m 134
sound-and-light show spettacolo m suoni e luci
sour acido(-a) 41

south sud m 95
souvenir regalo m ricordo, souvenir m 98, 156; **~ guide** guida f ricordo 156
spa stazione f termale
space spazio m 30
spade *(shovel)* paletta f *(cards)* carta *f* di picche
speak, to parlare 11, 41, 67; **~ to someone** parlare con qualcuno 128; **do you speak English?** parla inglese? 11
special rate condizioni fpl speciali; tariffa speciale f 86
special requirements le richieste f particolari 39
specialist specialista m/f
specimen campione m 164
spectacles occhiali mpl
speed limit limite di velocità m
spell, to sillabare 11
spend, to spendere
spicy speziato(-a)
spin-dryer asciugatore m elettrico
spine spina f dorsale 166
sponge spugna f
spoon cucchiaio m 39, 41
sports club palestra f/associazione f sportiva
sports ground campo m sportivo
sprained, to be essere slogato(-a)
sprained muscle strappo m al muscolo
spring *(season)* primavera f 219; *(water)* fonte f
square *(shape)* quadrato(-a) 134; *(street)* piazza f
stain macchia f
stainless steel acciaio m inossidabile
stairs scale f
stale non fresco(-a)
stall: the engine stalls il motore s'inceppa
stalls *(orchestra)* platea f
stamp francobollo m 150, 154; **~ machine** distributore m automatico di francobolli 154
stand in line, to aspettare, fare la coda 112
standby ticket biglietto m non prenotato
start inizio m 109
start, to cominciare 112 **starter** antipasto m 37
stately home palazzina f
statement *(legal)* dichiarazione f, denuncia f 93
station stazione f 96
stay, to fermarsi, rimanere 23, 65
sterilizing solution soluzione f sterilizzante
stiff neck collo m rigido
still: I'm still waiting sto ancora aspettando
sting puntura f 162
stocking calze fpl 144
stolen, to be essere rubato(-a) 71
stomach stomaco m 166; **~ ache** dolore m allo stomco 163; **~ cramps** crampi mpl allo stomaco
stool *(feces)* feci fpl 164
stop *(bus, tram, metro)* fermata f 79, 80
stop, to femarsi 76, 77, 98; **please stop here** si fermi qui, per favore
stopover sosta f
store detective personale m di sicurezza
store guide guida f al magazzino 132
stove stufa 28
straight ahead (sempre) dritto 95
strange strano(-a) 101
straw *(drinking)* cannuccia f
strawberry *(flavor)* fragola f 40
stream ruscello m, torrente m 107
string cordino m
stroller passeggino m
strong *(potent)* forte
stuck: the key's stuck chiave è bloccata
students studenti pl 74, 100
study, to studiare 121
stunning magnifico(-a)
stupid: how stupid! che stupidaggine!
style stile m
styling mousse schiuma f per messa in piega
subtitled, to be avere i sottotitoli 110
subway metropolitana 80
subway station stazione f (della) metropolitana 80, 96
suede pelle f scamosciata
sugar zucchero m 38, 39, 160
suggest, to suggerire 123

suit completo m 144
suitable for adatto(-a) per
summer estate f 219
sun block blocco m antisolaro
sun lounger sedia f a sdraio
sunbathe, to prendere il sole
sunburn scottatura f solare
suncare prodotti solari
Sunday domenica 218
sundeck *(ship)* ponte m superiore
sunglasses occhiali mpl da sole
sunshade *(umbrella)* ombrellone m 116
suntan lotion crema f/lozione f abbronzante 142
sunstroke colpo di sole m 163
super *(gas/petrol)* super 87
superb stupendo(-a) 101
supermarket supermercato m 158
supervision sorveglianza f
supplement supplemento m 68, 69
suppositories supposte fpl 165
sure: are you sure? è sicuro(-a)?
surfboard tavola f da surf 116
surname cognome m
suspicious sospettoso(-a)
swallow, to inghiottire
sweatshirt felpa f 144
sweet *(taste)* dolce
sweets *(dessert)* dolci mpl 150; *(candy)* caramelle f
swelling gonfiore m 162
swim, to nuotare 116
swimming *(activity)* nuoto
swimming pool piscina f 22, 26, 116
swimming trunks calzoncini mpl da bagno 144
swimsuit costume m da bagno 144
Swiss *(person)* svizzero(-a) m/f
switch interruttore m
switch on/off, to accendere/spegnere
Switzerland Svizzera f
swollen, to be essere gonfio
symptoms sintomi 163
synagogue sinagoga f
synthetic in fibra sintetica

T-shirt maglietta f 144, 156
table tavolo m 36
tablecloth tovaglia f da tavola
table tennis tennis m da tavolo
tablet pastiglia f 140
take away, to da asporto
take photographs/pictures, to prendere fotografie 98; fare fotografie 100
take someone home, to riaccompagnare
take, to *(room, bus, medicine)* prendere 140 *(carry)* portare 71, 165;
taken *(occupied)* occupato(-a)
talcum powder borotalco m
talk, to parlare
tall alto(-a) 14
tampons tamponi mpl
tan abbronzatura f
tap *(faucet)* rubinetto m 25
tape measure metro m a nastro
tarpaulin telo m per il terreno
taste gusto m
taxi tassì m 70, 71, 84
taxi driver autista m/f di tassì
taxi stand posteggio m tassì 96
tea tè m 40
tea bags bustine fpl di tè
teacher insegnante m/f
team squadra f
teaspoon cucchiaino m 140
teat *(for baby)* tettarella f
teddy bear orsacchiotto m
teenager adolescente m/f
telephone telefono m 22, 70, 92, 127
telephone bill *(in hotel)* conto m del telefono 32
telephone booth cabina f telefonica, telefono m pubblico 127
telephone directory elenco m telefonico
telephone kiosk cabina f telefonica
telephone number numero m di telefono 127
telephone token gettone m telefonico
telephone, to telefonare 128
television televisione f
telex telex m
tell, to dire 18, 79; **tell me** dirmi
temperature temperatura f 164
temporary provvisorio(-a) 89
tendon tendine m
tennis ball palla f da tennis
tennis court campo m da tennis

tent tenda f 30, 31
tent pegs picchetti mpl 31
tent pole palo m della tenda 31
terrible terribile 101
tetanus tetano m
thank you grazie 10, 94
that quello(-a)
that one quello(-a) 16, 134
that's all è tutto 133
thawing snow neve f fondente
theater [theatre] teatro m 96, 99, 110
theft furto m 153
their loro 16
theirs loro m/f 16
them loro 16
theme park parco m a tema
then *(time)* poi 13
there là 12
there is ... c'è 17
thermometer termometro m
thermos bottle [flask] termos m
these questi 134
they loro
thick spesso(-a) 14
thief ladro m
thigh coscia f 166
thin sottile 14
think, to credere 77; **I think** penso 42
think about it, to pensarci 135
third terzo(-a) 217; **a ~** un terzo 217
thirsty assetato(-a)
this one questo(-a) 16, 134
those quelli 134
thread filo m
throat gola f 166
throat lozenges pastiglie fpl per la gola
thrombosis trombosi f
through per, attraverso
thumb pollice m 166
ticket biglietto m 68, 69, 74, 75, 77, 79, 80, 114, 153
ticket agency/office biglietteria f 73
tie cravatta f 144
tie pin spillo m per cravatta
tight *(clothing)* stretto(-a) 117, 146
tights collant m 144
till receipt ricevuta f di cassa
time *(of day)* ora f 76, 220; **on ~** in orario 76; **free ~** tempo m libero 98; **at what ~?** a che ora?
timetable orario m 75
tin (can) lattina f; **~ opener** apriscatole m 148
tin foil carta f stagnola
tint, to fare il colore 147
tinted *(glass/lens)* colorati (e)
tip mancia f 32
tipping dare la mancia 42
tire pneumatico m 83, 88
tired, to be essere stanco(-a)
tissues fazzoletti mpl di carta 142
to *(place)* a 12
toaster tostapane m
tobogganing andare in toboga
today oggi 68, 124, 218
toe dito m del piede 166
toilet gabinetto m 26, 87
toilet paper carta f igienica 25, 142
toilets toelette fpl/gabinetti mpl 26, 98
tomorrow domani 84, 124, 218
tongue lingua f
tonic water acqua f brillante
tonight questa sera 110, 124; **for ~** per questa sera 108
tonsillitis tonsillite f 165
tonsils tonsille fpl 166
too *(also)* anche; *(extreme)* troppo 17, 93
too much troppo 15
tooth dente m 168
toothache mal m di denti
toothbrush spazzolino m da denti
toothpaste dentifricio m 142
top cima f
top floor ultimo piano m
torch torcia f 31
totally totalmente 17
tough *(food)* duro(-a) 41
tour giro m, gita f 97
tour guide guida m/f turistica
tour operator agente m di viaggio 26
tour representative rappresentante m/f dell'agenzia viaggi 27
tourist turista m/f
tourist office Ufficio Turismo m/Ente Turismo m 97
tow, to trainare
tow rope fune f da traino
towards verso 12

towel asciugamano m
towelling tela f per asciugamani
tower torre f 99
town città f 70, 94
town hall Municipio m 99
town plans
toy giocattolo m 157
track sentiero m
tracksuit tuta f da ginnastica
traditional tradizionale
traffic traffico m
traffic jam ingorgo stradale m
traffic light semaforo m
traffic offense/violation infrazione f stradale
tragedy tragedia f
trail sentiero m
trailer roulotte f 30
trailer park parco m roulotte
train treno m 75, 77, 80
train times orario m ferroviario 75
training shoes scarpe fpl da ginnastica
tram tram m
transfer *(transport)* trasferta f
transfer, to trasferire
transit, in durante il viaggio
translate, to tradurre 11
translation traduzione f
translator traduttore m, la traduttrice f
trash rifiuti mpl
trash bags sacchetti mpl per i rifiuti 148
trash cans cassetoni m per i rifiuti
travel agency agenzia f di viaggio 131
travel sickness *(car/air/sea)* mal d'auto/d'aria/di mare 141
travel, to viaggiare, partire 74
traveler's checks assegni turistici mpl 136, 138
tray vassoio m
tree albero m 106
tremendous straordinario(-a)
trim *(hair)* spuntatina f 147
trip gita f 97
trolley carrello m 158
trouble: I'm having trouble with ... ho difficoltà con ...
trouser press stirapantaloni m
trousers pantaloni mpl 144
truck camion m
true: that's not true non è vero
try on, to provare 146
tube tubo m
tumor tumore m 165
tunnel sotterraneo m
turn, to girare
turn down (volume, heat), to abbassare (il volume, il riscaldamento)
turn off, to spegnere 25
turn on, to accendere 25
turn up, to *(volume, heat)* alzare
turn(ing) svolta f 95
TV room sala f televisione
tweezers le pinzette fpl
twice due volte 217
twin bed due letti mpl 21
two-door car auto a due porte f 86
type: what type? che tipo? 112
typical tipico(-a) 37
tyre pneumatico m 83, 88

U

ugly brutto(-a) 101
UK Regno m Unito
ulcer ulcera f
umbrella ombrello m
uncle zio m 120
unconscious, to be perdere conoscenza 92, 162
under *(place)* sotto
underdone *(adj)* non abbastanza cotto(-a) 41
underpants mutande fpl 144
underpass sottopassaggio m 96
understand, to capire 11; **do you understand?** capisce? 11; **I don't understand** non capisco 11, 67
undress, to spogliarsi 164
uneven *(ground)* in dislivello
unfortunately sfortunatamente 19
uniform uniforme m/f
United States gli Stati Uniti mpl
university università f
unleaded gasoline benzina f senza piombo
unlimited mileage chilometraggio m illimitato
unlock, to aprire a chiave, sbloccare
unpleasant sgradevole 14
unscrew, to svitare

until fino a 221
up to fino a
upmarket elegante m/f
upper berth cuccetta superiore f 74
upset stomach mal m di stomaco 141
upstairs al piano superiore
urgent urgente 161
us: for/with ~ per/con noi
U.S. Stati fpl Uniti 119
use, to usare 139
use: for my personal use per mio uso personale 67
useful utile m/f
utensils stoviglie fpl 148

V

vacancy camere libere 21
vacant libero(-a) 14
vacate, to lasciare lbero(-a) 32
vacation vacanza f
vaccinated against, to be essere vaccinato(-a) contro
vaccination vaccinazione f
vaginal infection infezione f vaginale 167
valet service servizio m di pulizia
valid valido 75
validate, to *(ticket)* convalidare 79
valley valle *f* 107
valuable prezioso(-a)
value valore m 155
vanilla *(flavor)* vaniglia f
VAT *(sales tax)* I.V.A. (Imposta Valore Aggiunto) f 24
VAT receipt Ricevuta f Fiscale
vegan, to be seguire una dieta macrobiotica
vegan: suitable for vegans adatto(-a) per chi non consuma prodotti derivati da animali
vegetables i legumi m/le verdure f 38
vegetarian vegetariano(-a)
vegetarian *(n)* vegetariano m la vegetariana f
vehicle veicolo m
vehicle registration (document) documenti del veicolo
vein vena f 166
velvet velluto m
vending machine distributore m automatico
venereal disease malattia f venerea 165
ventilator ventilatore m
very molto 17
vet veterinario m
video arcade sala f giochi
video game videogioco m
video recorder videoregistratore m
view: with a view of the sea con vista sul mare
viewing point punto m panoramico 107
village paese m 107
vineyard vigne fpl 107
visa visto m
visit visita f 119
visit, to visitare 123
visiting hours ore fpl di visita 167
vitamin pills vitamine fpl
voice voce f
volleyball pallavolo 114
voltage voltaggio m
vomit, to vomitare

W

wading pool piscina per bambini
waist vita f **~ pouch** borsello m a cintura
wait attesa f
wait for, to aspettare 41, 76, 89, 126, 140; **wait!** aspetti! 98
waiter/waitress cameriere(-a) m/f 37
waiting room sala f d'aspetto 73
wake, to *(self)* svegliarsi
wake someone, to svegliare qualcuno 27
wake-up call chiamata f sveglia
Wales Galles m
walk: to go for a walk andare a fare una passeggiata
walk home, to rientrare a piedi
walking passeggiare, camminare
walking boots scarponi mpl 145
walking distance, within raggiungibile a piedi
walking route percorso m a piedi
walking gear abbigliamento m escursionismo 145
wall muro m
wallet portafoglio m 42, 153
want, to volere 18
ward *(hospital)* reparto m, corsia f 167

warm *(weather)* caldo(-a)
warm, to riscaldare
warmer più caldo(-a)
wash basin lavello m
wash, to lavare
washbasin lavabo m
washing, to do fare il bucato
washing instructions istruzioni di lavaggio
wasp vespa f
watch orologio m da polso 153
watch band cinturino m dell'orologio
watch battery pila f per orologi
watch maker orologeria f
watch TV, to guardare la televisione
water acqua f
water carrier bidone m dell'acqua
water heater boiler m 28
waterfall cascata f 107
waterproof impermeabile m/f
waterskiing sci m d'acqua
waterskis sci mpl d'acqua 116
wave onda f
way *(direction)* strada f 94; **I've lost my ~** mi sono smarrito 94; **it's in the ~** blocca il passaggio; **on the ~ to** sulla strada di 83
we noi
weak coffee caffè m lungo
weak: I feel weak mi sento debole
wear, to indossare
weather tempo m 122
weather forecast previsioni fpl del tempo 122
wedding matrimonio m
wedding ring fede f nuziale
week settimana f 23, 97, 218
weekend fine f settimana; **on [at] the ~** al fine settimana 218
weekend rate tariffa f per fine settimana
weekly *(ticket)* settimanale 79
weight: my weight is ... peso ...
welcome to ... benvenuto(-a) a
well-done *(steak)* ben cotta
Welsh *(person/adj)* gallese m/f
west ovest m 95
wetsuit tuta f per immersione
what? cosa? 18
what kind of ...? che tipo di ... ? 37, 106
what time ...? a che ora ...? 68, 76
what's the time? che ora è? 220
wheelchair carrozzella f
when? quando? 13
where? dove? 12; **~ is ...?** dov'è ...? 99
where are you from? da dove viene?
where else? in quale altro negozio
which? quale? 16; **~ stop?** quale fermata? 80
while mentre
whist *(cards)* gioco m del whist
white bianco 143
who? chi? 16
whole: the whole day tutto il giorno
whose di chi 16
why? perchè? 16
wide largo(-a) 14
wife moglie f 120, 162
wildlife fauna f
windbreaker giace f a vento
window finestra f 25; finestrino m 77; *(shop)* vetrina f
window seat posto m accanto al finestrino 69, 74
windshield [windscreen] parabrezza m 88
windy, to be essere ventoso(-a) 122
wine vino m 40; **~ bottle** bottiglia f di vino
winery vigne fpl 107
wine list lista f dei vini 37
winter inverno m 219
wishes: best wishes to ... migliori auguri mpl a ...
with con 17
withdraw, to fare un prelievo
without senza 17
witness testimone m/f 93
wood *(forest)* bosco m 107; *(material)* legno m
wool lana f 146
work, to lavorare 121; *(operate)* funzionare 28, 83, 89; **it doesn't work** non funziona 25
worry: I'm worried sono preoccupato(-a)
worse peggiore; **it's gotten [got] ~** è peggiorato(-a)
worst *(adv./adj.)* peggio, peggiore m/f
worth: is it worth seeing? vale la pena vederlo?

wound ferita f
wrap up, to impacchettare
write-off *(car)* inservibile
write: write soon! scriva presto!
writing pad carta f da lettere
wrong sbagliato(-a) 136; *(not right)* non funziona 88; **~ number** numero m sbagliato 128; **there's something ~ with ...** c'è qualcosa che non va con ...; **what's ~?** che guasto ha?

x-ray radiografia f 164
yacht yacht m
year anno m 218
yellow giallo 143
yes sì 10
yesterday ieri 218
yield *(give way)* dare la precedenza
yogurt yogurt m
you *(sing/plur/formal)* tu/voi/Lei
young giovane 14
your(s) *(formal)* Suo(-a), *(familiar)* tuo(-a) 16
youth hostel ostello m della gioventù 29
zero zero
zip(per) cerniera f
zone zona f
zoo zoo m 113
zoology zoologia f

A-Z Dictionary
Italian – English

This Italian-English Dictionary covers all the areas where you may need to decode written Italian: hotels, public buildings, restaurants, shops, ticket offices and transportation. It will also help with understanding forms, maps, product labels, road signs and operating instuctions (for telephones, parking meters etc.). If you can't locate the exact sign, you may find key words or terms listed separately.

A

a passo d'uomo dead slow
a proprio rischio at the owner's risk
a scelta at your choice …
a stomaco vuoto on an empty stomach
abbazia abbey
abbigliamento per bambini children's wear
abbigliamento per signora ladies wear
abbigliamento per uomo menswear
abbigliamento sportivo sportswear
abiti per uomo menswear
accendere i fari/luci switch on headlights
accettazione admissions
acciaio steel
accostarsi a sinistra/destra keep to the left/right
aceto vinegar
acqua non potabile do not drink water
acqua potabile drinking water
aereo plane
affitasi camere rooms to rent
affitasi appartamento apartment to let
agenzia di assicurazioni insurance agency
agenzia di viaggi travel agency
agenzia immobiliare real estate agency
aggiornato updated
agitare prima dell'uso shake well before use
ai binari to the platforms
al coperto indoor
albergo hotel
alianti gliding
alimentari grocer's
alimenti surgelati frozen foods
aliscafo hydrofoil
all'aperto outdoor/open-air
allacciare le cinture fasten your seatbelt
alle cabine cabin decks
alotto lounge
alpinismo mountaineering, abseiling
alpinismo da roccia rock climbing
alt stop
alta tensione high voltage
altezza height
altezza massima … metri headroom
altitudine altitude
alzare il ricevitore lift receiver
ambasciata embassy
ambulatorio oculistico eye infirmary
ancora meglio improved
andata one-way/single
andata e ritorno round trip
andata semplice one-way
anti-urto shock-proof
antiquario antiques store/shop
aperto open
aperto tutti i giorni anche la domenica open every day including Sundays
aprire qui open here
area di ristoro rest area
area di servizio service area
argenteria silver shop
argento silver
aria condizionata air conditioning
aromi (naturali) (natural) flavoring
arredi per arredamento furnishings
arrivi arrivals

articoli di bellezza e profumeria makeup and perfume
articoli per cucina kitchen equipment
articoli per il bagno bathroom accessories
articoli per la camera di letto bedroom accessories
ascensore elevator
aspettare il proprio turno please wait your turn
aspettare il tono wait for tone
attendere prego please wait
attenti ai ladri beware of pickpockets
attenti al cane beware of the dog
attenzione ghiaia loose gravel
attenzione non scendere il gradino prima dell'apertura della porta do not descend steps before doors open *(on buses)*
attenzione, prego please be careful
attenzione, questa macchina non da resto this machine does not give change
attenzione, ... avviso/avvertimento warning
attesa di ... minuti circa wait approx ... minutes
attrezzatura per pesca subacquea underwater fishing equipment
attrezzatura per scuba scuba diving equipment
autonoleggio car rental
autostrada expressway
autunno fall/autumn
avanti cross now

B

bagno restroom/toilets
bagno schiuma foambath
baia bay
balconata balcony, dress circle
balcone balcony
ballo dance
bambini children
bambini solo se accompagnati no unaccompanied children
banca bank
banco di pesce fishstall *(at market)*
bancomat cash dispenser
barca a remi rowboat
barca a vela sailboat, yacht
batelli di salvataggio lifeboats
batello a vapore steamer
belvedere view point
benvenuti! welcome
benzina gas
bevande analcoliche soft drinks
bevande extra drinks not included
bevande incluse drinks included
bibite fresche e snacks refreshments available
biblioteca library
biglietteria ticket office
biglietti tickets
biglietti per oggi tickets for today
biglietto di andata e ritorno return ticket
biglietto ordinario day ticket
biglietto settimanale weekly ticket
binario platform
biodegradabile disposable
birra beer
borse handbags
bracciole waterwings
bretella expressway junction
burrone profondo canyon

C

cabina bathing cabana/hut
cabina di ponte deck cabin
caduta massi falling rocks
caduta slavine avalanche danger
calcio soccer
calle street *(in Venice)*
calzolaio shoe repairs/cobbler's
cambiare a change at
cambiare per change *(to other metro lines)*
cambio exchange rate
cambio valute bureau de change
Camera dei Deputati parliament building
camere libere vacancies/accommodations available
camerini fitting rooms
camion truck
campeggio campsite
campi di tennis tennis courts
campo field
campo di battaglia battle site
campo giochi/sportivo sports ground

cancellato cancelled
cancello gate
canna da pesca fishing rod
canoa canoe
canottaggio canoeing, rowing
cantante singer
cantante lirica opera singer
canto Gregoriano Gregorian chant
capella chapel
Capodanno New Year's Day
capolinea terminal
capsule capsules
carne meat
carozza coach
carozza non fumatori (non)smokers compartment
carozza/vagone ristorante dining-car
carrelli carts/trolleys
carta d'imbarco embarkation card
carta riciclata recycled paper
cartelle cliniche medical records
cartoleria stationer's
casa house
casa di cura privata health clinic
casa patrizia stately home
cascata waterfall
casco crash helmet
cassa cashier, checkout
cassa di risparmio savings bank
cassa rapida express checkout
cassette luggage lockers; cassettes
cassieri cashiers
castello castle
catena di montagne mountain range
cavalcavia road bridge
centralino/centralinista operator
centrifuga dry spin
centro città downtown area
centro commerciale shopping area
centro congressi convention hall
centro direzionale business district
centro sportivo sports center
ceriali cereals
check-in check-in counter
chiamare ... per il ricevimento dial ... for reception
chiamare ... per una linea esterna dial ... for an outside line
chiesa church
chilometro kilometer
chirurgia surgery
chiudere il cancello keep gate shut
chiudere la porta please shut the door
chiuso (per restauro) closed (for restoration)
chiuso al traffico closed to traffic
chiuso fino a ... closed until ...
chiuso per ferie closed for holiday
chiuso per pranzo closed for lunch
chiuso per rinnovo locali closed for repairs
chiusura festiva closed for holidays
chiusura settimanale closed/day off
ciambella rubber ring
ciclismo cycling
ciniglia chenille
cinte belts
cintura di salvataggio lifebelt
cioccolateria confectioner's
circo circus
circonvallazione ring road
città city
città universitaria university
città vecchia old town
cittadini extracommunitari non-EU citizens
cognome surname
collina/colle hill
colonna sonora soundtrack
colori resistenti colorfast
comando polizia/comando Carabinieri police station
comincia alle ore ... begins at ...
commissioni bank charges
completo full
compreso inclusive
compreso nel prezzo included in the price
compresse tablets
compri due paghi uno buy 2 get 1 free
compriamo a ... currency bought at ...
compro e vendo ... we buy and sell ...
comunicazioni interurbane/internazionali/intercontinentali (con operatore) long distance calls (with operator): intercity/international/intercontinental
con bagno with private bathroom

con sottotitoli subtitled
con vista sul mare with sea view
concerto concert
conservanti preservatives
consiglio per la consumazione serving suggestion
consultare il proprio medico prima dell'uso consult your doctor before use
consumare entro il ... best before ...
contatore della luce electric meter
contenitore per batterie vetro/aluminio/latta/plastica container for battery/bottle/aluminum/tin/plastic/paper recycling
conto account
conto corrente current account
contorni vari choice of vegetables
contro la forfora against dandruff
controcoperta upper deck
controllo please show your bags before leaving *(in shop)*; check/control
controllo valuta currency control
convalidare il biglietto (prima della prossima fermata/prima di salire sul treno) validate your ticket (before next bus stop/before getting on train)
coperto cloudy
corsia d'emergenza emergency lane
corsa di levrieri greyhound racing
corsi di cavallo horseracing
corsia lane
corsia ciclabile cycle track
corsia di sorpasso passing lane
corsia preferenziale do not walk
corso semplice one-way
costa coast
costiera cliff
costo per chilo (Kg)/etto/litro/metro price per kilo/330 grams/liter/meter
cotone cotton
crema per le mani hand cream
crociere cruises
cucina cookery
cuffie obbligatorie bathing caps must be worn
cuoio leather
cura intensiva intensive care
curva pericolosa dangerous bend
curve per ... Km bends for ... kilometers

D

da consumarsi entro il ... best before ...
da non prendere per via orale not to be taken orally
da ... a .../dalle ore... alle ore ... from ... to ...
danza dance
danza classica ballet
danza folcloristica folk dancing
dare la precedenza yield/give way
darsena docks
data di nascita date of birth
degustazione vini winetasting
della casa homemade
della stagione in season
deltaplano hang gliding
depositi deposits
deposito ambulanze ambulance station
deposito bagagli left-luggage office
deviazione alternative route, detour/diversion
deviazione per camions/TIR truck route/alternative lorry
di giornata fresh daily
diagnosi e cura treatment room
diapositive slides
diga dam
diocesi diocese
diretto direct
direttore manager
disco orario parking disk
dissolvere in acqua dissolve in water
divieto d'attracco no anchorage
divieto di balneazione no swimming/bathing
divieto di campeggio no camping
divieto di ingresso esclusi i mezzi degli handicappati access for disabled person vehicles only
divieto di ingresso escluso veicoli autorizzati authorized vehicles only
divieto di scarico no dumping
divieto di sorpasso no passing
divieto di sosta no stopping
docce showers
dogana customs control

domani tomorrow
domenica Sunday
Domenica delle Palme Palm Sunday
domicilio home address
donne women only, women (toilets)
dopo i pasti after meals
dopobarba aftershave
doposole aftersun
doppiato dubbed
doppio senso two-way traffic
durante i pasti with meals

E

edicola newsagent's
edificio pubblico public building
elenco telefonico telephone directory
elicottero helicopter
emergenza emergency
emergenza sanitaria medical (health) emergency
entrata entrance
Epifania Epiphany (January 6)
equitazione horseback riding
esaurito sold out
esibire documenti/carta d'identità/passaporto proof of identity required
esibire la ricevuta sul paravento place ticket on windshield
espresso made to order
estate summer
estero foreign
estintore fire extinguisher
estuario estuary
etto 330 grams
extra extra charge/supplement

F

fabbrica factory
fantascienza science fiction
farina wheat flour
farina integrale fermenti lattici vivi whole wheat flour
farmacia drugstore
faro marina lighthouse
fatto su misura made to measure
fattore 8 factor 8 (sunlotion)
fattoria farm
febbraio February
fermata bus stop
fermata a richiesta request stop
fermata del tram tram stop
fermata service stopping
Ferragosto Assumption Day (August 15)
ferro iron
ferrovia railroad
Festa del Lavoro Labor Day (May 1)
Festa dell'Assunzione Assumption Day (August 15)
Festa dell'Immacolata Concezione (8 dicembre) Immaculate Conception (December 8)
Festa della liberazione (25 aprile) Liberation Day (April 25)
festa nazionale national holiday
fibre alimentari fibre *(food)*
fiera fair
fila row
film d'orrore horror film
film per famiglia universal *(film classification)*
filobus trolleybus
filosofia philosophy
fine autostrada/superstrada end of expressway/motorway
fine deviazione end of detour/diversion
fine lavori stradali end of roadworks
finestrino window seat
finire la cura/il trattamento finish the course
fino a ... until ...
fioraio florist's
Firenze Florence
firma signature
fiume river
fon hairdryer
Fondamenta canal-side *(Venice)*
fontana fountain
formaggio cheese
fortezza fortress
fototttico photographic store
fragile – vetro fragile – glass
frana landslide
francobolli stamps
franchigia bagagli luggage allowance
freno d'emergenza emergency brake
fresco fresh
frontiera border crossing

frutta fruit
fruttivendolo greengrocer's
fumetti comics
funivia cable car/gondola
funzione religiosa church service
fuochi d'artificio fireworks
fuori servizio out of order

G

gabinetti restrooms [toilets]
gabinetti pubblici public restrooms [toilets]
galleria shopping mall (dress) circle; gallery
galleria chiusa (mountain) tunnel closed
galleria d'arte art gallery
gara contest
gas per campeggio camping gas
gennaio January
Genova Genoa
genuino genuine
ghiaccio icy snow
ghiaccio nero black ice
giardini pubblici park
giardino garden
giardino botanico botanical garden
gift omaggio free gift
ginocologo gynecologist
gioaccatoli toystore
giornalaio newsagent's
giorni feriali weekdays
giovedì Thursday
giugno June
gocce drops
goielleria jeweler's
gola gorge
gomma rubber
grassi fat content
grassi vegetali vegetable fats
grotta cave
gruppi groups welcome
guanti, cinte e sciarpe gloves, belts and scarves
guardaroba cloakroom
guida ai piani store guide

H

hockey su ghiaccio ice hockey

I

il cuoco suggerisce ... the chef suggests ...
il migliore del mondo world's best
imbarco ad uscita n° ... boarding at gate no. ...
imbarco immediato boarding now
immigrazione immigration control
in casi di guasti telefonare al numero ... in case of breakdown, phone/contact ...
in funzione sistema di vigilanza/allarme surveillance/alarm system in operation
incrocio crossing
indirizzo address
indirizzo di casa home address
industria cinematografica movies/cinema
informazioni information desk, reception
informazioni elenco abbonati enquiries
informazioni nutirizionali nutritional information
ingoiare intere swallow whole
ingrandimento enlargement service
ingresso access only, entrance
ingresso libero admission free
ingresso per gli handicappati entrance for disabled persons
ingresso per soli residenti access to residents only
inizia alle ore ... commencing ...
inizio autostrada freeway entrance
inizio spettacolo curtain up
innestare la prima marcia prima di lasciare la macchina leave your car in first gear
inserire monete insert coin
inserire carta di credito insert credit card
inserire il denaro nella macchina e ritirare il biglietto insert money in machine and remove ticket
inverno winter
inversione di marcia change direction
irritante per gli occhi e la pelle harmful for eyes and skin

isola pedonale pedestrians only/ pedestrian zone
istituto di credito bank
istruzioni per l'uso instructions for use
itinerario naturale nature trail
itinerario panoramico scenic route
itinerario turistico tourist route
IVA VAT/sales tax
IVA compreso/incluso VAT included

L

l'originale the original
La Befana (6 gennaio) Epiphany (January 6)
la merce non può essere cambiata goods cannot be exchanged
lago (artificiale) (artificial) lake
lana wool
lastri x-ray
latte e latticini dairy products
latteria dairy
lavaggio macchine car wash
lavanderia laundry, washing facilities
lavare a mano hand wash only
lavare in acqua fredda/tiepida wash in cold/warm water
lavori in corso (a ... metri) construction (... m) ahead
leggere attentamente le istruzioni prima dell'uso read instructions carefully before use
legno wood
lettino sun lounger
lettura di poesie poetry reading
levate alle ore ... times of collection
libero vacant, for rent
libreria bookstore
libretto di circolazione/documenti registration papers
lino linen
liquidazione clearance sale
liquori liqueurs
lista menu
Livorno Leghorn
lo chef suggerisce ... the chef suggests ...
locanda guest house
luna park amusement park
lunedì Monday
Lunedì dell'Angelo Easter Monday
luogo di nascita place of birth

M

macchina car
macelleria butcher's
magazzino department store
maggio May
mare sea
mare mosso rough sea
marionette puppets
marmellate e conserve preserves
martedì Tuesday
marzo March
maternità maternity
mattina a.m.
medico doctor
meglio se servito fresco best served chilled
meno di 8 articoli 8 items or less
menù fisso set menu
menù turistico tourist menu
mercato market
mercato coperto covered market
merce da dichiarare goods to declare
mercoledì Wednesday
messa mass
messa vespertina Evensong
metallo metal
metropolitana/metro subway
mezza pensione half board
mimo mime
miniera mine
misura unica one size fits all
mittente sender
mobili ed arredamenti furniture
mobilificio furniture warehouse
molo dock (boarding)
molta neve heavy (snow)
monastero monastery
monsignore monseignor
montagna mountain
monumenti antichi ruins
monumento (ai caduti) (war) memorial
monumento di interesse turistico tourist feature
monumento storico ancient monument
mulino mill
mulino a vento windmill
multicine multiplex cinema

municipio town hall
muro wall
museo museum
musica music
musica da camera chamber music
musica dal vivo live music
musica lirica opera

N

Napoli Naples
Natale Christmas
nave ship
nazionalità nationality
nebbia fog
negozio di musica music store/shop
neve snow
neve artificiale artificial snow
neve bagnata wet snow
neve fresca fresh snow
neve ghiacciato icy snow
neve leggera powdery snow
niente flash no flash
niente resto exact change/no change given
niente rimborsi no refunds
nocivo harmful
noleggio for rent
noleggio abiti/vestiti dress rental
nome name
nome dei figli name of children
nome del coniuge name of spouse
nome di famiglia surname
nome di ragazza maiden name
non allacciato disconnected
non appoggiarsi alla porta do not lean against door
non asciugare al sole do not dry in direct sunlight
non avvicinarsi keep clear
non bruciare do not burn
non calpestare il prato/l'erba keep off the grass
non compreso exclusive
non danneggia le pellicole film safe
non esporre a fonti di calore do not expose to heat
non gettare rifiuti do not litter
non incluso not included
non lasciare bagagli incustoditi do not leave baggage unattended
non lasciare oggetti di valore nell'automobile do not leave valuables in your car
non parlare al conducente do not talk to the driver
non più di 4 persone no more than 4 persons
non scongelare prima di cucinare do not defrost before cooking
non si accetta nessuna responsabilità per danni o furto the owners can accept no responsibility for any damage or theft
non si accettano assegni no checks
non si accettano carte di credito no credit cards
non stirare do not iron
non superare 375 kg do not exceed 375 kilos (in elevators)
non toccare do not touch
non usare candeggia do not bleach
nulla da dichiarare nothing to declare
numero di targa license plate number
numero verde toll free number
numeri di emergenza emergency telephone numbers
numeri utili useful numbers
numero del passaporto passport number
numero della carta di credito credit card number
numero di soccorso pubblico di emergenza general emergency number
numero di volo flight number
nuoto swimming

O

occupato occupied/engaged
offerta speciale special offer
officina meccanica car repairs
oggetti elettrici electrical shop/store/appliances
oggetti smarriti lost property
oggi today
ogni ... ore every ... hours
Ognissanti All Saints' Day (November 1)
olio oil; sauces
ombrellone sun umbrella [sunshade]

omeopatico homeopath
ommaggio ...% se spendi più di ... % discount if you spend more than ...
operatore operator
orari timetables
orario opening/business/visiting hours
orario continuato open all day
orario di visite visiting hours
orchestra sinfonica symphony orchestra
24 ore su 24 24-hour service
oreficeria jeweler's
oro gold
ospedale hospital
ospizio hospice
osservatoria observatory
ostello della gioventù youth hostel
ottico optician
ottobre October
ottone brass

P

pacchi packages
padiglione pavilion
padre Father
pagare alla cassa please pay at cash desk
pagare qui please pay here
pagato (grazie) paid (with thanks)
pagine gialle yellow pages
palco (pl. **palchi**) box
palude marsh, swamp
pane bread
panificio bakery/baker's
paracadutismo parachuting
parcheggio parking (permitted); parking lot
parcheggio libero free parking
parcheggio per biciclette parking for bicycles
parcheggio per soli residenti parking for residents only
parcheggio riservato ai clienti customer parking lot
parcheggio sotterraneo underground garage
parcheggio vietato/divieto di sosta no parking
parrucchiere hairdresser's/hairstylist's
partenze departures
partita match
Pasqua Easter Sunday
passaggio a livello railroad/level crossing
passaggio sotteraneo underground passage
passo carrabile do not block entrance
pasticceria pastry shop
pattini skates
pedaggio toll
pedoni pedestrians
pelle leather
pellicola film
pendenza incline [gradient]
penisola peninsula
pensione completa full board
pensione guest house
per vegetariani suitable for vegetarians
per ... giorni for ... days
percorso del traghetto ferry route
percorso per autobus/pullmans bus route
pericolo danger
pericolo di bufere storm warning
pericolo di burrasche gale warning
pericolo di ghiaccio icy road
pericolo di slavine danger of avalanches
pericoloso dangerous
personale staff only
pesce fish; angling
pesce fresco fresh fish
pesce surgelato frozen fish
pescheria fish store
pesistica weight-lifting
piatti pronti oven to table
piatto del giorno dish of the day
piazza square
picco peak
piccola colazione breakfast
piccoli prezzi grande qualità low prices, top quality
pillole pills
pinacoteca art gallery
pioggia rain
piscina swimming pool
piscina per tuffi diving pool
pista bianca (ski trail)for beginners

pista blu e pista rossa for intermediates *(ski trail)*
pista chiusa closed
pista ciclabile cycle lane/track
pista nera for advanced skiers
pista per principianti for beginners *(ski trail)*
pista pericolosa dangerous trail
platea stalls
polizia police
polizia stradale highway/traffic police
pollame poultry
poltrona n° seat no.
pomata ointment
pomeriggio p.m.
pompa pump
ponte bridge
ponte bassa (altezza ... m.) low bridge (height ... m.)
ponte di coperta upper deck
ponte di passeggiate promenade deck
ponte levatoio drawbridge
porta gate (to town/city); door
porta antincendio fire door
porta automatica automatic door
portiere notturno night porter
porto harbor
posta post office
posto corridoio aisle seat
posto fumatore smoking
posto non fumatore no smoking
posto n° seat no.
posto riservato agli invalidi please give up this seat to the disabled
pozzo well
PP.TT. post office
prato (campeggio) grass (camping site)
prefisso area code
preghiera prayers
prelievi withdrawals
prelievi di sangue blood tests
prendere il biglietto take ticket
prendere la ricevuta dalla cassa automatica pay at the meter
prenotazione biglietti ticket reservation
prenotazioni reservations, advance bookings
prezzi fissi no discounts
prezzi speciali per gruppi special price for groups
prezzo rate
prezzo al litro price per liter/litre
prezzo per chilo (Kg)/etto price per kilo/330 grams
prima classe first class
prima dei pasti before meals
prima di coricarsi before going to bed (medicine dose)
primavera spring
primo piano first floor
prodotti antiallergici antiallergic products
prodotti di bellezza beauty products
proibito circolare nella chiesa durante le funzioni liturgiche/durante la santa messa no entry during services
pronto intervento emergency services
pronto soccorso accident and emergency; medicine box
proprietà privato private property
prossima levata alle ore ... next collection at ...
prossima visita guidata alle ore ... next tour at ...
punto d'imbarco embarkation point
punto d'incontro meeting point
punto di raduno muster station

Q

questa macchina non da resto this machine does not give change
questa sera/stasera this evening
qui si vendono carte telefoniche phone cards on sale here

R

racchetta racket/raquet; ski poles/sticks
raccordo anulare ring-road
rallentare slow down
rallentare, scuola/bambini caution, school/children
reclamo bagagli baggage claim
referti test results
regali gifts
reggersi ai corrimano hold on to the side (escalator)
resto massimo (L.2000) maximum change given (L.2000)

ricambi per auto car accessory/spares shop/store
ricevimento reception
riduzioni reductions
rifugio ski shelter
rilasciato il ... da ... issued on ...by ...
rimozione forzata unauthorized vehicles will be towed away
rio stream
riparazioni repairs
riserva d'acqua reservoir
riserva naturale nature reserve
riservato reserved
ritardo delayed
rocca castle, fortress
roccia (campeggio) stone (camping site)
romanzi novels
rompere il vetro in caso di pericolo break glass in case of emergency
rotatoria (a ... metri) roundabout/circle (... m. ahead)
roulotte trailer/caravan
rubinetto water tap
rupe cliff

S

sabato Saturday
sabbia mobile quicksand
sala banchetti reception facilities
sala congressi/conferenze conference room
sala d'attesa waiting room
sala da pranzo dining room
sala giochi games room
sala operatoria operating theater
sala passaggeri passenger lounge
sala TV television room
saldi clearance sale
sale salt
salita entrance (get on)
salotto lounge
salvagenti lifejackets
San Gennaro St. Januarius (September 19, Naples)
San Giovanni Battista St. John The Baptist (June 24, Florence)
San Marco Saint Mark's Day (April 25, Venice)
San Pietro e Paolo Saint Paul's and Peter's Day (June 29, Rome)
San Silvestro New Year's Eve
Sant'Ambrogio Saint Ambrose's Day (December 7, Milan)
Santo Stefano Boxing Day (December 26)
sanzioni per i trasgressori trespassers will be prosecuted
sanzioni per i viaggiatori senza biglietto penalty for traveling without a ticket
sanzioni se viaggiate senza biglietto penalty for traveling without ticket
saporito tasty
scadenza della carta di credito credit card expiration date
scala d'emergenza emergency stairs
scala mobile escalator
scarico merci deliveries only
scarpata escarpment
scarponi da sci ski boots
schiuma per la barba shaving cream
sci skis, skiing
sci di fondo cross-country skiing
sci nautico waterskiing
sciovia tow (ski) lift
sconto di ...% se spendi più di ... ... % discount if you spend more than ...
scuola school
scuola rallentare slow, school
sdraia deck-chair
se i sintomi persistono consultare il proprio medico if symptoms persist, consult your doctor
seconda scelta sale
secondo piano second floor
segale rye
seggiovia chairlift
selezionare destinazione/zona select destination/zone
semaforo provvisorio temporary traffic light
senso unico one-way street
sentiero footpath, track
senza grassi fat-free
senza intervallo no intermission
senza piombo unleaded
senza zucchero sugar-free
sereno sunny weather
servizio service charge

servizio compreso/incluso service included
servizio di camera room service
servizio diretto direct service
servizio immediato while you wait
servizio non incluso service not included
servizio notturno night service
seta silk
si accettano gruppi parties welcome
si accettano carte di credito we accept credit cards
si prega consegnare le borse please leave your bags here
si prega controllare il resto please check your change
si prega di aspettare dietro la linea please wait behind barrier
si prega di non consumare cibo nella camera no food in the room please
si prega fare un contributo please make a contribution
si prega mantere il silenzio durante le funzioni religiose quiet, service in progress
si prega pulire la camera make up this room please
si prega rispettare questo luogo sacro please respect this place of worship
si prega tenere il biglietto please retain your ticket
sicurezza security
signore women only; ladies (toilets)
signori gentlemen (toilets)
slittino sledge
soccorso stradale breakdown services
solista soloist
solo ciclisti cyclists only
solo contanti cash only
solo giorni feriali weekdays only
solo giorni festivi Sundays only
solo per gli abbonati season ticket holders only
solo per uso esterno not for internal consumption
solo rasoi shavers only
solo residenti residents only
solo stasera/una serata for 1 night only
solo uso esterno for external use only
sono previste sanzioni per chi non può esibire lo scontrino fiscale/il biglietto you are liable to be fined if you don't keep your receipt/ticket
sopra il livello del mare above sea level
sopraelevata flyover
sorgente spring
spegnere il motore turn off engine
spettacolo spectacular
spettacolo serale evening performance
spettatori spectators
spiaggia beach
spiaggia per nudisti nudist beach
spingere push
spogliatoi changing rooms
SQ subject to availability
squisito delicious
staccare la corrente prima di (togliere) disconnect from electric mains before (removing)
stampa e sviluppo photographic store
stampe prints
stazione degli autobus bus station/terminal
stazione di pedaggio toll booth
stazione di servizio service/filling station
stazione ferroviaro train station
stirare a temperatura bassa cool iron
storia history
storia dell'arte art history
strada road
strada a doppia corsia dual highway
strada a doppio senso traffic from the opposite direction
strada a senso unico one-way street
strada bianca gravel/unpaved road
strada chiusa road closed
strada dissestata uneven road surface
strada in costruzione road under construction
strada nazionale main road/highway
strada principale main street
strada senza uscita cul-de-sac; no through traffic
strada stretta narrow road

straniero(-a) foreign
strappare qui tear here
strisce pedonali pedestrian crossing
studio medico doctor's office [surgery]
succhi di frutta fruit juices
suonare la campanella ring the bell
super four-star (gas)
superstrada expressway
supplemento (notturno, aeroporto, bagagli, festivo) supplement (night-time, airport, baggage, Sunday, holiday)
surgelato frozen
sviluppo developing
svincolo junction/interchange

T

tagliare qui cut here
tangenziale bypass
tavola da sci snowboard
tavola da surf surfboard
tavoli al piano superiore seats upstairs
tassì taxi
teatro per ragazzi children's theater
telefono per solo carte card phone
telefono SOS/di emergenza emergency telephone
teleselezione direct dialing
tenere in frigo keep refrigerated
tenere in un ambiente fresco keep in a cool place
tenere lontano dagli occhi keep away from eyes
tenere lontano dai bambini keep out of reach of children
tenere lontano dal sole do not expose to sunlight
tennis da tavola table tennis
terme baths
tessera season ticket
tessera mensile monthly ticket
tessuti per arredamento upholstered [soft] furnishings
tier tribuna stand/grandstand
tintoria dry cleaner's
tintura per capelli hair dye
tipografia printing & copying
tirare pull
tiro all'arco archery
tomba grave, tomb
Torino Turin
torre tower
tossico poisonous, toxic
traffico intenso delays likely
traffico lento slow traffic
traghetto passenger ferry
transito con catene chains required
transito con catene o pneumatici da neve use chains or snow tires
treno train
trotta harness racing
tuffo deep water diving
tutte le operazioni all transactions

U

ufficio cambi exchange office
ufficio informazioni information office
ufficio postale post office
ufficio prenotazioni ticket reservations
ultima novità brand new
ultima stazione di servizio per ... chilometri last gas station for ... kilometers
ultima vista alle ore ... last entry at ...
una bibite inclusa includes 1 complimentary drink
uomini men only; men (toilets)
usare con cautela take care when using
uscita exit, way out; gate
uscita autostrada freeway/motorway exit
uscita camions truck/lorry exit
uscita d'emergenza emergency/fire exit
uso della cucina cooking facilities

V

vaccinazioni ecografie vaccinations
vaglia postali/telegrafici postal money order and electronic transfers
vagone letto sleeper (train)
validità del passaporto passport expiration date
validità della carta di credito credit card expiration date
valido per (75 minuti) valid for (75 minutes)
valido per le fasce ... valid for zones ...

veicoli lenti slow vehicles
veicoli pesanti heavy vehicles
vela sailing
veleno(so) poison(ous)
velocità massima ... km/ora maximum speed
vendere entro il ... sell by ...
vendiamo a ... currency sold at...
venerdì Friday
venti forti strong winds
venti moderati light winds
verdura vegetables
vernice fresco wet paint
vero genuine
vetro glass
vetro riciclato recycled glass
via street
viaggi/viaggiare travel
viale avenue, boulevard
vicino al mare within easy reach of the sea
vicolo alley
vicolo cieco dead end
videogiochi video games
vietato forbidden
vietato a veicoli con peso superiore a closed to heavy vehicles
vietato accendere il fuoco no fires
vietato ai minori di ... anni no children under ...
vietato ai pedoni no pedestrians
vietato avvicinarsi alle macchine durante la traversata no access to car decks during crossing
vietato di sosta no waiting
vietato fermarsi fino a ... no stopping (between ... and ...)
vietato fotografare no photography
vietato fumare no smoking
vietato gettare rifiuti don't dump rubbish
vietato giocare con la palla no ball games
vietato l'ingresso no entry
vietato l'ingresso dopo l'inizio dello spettacolo no entry once the performance has begun
vietato pescare no fishing
vietato pescare senza autorizzazione fishing by permit only
vietato salire no entry
vietato scendere no exit
vietato sporgersi dalla finestra do not lean out of windows
vietato suonare il clacson use of horn prohibited
vigili del fuoco fire brigade
vigili di fuoco fire station
vigneti vineyards
visite guidate guided tours
vivaio garden center
voi siete qui you are here
voli internazionali international flights
voli nazionali domestic flights
volo numero ... flight number
... volte al giorno ... times a day

WX YZ

zona a parcheggio limitato giorni feriali limited parking zone on weekdays
zona non fumatore no smoking
zona pedonale pedestrian zone/precinct
zona riservata a carico e scarico loading bay
zone fumatore smoking
zucchero sugar

Reference

Numbers 216
Days/Months/ Dates 218
Greetings 219
Public holidays 219
Time 220
Maps 222
Quick reference 224

Numbers Numeri

GRAMMAR

Larger numbers are built up using the components below: e.g.

3 456 789 **tremilioniquattrocentocinquantaseimila e settecentoottantanove**

Mille, **milione** and **miliardo** have plural forms (**mila**, **milioni**, **miliardi**). Note that **e** can be used to break larger numbers up.

0 **zero** *dzehro*
1 **uno** *oono*
2 **due** *doo-ay*
3 **tre** *tray*
4 **quattro** *kwattro*
5 **cinque** *cheengkweh*
6 **sei** *sayee*
7 **sette** *sehttay*
8 **otto** *otto*
9 **nove** *novay*
10 **dieci** *dee-ehchee*
11 **undici** *oondeechee*
12 **dodici** *dodeechee*
13 **tredici** *traydeechee*
14 **quattordici** *kwattordeechee*
15 **quindici** *kooendeechee*
16 **sedici** *saydeechee*
17 **diciassette** *deechassehttay*
18 **diciotto** *deechotto*
19 **diciannove** *deechanovay*
20 **venti** *vayntee*
21 **ventuno** *vayntoono*
22 **ventidue** *vaynteedoo-ay*
23 **ventitre** *vaynteetray*
24 **ventiquattro** *vaynteekwattro*
25 **venticinque** *vaynteecheengkweh*
26 **ventisei** *vaynteesayee*
27 **ventisette** *vaynteesehttay*
28 **ventotto** *vayntotto*
29 **ventinove** *vaynteenovay*
30 **trenta** *traynta*

31 **trentuno**
trayntoono

32 **trentadue**
trayntadoo-ay

40 **quaranta**
kwaranta

50 **cinquanta**
cheengkwanta

60 **sessanta**
sayssanta

70 **settanta**
sayttantta

80 **ottanta**
ottanta

90 **novanta**
novanta

100 **cento**
chaynto

101 **centouno**
chaynto-oono

102 **centodue**
chayntodoo-ay

200 **duecento**
doo-aychaynto

500 **cinquecento**
cheenkwehchaynto

1000 **mille** *meellay*

10 000 **diecimila**
deeaycheemeela

35 750 **trentacinquemilasette centocinquanta**
trayntacheengkweh meelasehttaychayn to cheengkoo-anta

1 000 000 **un milione**
oon meelyonay

first **primo**
preemo

second **secondo**
saykondo

third **terzo**
tayrtso

fourth **quarto**
kwarto

fifth **quinto**
kooeento

once **una volta**
oona volta

twice **due volte**
doo-ay voltay

three times **tre volte**
tray voltay

a half **mezzo**
maytso

half a(n) hour **mezz'ora**
maytsora

half a tank **mezzo serbatoio**
maytso sayrbatoeeo

half eaten **mezzo mangiato**
maytso manjaato

a quarter **un quarto**
oon kwarto

a third **un terzo**
oon tayrtso

a pair of … **un paio di …**
oon paa-eeoo dee

a dozen … **una dozzina …**
oona dotseena

1997 **millenovecento-novantasette**
meellaynovay-chayntonovanta-sehttay

2001 **duemilauno**
doo-aymeela-oono

the 1990s **gli anni novanta**
lyee annee novanta

Days Giorni

Monday	**lunedì** *loonaydee*
Tuesday	**martedì** *martaydee*
Wednesday	**mercoledì** *mayrkolaydee*
Thursday	**giovedì** *jovaydee*
Friday	**venerdì** *vaynayrdee*
Saturday	**sabato** *sabato*
Sunday	**domenica** *domayneeka*

Months Mesi

January	**gennaio** *jaynnaaeeo*
February	**febbraio** *faybbraaeeo*
March	**marzo** *martso*
April	**aprile** *apreelay*
May	**maggio** *madjo*
June	**giugno** *jooño*
July	**luglio** *loolyo*
August	**agosto** *agosto*
September	**settembre** *sehttehmbray*
October	**ottobre** *ottobray*
November	**novembre** *novehmbray*
December	**dicembre** *deechehmbray*

Dates Date

It's ...	**È ...** *eh*
July 10	**il dieci luglio** *eel dee-ehchee loolyo*
Tuesday, March 1	**martedì, primo marzo** *martaydee preemo martso*
yesterday	**ieri** *ee-ehree*
today	**oggi** *odjee*
tomorrow	**domani** *domaanee*
this/last ...	**questo(-a)/l'ultimo(-a) ...** *kwaysto(-a)/loolteemo(-a)*
next week	**la prossima settimana** *la prosseema saytteemaana*
every month/year	**ogni mese/anno** *oñee maysee/anno*
on/during the weekend	**al fine settimana** *al feenay sayteemaana*

Seasons Stagioni

spring	**la primavera** *la preemavayra*
summer	**l'estate** *laystaatay*
fall/autumn	**l'autunno** *lowtoonno*
winter	**l'inverno** *leenvayrno*
in spring	**in primavera** *een preemavayra*
during the summer	**durante l'estate** *doorantay laystaatay*

Greetings Saluti

Happy birthday!	**Buon compleanno!** *bwon komplayanno*
Merry Christmas!	**Buon Natale!** *bwon nataalay*
Happy New Year!	**Felice Anno Nuovo! Buon anno!** *fayleechay anno noo-ovo/bwon anno*
Happy Easter!	**Buona Pasqua!** *bwona paskwa*
Best wishes!	**I migliori auguri!** *ee meelyoree owgooree*
Congratulations!	**Felicitazioni!/Congratulazioni!** *fayleecheetatseeonee/kongraatoolatseeonee*
Good luck!/All the best!	**Buona fortuna!** *bwona fortoona*
Have a good trip!	**Buon viaggio!** *bwon veeadjo*
Give my regards to ...	**Saluti ... da parte mia.** *salootee ... da partay meea*

Public holidays Giorni festivi

There are a number of regional holidays observed in Italy, such as **Festa del patrono** (the local patron saint's day); this sees Rome close down for St. Peter and Paul on June 29. National holidays are listed below.

January 1	**Capodanno or Primo dell'Anno**	New Year's Day
January 6	**Epifania/Befana**	Epiphany
April 25	**Anniversario della Liberazione (1945)**	Liberation Day
May 1	**Festa del Lavoro**	Labor Day
August 15	**Ferragosto**	Assumption Day
November 1	**Ognissanti**	All Saints' Day
December 8	**L'Immacolata Concezione**	Immaculate Conception
December 25	**Natale**	Christmas
December 26	**Santo Stefano**	St Stephen's Day
Movable dates:	**Lunedì di Pasqua/Pasquetta**	Easter Monday

Except for April 25, all Italian holidays are celebrated in the **Ticino** (Italian-speaking Switzerland), as well as: March 19 (**San Giuseppe**), August 1st (National Holiday), and the holidays of **Ascensione** (Ascension Day) and **Corpus Domini**.

Time Ora

The official time system uses the 24-hour clock. However, in ordinary conversation, time is generally expressed as shown below, often with the addition of **di mattina** (morning), **di pomeriggio** (afternoon) or **di sera** (evening).

Excuse me. Can you tell me the time?	**Scusi, può dirmi che ora è?** *skoozee pwo deermee kay ora eh*
It's five past one.	**È l'una e cinque.** *eh loona ay cheenkway*
It's …	**Sono le …** *sono lay*
ten past two	**due e dieci** *doo-ay ay dee-ehchee*
a quarter past three	**tre e un quarto** *tray ay oon kwarto*
twenty past four	**quattro e venti** *kwattro ay vayntee*
twenty-five past five	**cinque e venticinque** *cheenkway ay vayntecheenkway*
half past six	**sei e trenta** *seh-ee ay traynta*
twenty-five to seven	**sette meno venticinque** *sehttay mayno vayntecheenkway*
twenty to eight	**otto meno venti** *otto mayno vayntee*
a quarter to nine	**nove meno un quarto** *novay mayno oon kwarto*
ten to ten	**dieci meno dieci** *dee-ehchee mayno dee-ehchee*
five to eleven	**undici meno cinque** *oondeechee mayno cheenkway*
It's twelve o'clock (noon/midnight).	**È mezzogiorno/mezzanotte.** *eh maytsojorno/maytsanottay*

at dawn	**all'alba** *allalba*
in the morning	**al mattino** *al matteeno*
during the day	**durante il giorno** *doorantay eel jorno*
before lunch	**prima di pranzo** *preema dee prandzo*
after lunch	**dopo pranzo** *dopo prandzo*
in the afternoon	**nel pomeriggio** *nayl pomayreedjo*
in the evening	**di sera** *dee sayra*
at night	**di notte** *dee nottay*
I'll be ready in five minutes.	**Sarò pronto(-a) fra cinque minuti.** *saro pronto(-a) fra cheenkway meenootee*
He'll be back in a quarter of an hour.	**Ritorna fra un quarto d'ora.** *reetorno fra oon kwarto dora*
She arrived half an hour ago.	**È arrivata mezz'ora fa.** *eh arreevaata maytsora fa*
The train leaves at …	**il treno parte …** *eel trayno partay*
13:04	**alle tredici e zero quattro** *allay traydeechee ay dzayro kwattro*
0:40	**alle zero e quaranta** *allay dzayro ay kwaraanta*
10 minutes late/early	**con dieci minuti di ritardo/di anticipo** *kon dee-ehchee meenootee dee reetaardo/dee anteecheepo*
5 minutes fast/slow	**cinque minuti avanti/indietro** *cheenkway meenootee avaantee/eendeeaytro*
from 9:00 to 5:00	**dalle nove alle cinque** *dallay novay allay cheenkway*
between 8:00 and 2:00	**fra le otto e le due** *fra lay otto ay lay doo-ay*
I'll be leaving by …	**Partirò entro …** *parteero ayntro*
Will you be back before …?	**Ritornerà prima di …?** *reetornayra preema dee*
We'll be here until …	**Saremo qui fino alle …** *saraymo kwee feeno allay*

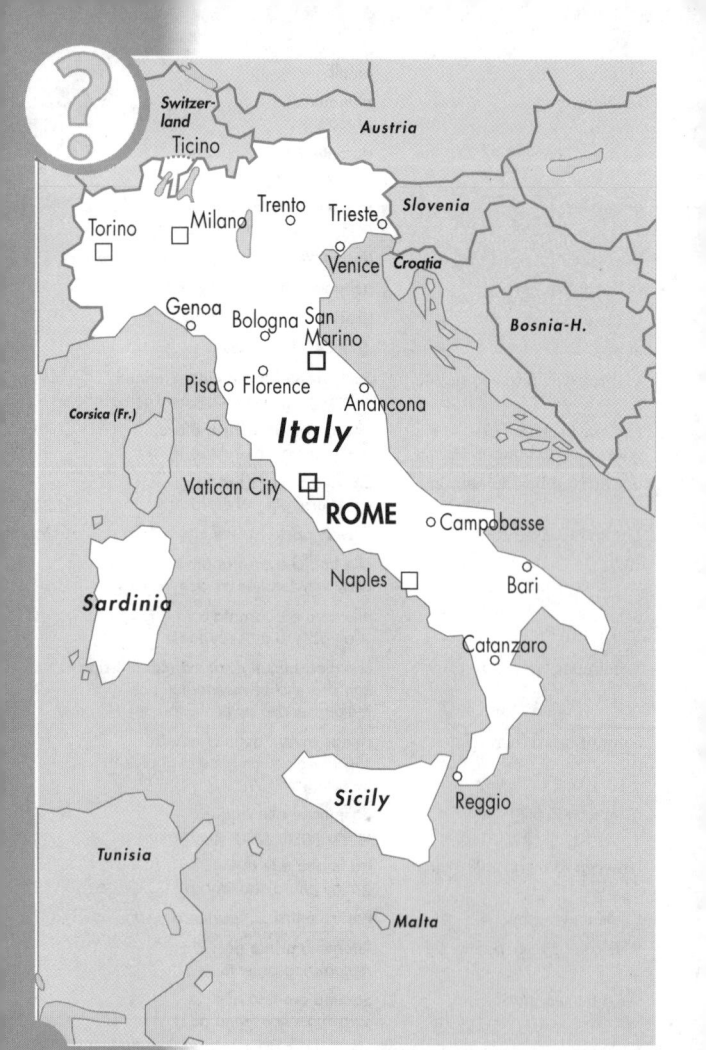
Switzer-
land
Austria
Ticino
Trento
Trieste
Slovenia
Torino
Milano
Venice
Croatia
Genoa
Bologna
San
Marino
Bosnia-H.
Pisa
Florence
Ancona
Corsica (Fr.)
Italy
Vatican City
ROME
Campobasse
Naples
Bari
Sardinia
Catanzaro
Sicily
Reggio
Tunisia
Malta

Italy
Sassari
Nuoro
Sardinia
Oristanto
Cagliari
Palermo
Messina
Trapani
Sicily
Catania
Arigento
Ragusa
Siracuse
Tunisia

Quick reference Consultazione rapida

Good morning	**Buongiorno** *bwonjorno*
Good afternoon	**Buongiorno** *bwonjorno*
Good evening	**Buona sera** *bwona sayra*
Hello	**Ciao** *chaao*
Good-bye	**Arrivederci** *arreevaydayrchee*
Excuse me (getting attention)	**Scusi.** *skoozee*
Pardon?	**Prego?** *praygo*
Sorry!	**Scusi!** *skoozee*
Please.	**Per favore.** *pehr favoray*
Thank you.	**Grazie.** *graatseeay*
Do you speak English?	**Parla inglese?** *parla eengglayzay*
I don't understand.	**Non capisco.** *non kapeesko*
Where is ...?	**Dov'è ...?** *doveh*
Where are the restrooms [toilets]?	**Dove sono i gabinetti?** *dovay sono ee gabeenayttee*

Emergency Emergenze

Help!	**Aiuto!** *aaeeooto*
Go away!	**Se ne vada!** *say nay vada*
Leave me alone!	**Mi lasci in pace!** *mee lashee een pachay*
Call the police!	**Chiami la polizia!** *keeaamee la poleetseea*
Stop thief!	**Alladro!** *alladro*
Get a doctor!	**Chiami un dottore!** *keeaamee oon dottore*
Fire!	**Al fuoco!** *al foo-oko*
I'm ill.	**Sto male.** *sto malay*
I'm lost.	**Sono smarrito.** *sono smarreeto*
Can you help me?	**Mi può aiutare?** *mee pwo a-eeootaaray*

Emergency ☎

	Italy	Switzerland
	113 for Fire **(vigili del fuoco)** Ambulance **(ambulanza)**, and Police **(polizia)**	**118** for Fire **117** for Police

Embassies/Consulates ☎

	Italy	Switzerland
UK	**06-69923561, 06-4825551**	**031 352 50 21**
U.S.	**06-646741**	**031 357 70 11**